FIRST PERSON *PLURAL*

CAMERON WEST, PhD

FIRST PERSON *PLURAL*

My Life as a Multiple

BLACK STONE
PUBLISHING

Published in 2026 by Blackstone Publishing
Cover and book design by Alenka Linaschke

Printed in the United States of America

First edition: 2026
ISBN 979-8-228-70617-0
Biography & Autobiography / Medical (incl. Patients)

Version 1

Blackstone Publishing
31 Mistletoe Rd.
Ashland, OR 97520

www.BlackstonePublishing.com

MY GUYS

Soul is an ageless alter who emerged early on and whose job it was to give me hope so I could survive. His presence is still felt, but he rarely comes out, even in therapy.

Sharky is a primitive alter who at first couldn't form words at all. He would grunt and swing his head from side to side and bite things, like tables and clothes and plants. One of the other alters drew a picture of him as a limbless being with a huge toothy mouth. Sharky has learned to talk and eat with his hands or a fork. He doesn't come out too often, but he likes to share treats with the others.

Davy is four. He is sweet and sad. He was the first to emerge, but he doesn't come out much anymore.

Anna and *Trudi* are four-year-old twins. Anna is doe-eyed and happy, with a smile so big it makes my face hurt. She remembers her abuse, but feels no anger, no sadness. She loves a good cookie. Trudi is dark and brooding, a kid in the corner. She remembers, too, but only the pain and sadness and horror. Anna shares her cookies with her. Anna is a member of the core group of alters who come out with the most frequency.

Mozart is six years old. He is very quiet and fragile and has difficulty breathing. Mozart doesn't come out very often.

Clay is eight and comes out frequently. For a long time he had an awful stutter and tense muscles, and he couldn't look anyone in the eye. But he is much more relaxed now. The stutter is mostly gone, and he is learning to meet a person's gaze. Clay has a scarf we wear every day. We never go anywhere without it. Clay is also a member of the core group.

Switch is eight years old. He held incredible rage for being abused, but he also felt a powerful allegiance to one of our abusers and turned that rage toward me and some of the others. Switch harmed my body many times. He is not so angry anymore, and he has been accepted by everyone in the system. Switch has his own sheriff's badge now, which he likes to wear around. He is a member of the core group.

Wyatt is a bright ten-year-old who comes out frequently and likes to talk to people as he walks around the periphery of things. He is almost perpetually in motion, usually rocking, pacing, counting, or studying shapes and patterns. Wyatt likes words and describes things in unusual ways. Wyatt is also in the core group.

Tracy, Kit, Nicky, Lake, Toy, and *Casey* are "The Boys." They all appeared in the early months, each locked somewhere in the time when Kennedy was president and only baseball games and Bonanza were in color. Over time the boys blended until they eventually merged and faded back. They are no longer accessible.

Dusty is a twelve-year-old girl. She is gentle and kind and comes out often to go food shopping and cook. Dusty takes care of the little ones, sometimes reading children's books to them. She is disappointed that she exists in the body of a middle-aged man. Dusty is a member of the core group.

Gail is the newest member of the system, having only fully emerged as this book was being completed. She was very quiet at first, but now she is close to Dusty, and they do most things together. Dusty taught Gail how to make bread. At some point they will probably integrate. Gail is also in the core group.

Keith is fifteen. He is quiet, self-effacing, and rarely comes out.

Bart is twenty-eight, easygoing, and funny. His role in the system has changed from scaring everyone into keeping their secrets to protecting the young ones and helping to keep things light. Along with Per, he takes control when crises arise or when my world gets too dark. Bart's levity has kept us afloat many times. He wishes he were more sophisticated and half-jokingly refers to me as "The Doc" or sometimes "The Stiff."

Kyle emerged shortly after Bart. He was Bart's age, his buddy and sidekick. Over time Kyle got closer and closer to Bart until they blended together and finally merged.

Leif is in his thirties, with an incredible focus and force. He embodies action, productivity, and accomplishment, with an utter lack of emotion or concern for a second of pleasure. Leif usually stayed just behind me, not taking over completely, but relentlessly driving me to keep moving. He now works with Bart and Per to help me get things done, but at a human pace, and with some cheer and calm. Leif is in the core group.

Sky is in his thirties. He appeared early on to help regulate the flow of emotions and memories so my alters and I wouldn't overload. The more the system learned to communicate and work together, the less we've had to rely on Sky. He never comes out anymore.

Stroll is about thirty. He was a serpentine, sexual tool, existing solely for the pleasure of women, emerging any time a woman of any age showed me any kindness at all. Although he is still triggered by women's attention, Stroll has changed his role to one of support for the younger alters. He comes out only in therapy now, and even there, infrequently.

Per is a gentle, spiritual soul. He is a poet, an artist, a connection to the forces of balance and nature. He is peace and relief. He holds us tenderly in his arms and keeps us safe. Per, a member of the core group, is the father figure to everyone in the system.

Author's Note: After the publication of *First Person Plural*, one more alter named *Roger* appeared. He is five years old and holds the memories of an incident of abuse in which he was held down and couldn't breathe. When he comes out, the right side of my face droops as if I've had a stroke, and Roger's brain wave patterns, as tested by an electroencephalogram, indicate signs of brain damage, though mine do not.

PROLOGUE

Looking out my upstairs bedroom window through a curtain of fog, I see a vague image under a street lamp. I squint my eyes, and as the image slowly becomes clearer, I can distinguish a human outline. I take a step closer and lean forward, placing my hands on the windowsill, pressing my forehead against the cool pane. *Who is that?*

It's a slim, dark-haired man in a T-shirt and blue jeans. He's doing something, but I can't quite make it out. I rub my eyes and again press my face to the glass, straining to see. The darkhaired man is leaning over a white, free-standing sink with a mirror attached to the back of it. There appears to be something in his left hand—something sharp. *What's he doing?*

Then I see that his right arm is covered with blood. Blood is dripping off the tips of his fingers and into the sink. He looks up into the mirror and back down at his arm. I follow his gaze and see blood dripping from a five-inch incision on his forearm. Large drops of blood fall from the end of the short steel blade of a knife. He makes another pass with the knife, and fresh blood fills the wound, trailing down his arm, splattering in the sink.

Suddenly, a familiar force seizes me; a silent vacuum pulls my viscous self through the window and across the street. I'm now behind the man with the bloody arm, watching him lean over the sink. He spots me in the mirror, and like a balloon filling with molasses, I slowly expand and fill his body. Now I am inside. I look down at the left hand holding the bloody knife, then at the open flesh oozing red. The eyes peer into the mirror, and from an island in my mind, I realize that it's my face looking back at me, it's my hand holding the knife, my arm bleeding into the sink. *Oh my God!* The light intensifies, jabbing my eyes, and my face flushes hot crimson. Reality's insect creeps up the back of my neck into my right ear and whispers one long, drawn-out word.

"Welllcommme."

Oh no, not again. Who cut me? Who? Who's doing this?

A voice says, "It's Switch."

I look in the mirror at eyes that don't belong to me. *Switch cut my body. He's the one.*

I watch my left hand put the knife down on the edge of the sink, and a moist bubble of sadness passes from the back of my mind to my eyes and becomes a tiny tear that swells and finally falls, trickling down my left cheek. *Switch is so young and so hurt.*

With a jolt, I realize I've got to clean up the mess. I turn on the cold water and begin to wash away the blood. Using wads of toilet paper, I blot the gash on the inside of my right forearm and inspect the damage. The laceration is deep, exposing fatty tissue and muscle, but there's no pain, just a slight stinging sensation in my arm. I keep blotting the wound until it's only seeping a little and pinch the skin together to determine if I should go to the emergency room for stitches or if Steri-Strips will close it. I let go and the wound yawns open. *Damn! It's gotta be stitched.*

I don't want to go to the emergency room. They know me there. I shake my head, annoyed. *This is going to be embarrassing.* I'll have to make up some transparent lie about cutting myself on something sharp. *Hmm . . . my linoleum knife slipped while I was replacing the kitchen floor?* It's all bullshit. I'll be convincing, but they'll know I'm lying. And they'll know that I know that they know I'm lying.

"Fuck!" I shout, and the sound of my voice startles me. Nobody gets hurt so many times in the same place. Nobody. I mean, Jesus, you could play tic-tac-toe on my right arm. They'll look at each other, eyebrows raised, and wonder if they should fifty-one-fifty me, but they won't. They won't commit me for observation, because I'm so goddamn good at seeming normal.

They're just ER interns and nurses, not psychiatrists. They don't know about multiples, and I'm too poised to be a cutter. I don't fit the profile. Distinguished-looking, middle-aged men just don't come into suburban emergency rooms with their arms sliced up, unless it's some kind of accident. They'll let me slide.

But I wonder how I'll hide this wound from Kai. I know I'm going to have to call Rikki at work and tell her I've been cut again. Last time it happened, she walked in and discovered me just after the cutting, before all the blood had been cleaned up. We were about to leave for a dinner party at our neighbors' house. In frustration, she had burst into tears and angrily spat, "Drive yourself to the emergency room!" This time I'll make the phone call to prepare her before she gets home. I owe her that.

A dark blue sadness gathers in my chest while I wrap gauze around my arm and clean up the blood. I hear the confused voices of some of the others in my head; they're wondering what's going on. As I drive to the hospital, my only concern is to play the emergency room scene and escape discovery. Later, when I get home, I'll allow myself to feel the odd, but familiar, calmness that seeps through me after I've been cut. The usual fatigue will come, too. Not mine, but Switch's.

"When we get home from the hospital we'll all lie down," I say out loud as authoritatively as I can. My words sound strange in the empty car. After I've been stitched up and bandaged, when I'm home again, a gentle wave of peacefulness will wash over me. But even as it does, I'll know—we'll know—this hasn't been a good day.

PART ONE
MY SAD HOTEL

Three years earlier

ONE

I was lying on my back on our white Berber living room carpet, admiring the self-portraits in a luxuriously detailed book called *Rembrandt: The Human Form and Spirit.* The Rembrandt book was one of several wonderful art books Rikki and I had given to my dad. After he died, at the age of fifty-nine, ownership of the books had reverted to us, and I was glad about that, even though I would have been gladder had I not gotten them back so soon.

Every time I look at Rembrandt's self-portraits I get a feeling inside that's hushed and private and kind of sad, like a solitary stretch of river at night, and I know I'm looking directly into the man's soul. And for some reason, when I look at those paintings I feel a little closer to my dad, even though Rembrandt probably knows him better than I ever did.

It was early evening in the middle of October. The days were getting shorter, and outside you could see your breath. The leaves on the trees surrounding our small fieldstone house on our four-acre hill were turning, and soon they'd fall off and we'd have to surrender the cocoon-like feeling that had originally attracted us to the old place. Before long, through the bony trees, we'd be able to see our nearest neighbor's home down the hill and across the street, maybe six hundred feet away. Autumn in New England.

Rikki was standing at the white Formica counter in our small, bright kitchen that opened to the living room. The counter was a happy sight, covered with all the fixings for a homemade pizza, one of my two favorite meals along with homemade ravioli with pesto sauce. The dough had risen and was stretched out on a perforated pizza pan, a tasty sauce simmered on the stove, and a big chunk of mozzarella sat next to a yellow-handled stainless steel grater. Black olives, Crimini mushrooms, and a shiny red bell pepper were already cut up, and Rikki was expertly slicing a Vidalia onion with an eight-inch Henckels knife on a worn, round, teak chopping board we'd gotten as a wedding gift twelve years earlier.

The new L. L. Bean suede moccasins Rikki had just given me for my thirty-seventh birthday—actually *our* birthday, since we were born on the same day—were on the floor next to me, and five-year-old Kai was beside me on his belly, wearing his blue and red Spiderman pajamas with the matching cape. He'd made a fort out of my moccasins for some of his GI Joe figures and the battle was raging, with Kai providing excellent dialogue and sound effects, which at one point got overly juicy and he spit in my ear.

"Kylie, jeez!" I said, making a "yucchhh" face and wiping the saliva off my ear with my shoulder.

"Sorry, Dad," he apologized in his little voice. We looked at each other for half a second and both cracked up. I put Rembrandt down, rolled over to my left, and propped myself up on my elbow.

"Aw that's nothing," I said. "Once when you were a real midget, maybe three months old, I was lying on my back on the floor holding you up doing a 'Superman'."

Rikki pointed the knife at me and nodded without looking up from the cutting board. "Yup, I remember this," she said, grinning.

"Anyway," I continued, "I'm on my back flying you around singing 'Su—per—maaan,' swoopin' you back and forth and going 'nyowww,' and all of a sudden . . . are you ready for this? You puked, 'bluhhhhh,' right in my ear!" Kai burst out laughing and a load of snot blobbed out of his nose and hung on his lip.

"Quick!" I shouted. "Go to Mom!" He jumped up and tooled into the kitchen, still laughing and trying to snort the mucus back up his little nose. Rikki put the knife down, grabbed a paper towel, and held it to Kai's face while he blew.

"Right in my ear," I said, chuckling. "Hot baby puke right in my ear."

Rikki tossed the paper towel in the garbage can under the sink, rinsed her hands off, and picked up the knife and another onion. "You think that's funny, Kai," she said, leaning forward against the counter. "Tell him, Dad."

I nodded, knowing right away what she was referring to. Parenthood and twelve years of marriage provided us with the comfortable, unspoken understanding and knowledge that comes from thousands of shared experiences. I shook my head, laughing. "You're really gonna like this, Little Man."

"What, Daddy?" Kai asked, as he padded back, plopped down, and resumed the moccasin wars. "What am I gonna like?"

"Okay," I said. "You were even littler than you were when you ralphed in my ear,"

"Ralphed," he giggled. "Daddy, you're funny."

"Hey," I said, giving him the Groucho eyebrows and air cigar. "Nobody calls me funny and gets away with it."

Now Rikki was giggling. I paused and watched her snickering and chopping vegetables. I loved seeing her laugh. Loved the sound of her laugh. Such an easy laugh. Such a good person—a good friend. And sexy as hell, too. I never got tired of looking at her. Thirty-seven-years old. Five feet six and slender. Long shapely legs that went all the way up to the buns of Navarone. Straight honey-brown hair cut just below her shoulders and large, deep blue eyes. Everyone who met her loved those eyes.

Kai poked me with his finger and whined, "C'mon, Dad."

I snapped out of my reverie. "Okay, where was I . . . oh, yeah. You were tiny, maybe four weeks old . . ." I looked up at Rikki, raising my eyebrows quizzically.

"Mm-hmm," she said. "Four weeks to the day."

"Right," I said. "Anyway, we were shooting some videotape on this old, beat-up video camera . . ." I looked up at Rikki again. "Remember that camera?" She nodded.

"Old camera," I said. "Made everything look green. So, Mom had the camera, we were sitting in the living room in our house in Nashville. You're on my lap—nude—or maybe you had a shirt on. I forget."

"He was wearing a T-shirt," Rikki piped up. "Why wasn't he wearing a diaper?"

"I don't know," she shrugged. "Airing him out?"

"Anyway," I continued, "you were sitting on my lap and Mom was shooting some video of us. And all of a sudden, 'pftthhdd,' you took a crap—on my leg!" That cracked Rikki up, and Kai fell over laughing hysterically, holding his little belly. "Right there on the video," I said, shaking my head. "Recorded for all time. The first time my kid ever crapped on me."

"Won't be the last, either," Rikki said, still laughing. Her eyes were tearing and she was sniffling—not from the story, but from the onion. "Now that was classic," she said, wiping her eyes with the sleeve of her teal cotton jersey.

Kai put Joe's butt on top of my head, stuck his tongue out and went "pftthhdd," and cracked up some more. Then he said, "Hey, Dad. Let's do Buns in Space!"

Buns in Space was a game we played where I'd lie on my back on the floor with my knees up and my feet flat. Kai would straddle me and sit down on my stomach. With my palms facing up, I'd grab hold of him by the upper thighs and butt, one cheek in each hand, and support his weight. Then in his pipsqueak voice he'd announce—and this was my favorite part—"Ladies and gentlemen, boys and girls, once again it's time for . . . BUNS . . . I—IN . . . SPA—AAA—CE!!" And as soon as he said the words, I'd start to shake him and lift him and make a sound like a rocket launching. When my arms were extended, I'd shout, "Hit the button for hyperspace!" and with his finger he'd press an imaginary button on his left knee, and I'd make an even bigger launch noise and shake him some more, lifting him higher. After a few seconds I'd make him pitch and yaw, while I coughed and sputtered like Elmer Fudd's car. "Oh no, we're going dowwwn!" I'd yell, bucking him all over the place. "Look out belowww!" He'd laugh like hell and hang on to my wrists, totally exhilarated, and then I'd gently topple him over and we'd both crack up. A second later he'd jump up and say, "Again for it, Daddy," and we'd start all over.

Kai and I hadn't done Buns in Space in a long time—at least it seemed like a long time to me. I couldn't bench-press his forty pounds anymore, and it broke my heart.

I told Kai I was sorry, but I didn't feel up to it. He shrugged it off and went back to playing. I went back to Rembrandt. Before long, Rikki told us to get ready to eat.

Immediately after dinner I had to lie down again. As usual, I didn't feel well. I had a roaring sinus infection that always seemed to get worse right after I ate. Without even clearing the table, I ambled over to the living room couch and collapsed onto it.

Rikki ushered Kai up the stairs for his bath, and I lay there looking up at the ceiling, exhausted and pissed off. I noticed a cobweb in the corner of one of the built-in oak bookshelves. Entangled in it was the crunchy carcass of a captured fly that had already had all the juice sucked out of it. *I'm dying.* I shook it off. *Damn, I'm not missing this bath!*

"Wait guys," I called, "I'm coming." I groaned, struggling to get up from the couch.

Rikki looked back down the stairs at me. "You sure?"

"Yup." I grunted and stood up. Trying not to waste energy by bending over too far, I made a stab for the moccasins and missed. I took a deep breath and grabbed for them again, and this time I got them. I shook the soldiers out, dropped the slippers to the floor, and snaked my feet into them. Then I shuffled over to the L-shaped staircase, took hold of the wrought-iron railing, and pulled myself up the oak stairs.

Rikki and Kai were in the bathroom with the tub water running. Rikki gave my arm a gentle squeeze and looked at me worriedly. I kissed her cheek and looked over at Kai. "Guess what, Little Man," I said excitedly.

"What?" he asked.

"How would you like to take a bath with shaving cream?" I picked up a can and gave it a few shakes.

He balled his little fists and threw his arms up. "Yeahhh! You mean I can shoot it?"

"Sure!" I said, glancing sideways at Rikki.

She raised her eyebrows at me and said to Kai, "Just try to keep it in the tub, honey, okay?"

"Don't worry, I will," he said gleefully.

Rikki tested the water with her fingers and turned off the faucet. "Peel and hop in, Spiderman," she said. "I'll go get your guys."

I lowered the toilet lid and sat down, ready to watch Kai go at it. Using both hands, he sprayed the first shot of shaving cream into the built-in tiled soap dish. "Coool!" he said. I smiled, agreeing that it was indeed cool for a kid to be let loose with a full can of shaving cream. I leaned back against the water tank and watched him.

In a minute Rikki came back with a clear plastic tub of action figures, and Kai carefully chose a few with his left hand, holding the shaving cream can in his right, reluctant to put down his new favorite weapon. He held up Shredder, who looked like a gladiator with serrated knives on his helmet, and blasted him with enough lather for twenty shaves. He giggled devilishly.

Rikki stood next to me, gently massaging my back with her right hand, and the room filled with that synthetic lime shaving cream smell that's supposed to make women think men are manly.

Evening had succumbed to night, and the critters in our woods were making themselves busy under the cover of darkness. I guessed that somewhere nearby somebody was throwing another log on a fire. I shifted my gaze from Kai to the large mirror on the far wall and took in Rikki's profile beside me. She looked soft and radiant.

Then I caught a glimpse of my own reflection. The harsh yellow light was not nearly as kind to me. *In two days, he'll cut me open again. It won't work. I'm a dead man.*

An hour later Spiderman was fast asleep in his bed. The shaving cream had been rinsed off the bathroom walls and floor. Rikki had cleared the table and washed the dishes, buttoned up the house, turned down the thermostat, and climbed in bed next to me.

She was wearing nothing but an oversized white T-shirt with a silk screen of the Beatles' *Let It Be* album cover on the front. Paul's picture covered her right breast and John's covered her left. George and Ringo were underneath. John and Paul were the lucky ones. Rikki and I lay facing each other, holding hands. Her skin felt warm and feminine, and she smelled like a bowl of fresh fruit from the Caswell-Massey soaps I'd bought her for our birthday.

I inhaled deeply through my nose. "Mmm," I sighed. "Strawberry?"

"Mm-mm. Pomegranate."

We lay in silence for a couple of minutes, looking into each other's eyes. Rikki spoke first. "I know you're scared about the operation," she said, squeezing my hand. "It's gonna be all right, Cam. We're going to get through this and you're going to get better."

She was talking about the dual maxillary and ethmoid sinusotomy—my fourth sinus operation, the third in four years—I was going to undergo in two days. I looked deeply into her eyes but didn't say anything.

"You've been sick for so long. You deserve to get better." She ran a hand through my hair and kissed me. "You're going to make it. I won't let you go down, you know. I won't."

"These operations never seem to work for too long, Kid," I said softly. "I don't know why. It feels like it's in my bones. Like I'm sick all the way to my bones and I can't stop it. Mercer can't help me. He's just a guy with a knife." I shook my head. "It's deeper. Something's not right. It's never been right."

We looked at each other some more. "You've been a good friend and you're a great mom," I said. Rikki squeezed my hand harder, and a tear ran down her cheek and fell onto the light blue pillowcase. "I feel like you married a lemon," I said, and then my composure crumbled and I began to cry, too. "I'm so sorry, Rik."

Rikki pulled me close to her and put my head on her shoulder. She stroked my hair and we cried together. "We'll make it," she whispered. "You'll see. Everything'll be all right."

But in my heart, I didn't really think it was true.

TWO

I pulled my silver-blue Mercedes 450SLC into a parking space in front of my office and, with grunting effort, extracted myself from the car. My brother Tom and I co-owned a company that sold custom advertising specialty products. The quantities were huge and our competitors were sharper than rats' teeth.

I'd been putting together a deal for Anson Laboratories, a client that was launching a new pharmaceutical product. I'd developed a custom promotional item for them—a futuristic-looking, plastic dosage spoon that sales reps could hand out to doctors, nurses, and pharmacists when they called on them. Anson had maybe three thousand reps and was considering buying over a million spoons. Because my design was proprietary, if the deal went down right we stood to make a couple hundred thousand dollars in profit.

I had a few things to clear up on the spoons deal before I went in for surgery the next day, if I could just focus for an hour or so. It wasn't going to be easy. For me, nothing was easy those days.

I left the crisp morning sunshine behind me and felt the buzz of busy people and fluorescent overhead lights as I walked in the glass front door of my office building. The receptionist and customer service rep were working at their computers, and my assistant, Diana, had a phone perched between her right ear and shoulder and was leaning over the fax machine, guiding an incoming fax out with both hands.

Diana was in her late twenties, pretty, with a freckled nose and straight auburn hair cut in a Dutch Boy. She was a jogger, and her face and hourglass figure probably drew a lot of whistles from men when she ran. She turned toward me, raised her eyebrows and smiled brightly, nodding and pointing at the fax. I gave her a weak smile, grunted a hello to everyone, and turned right into my office.

I closed the door, shuffled out of my jacket, and tossed it onto the maroon leather couch, narrowly missing the Raku flower vase on the coffee table. With a huff, I collapsed into my high-backed leather chair. From the other room I heard Diana's clear voice saying over the phone, "It's coming through now, Harry. Cam just got here. I'll take it right to him. Would you like to hold or should we call you back? Okay, bye."

My speakerphone intercom bleeped and Diana's voice came over it. "The fax came in from Harry," she said. "He had to take a call. I told him you'd call back. I'm coming in." Four seconds later she came briskly into my office, closed the door behind her, handed me the fax, and plunked herself down in one of the two client chairs in front of my desk, pad and pen at the ready on her lap.

The fax was a copy of the schematic of the dosage spoon that our graphic artist had drawn. There were two images, one from the top and one from the side. At the bottom of the page was a quote for a two-piece mold and a three-color imprint, with price breakdowns and turnaround times for different quantities.

I pressed Tom's intercom button. "Good morning."

"You again."

"That's what I say when I look in the mirror. The fax came in from Hairball. Diana's in here."

"I'm already there."

We were different, Tom and I, not just in age—he was older—but in most other ways. He was tall and thick, like my father, where I was of average height and wiry. He had an incredible memory, and I had to write everything down. He could wait till the last minute, trusting that whatever he was involved in would somehow come together, and I tried to be prepared for every eventuality and trusted no one. Except Rikki.

In a few seconds, Tom walked in and sat down in the other chair. I passed him the fax.

"You should be in bed," he said, without looking up.

"I'm leaving as soon as this is together," I said, taking my calculator out of my center drawer and punching in some numbers. "Oooh . . . this looks tasty."

Tom smiled a toothy smile and nodded, looking at the fax. "Scrumptious," he said.

I put the calculator down and sat up as straight as I could.

Diana grabbed her pen. I took a deep breath and began. "We're going to need a pre-pro sample, which Anson isn't going to pay for. I want Harry to split the sixty-two hundred for the mold with us—he'll do that; it's probably only two g's to him. He's got to turn the spec sample around—with the threecolor hit—in a week. No less than two dozen of 'em."

Tom said, "Have him send them to my attention, Diana, and label it urgent. They've got to be perfect."

"Handwerker's going to want to pass some around Purchasing," I said, "and tell everybody they were his idea. Harry says if we make a million of them he'll keep the overrun to 3 percent. We're going to tell Handwerker that plus or minus 5 percent constitutes a completed order, and we'll have Harry overrun 4, maybe 4½, percent depending on the quantity. I'll run the numbers again and call Handwerker, and then you can fax him the final quote. This is our deal, our turn to pillage. When this is over Genghis Khan is gonna want to join our fan club."

Diana finished jotting notes and looked up.

"That's it," I said, sinking back into my chair. "Thanks."

"Got it," Diana said, tapping her pen on her notepad. She got up and hustled out of my office, closing the door behind her.

Tom stood up. "Nice going, Killer," he chuckled, shaking his head. "Genghis Khan." He stopped at the door and turned to me. "Go home."

"Ten minutes," I told him, wiping a little sweat off my forehead with my shirt sleeve.

I worked out the final quote and called Handwerker with it.

He seemed pretty happy about the price, although I knew he'd beat on me some before it was over. I reminded him that my design was proprietary, and he assured me it wouldn't bid out. We hung up and I had Diana fax him the quote. That was it for me; I was done. I could go home and collapse.

Before leaving, I stopped in the restroom to splash some cold water on my face. I hunched over the sink, supporting myself with my left hand, ladling water onto my face with my right. With my eyes shut tightly I groped for some paper towels, wiped off my face, and tossed the wet towels into the trashcan. I fumbled for my wire-rimmed glasses, which I'd perched on the corner of the sink, and put them on. I opened my eyes and checked my reflection in the mirror, and as I did, something bizarre happened.

A sudden jolt shot through me like an electric shock, and my whole body trembled for just a second. Then I began to mumble gibberish, like I was trying to say something, but had lost control of my mouth.

Terrified, I looked in the mirror again and saw a reflection—mine—disconnected, staring blankly, mumbling. I tried to decipher my words but they were unintelligible. *What's happening to me?!* And then, with another jolt and shake, I was back and the mumbling stopped. I slumped to the floor, chest heaving, heart racing. The tile felt cold against my hands.

After a couple of minutes I pulled myself to a standing position, relieved that no one had walked in on me. *You're a very sick person. Go home.*

I shuffled to my office, shrugged on my jacket, and left without saying goodbye to anyone. I made it home without hitting anything, dragged myself upstairs, and passed out until dinnertime. I didn't tell Rikki what had happened.

The next morning at nine I went under the knife. Rikki stayed with me all day and through the night, holding my hand and feeding me ice chips to soothe my scorched throat, while I lay in a wretched hospital bed with packing up my nose and stitches in my gums, feeling like my face had been rolled over by a Case combine.

Dr. Mercer said the operation was a success, but a few days after I got home I developed a severe infection in my right maxillary sinus. The pressure from the infection burst open the sutures over my right upper teeth, where my gums had been cut to access the sinus cavity, and I was left with a gaping hole.

My immune system was in such a weakened state from the years of antibiotics, the illness, and the surgery itself, that battling the infection was like trying to hold back a tsunami with a parasol. Although I'd walked the rocky path of chronic illness for a long time, I'd never actually kicked a stone over the precipice of death. But now I felt like I was sliding over the edge, desperately clawing at the loose scree, scrambling for a foothold, while thick black smoke and searing embers belched from the reaper's fiery mouth as he beckoned me in.

About a week after I'd returned home, I was in my usual position, flat on my back under the covers, a cold, damp mist from the humming vaporizer blanketing my face to make swallowing easier. I couldn't breathe through my nose, and my throat felt like it had been worked over with a wire brush. A videotape of M*A*S*H reruns played endlessly in the background, and I stared at the white stucco ceiling, my head feeling like a hand grenade with the pin missing.

The phone rang. Kai was at school, and Rikki was out grocery shopping; it was just me, my misery, and the gang from the 4077th. I clicked the mute button on the TV gizmo with my right hand and pawed for the receiver with my left.

"Hello," I rasped.

It was Tom. "Hey pal, how're you feeling?" he asked, in the chipper way people do when they know you're suffering and don't really know what to say.

"Never better," I croaked, but it came out "nare bear." My face felt like I was wearing a thirty-pound mask lined with needles.

"The pre-pro samples came in," Tom said, "and Handwerker loved 'em. The deal's going down today, but I really think you're the guy to close it. You were right about Handjob. He's really hard to read." Tom paused. "I'm sorry to bug you with this, Cam, but it's your deal."

I sighed deeply, still looking at the ceiling. *Oh, brother.*

"Did you hear me?"

"Uh huh," I mumbled.

"Are you up to it?"

"Yeah," I lied. "Hold on." I put the receiver down and reached over to switch off the vaporizer. Now came the hard part. Like an ancient rusty crane, I slowly shifted to an upright position and placed my stockinged feet on the rug. I felt feverish and dizzy. My eyes focused on Rikki's open closet, and for half a second I wondered what she was wearing. I slowly and painfully turned my head toward the telephone and picked up the receiver again. It felt heavy. With a great effort to speak clearly, I said, "Okay. Where're we at?"

The deal was a phone call away from closing, which is the very point at which deals can go in the hopper.

"All right," I grunted. "Have Diana call Handwerker and patch me through. I don't think I'll be able to remember the number if you tell me, and I don't see a pencil." Tom said he'd do it right away and hung up. I put the receiver down and noticed a yellow-lined pad of paper and pencil right next to the phone. *Focus.*

The phone rang again less than a minute later. It was Diana.

She told me she was going to connect me. I said, "Mmff," and suddenly a very odd change took place. My body shook briefly, like a shiver, and instantly my head cleared. It was as if I were still lying on the bed buried under the rubble of my illness while someone else sat up, lucid and focused—as if I weren't alone. Gone, but not gone. A second later I heard Handwerker's game voice on the phone.

"Louis Handwerker."

"Hi, Louis, Cameron West. Sorry I'm talking funny. My mouth's not completely healed." He made a joke about my needing to stop having operations every time I wanted a vacation. I faked a chuckle and got down to business.

It took maybe three minutes to hammer out the specifics of the deal. I pushed him to take more of the dosage spoons than he needed then or would ever need. He balked, and I promised to take him to Rosie's Kitchen for the tamales and buy him a Baby Ruth afterward, which really meant that I'd buy him the top-of-the-line treadmill he'd hinted at and have it delivered to his house. In the end, we settled on 1.2 million spoons, and he gave me a purchase order number and asked me to fax him the deal. He told me to take care of myself and said goodbye. It was done.

I called the office and gave Tom the specifics. He was ecstatic and said he'd handle the rest. He called Handwerker a "chiselin' rat" and told me to take it easy, and we both hung up.

And then, just as quickly as it had emerged, the power I'd experienced disappeared. I was sweating and shaking. I switched on the vaporizer and leaned my face into the cold fog. Grunting, I gingerly lowered myself back down onto the pillow and pulled the comforter up to my chin. My face throbbed, and the inside of my head glowed and pulsed like an ambulance light. I pressed the mute button to get back to M*A*S*H and glanced at the television. Colonel Henry Blake was whooping it up because he'd just found out he was shipping out of Korea—he was going home. I'd seen this episode before and knew that the plane taking Henry back to the States would get shot down. In a week he'd be dead. I wondered if I would be, too.

THREE

Over the next six weeks Rikki shuttled me back and forth to Dr. Mercer's a total of seven times. The first few times Mercer rinsed my sinuses with saline solution. The rinsing wasn't like going to the dentist, where you swish around a teaspoonful of pink bubble-gum-tasting liquid and spit. Nope. This kind of rinsing involved jamming a tube connected to a syringe the size of a turkey baster through the hole in my gums into the hole in my face and blasting saline solution against the inner walls of my maxillary sinuses, while I hung my burning face over a big stainless steel bowl.

Mercer kept adjusting the antibiotic cocktail to get the infection under control until the rattler that had me by the throat finally let go and slithered away. Then he sewed up the gaping hole in my gums. There was so little gingiva left and he had to restitch three times just to get the sutures to hold.

I was in trouble. Traditional medicine had gotten me to a place where life wasn't life at all, but an arid and desolate outpost, where vultures hovered, waiting to turn what was left of me into bleached bones. My sweet Rikki's loving care and Kai's joyful laugh could reach me and soothe me, but they couldn't save me. I had to save myself.

It was 10:20 on a Thursday morning when I made the decision to live. Light from the fat December sun poured through our bedroom window, giving everything in the room a whitish glow. Kai was at school,

Rikki was at the gym, and the house was silent except for the hum of the heater. I threw the covers off, slid over to Rikki's side of the bed, and slowly got up. I looked out the front window, and the glare off the snow-covered lawn made me wince. I shook out my arms and tried jogging in place for two steps. That was enough.

I dressed quickly in old blue jeans, a heavy black cable-knit sweater, and my green-and-brown suede Avia low-top hiking shoes. I went to the bathroom, but didn't bother to shave or comb my hair. That required too much energy. I slowly creaked my way downstairs, went to the closet, and got out the gray wool overcoat and black gloves Rikki had bought for me at Louis of Boston. I worked my way into them and opened the front door.

Taking a deep breath, I stepped out onto the porch. The cold slapped me in the face like a ruler on a school desk, and I suddenly realized that I'd forgotten the keys. I turned around, went back to the kitchen, and plucked the keys to our silver Volvo station wagon from the key rack. If I'd gotten down to the car before realizing I didn't have the keys, I might not have been able to go at all. Just getting into my coat had sapped half my steam.

I walked back into the cold, down the stone steps and walkway, which Rikki had cleared of the few inches of snow that had fallen the night before, and down the ten railroad-tie steps to the car. I had a plan.

I hadn't driven in over two months and was actually worried that I might not have the energy to work the controls. I started the car and drove the two hundred feet down to the end of the driveway and stopped. *Good. Stopping is good.* I turned right onto our street and drove four miles into the center of town. Just before the Stop & Shop I took a right into the parking lot of a little strip mall that housed a deli, a hair salon, a realtor, an educational toy store, a wine shop, and a health food store. I pulled in front of Natural Selection Health Foods and parked without crashing. I grunted and slowly emerged from the car, stepped carefully up onto the sidewalk, and went into the store.

The shop was tiny, about 12 by 30, packed to the epaulettes with enough health food products to fill a supermarket. There was just enough room to move if no other customers came in. To the right, behind the counter, sat a scrawny girl about eighteen years old with long, stringy brown hair that looked like it hadn't been washed more than twice since George Bush puked on that Japanese guy. When I walked in she'd just taken a big bite of an Italian sub that I guessed had come from the deli. The girl stopped chewing for a second and put the sandwich down on its paper. She looked at me and shrugged as if to say, "Oops."

"Is that a healthy sandwich?" I said, managing a mini-grin with the half of my face that worked.

She flashed a smile that reminded me of wax fruit, then stared at me vacantly with the lump of food jammed in her cheek. "My boyfriend works at the sub shop," she mumbled and started chewing again. I glanced down at her sandwich. Next to it was a bag of chips and a grape soda. Mmm, health food.

I felt weak and wanted to lean on something, but was afraid if I touched anything a domino effect might take place and everything in the store would come crashing down.

"I need some help," I said. "Do you know if the owner has a list of holistic practitioners in the area?" My face hurt, and the stitches in my gums were digging into my cheek.

She shook her head, swallowed, and said, "We don't, but there's a lady named Hanna at Geneva Farm on Route 226 who knows everybody. She could probably help you."

She said it was only about five miles away and explained how to get there. I thanked her, sucked in my shoulders, and turned to walk out, careful not to hit anything.

The kid's directions were good, and in less than ten minutes I found the place. Geneva Farm was a small, single-story, rustic-looking house that stood about thirty feet from an identical, larger, single-story, rustic-looking house about a hundred feet down a gravel drive off a narrow two-lane road in a semirural section of town.

There was a white-and-red plastic sign that said OPEN on the raised-panel wood door. It was eleven-thirty in the morning and already past my bedtime, but I was on a mission, so I hobbled up to the door and went in. Some hanging bells jingled when I opened the door and again when I closed it. As I stepped into the room, I was immediately met with the cozy smell of orange and spices drifting off the steam curls rising from the spout of a teapot that stood on a small hot plate on the counter.

Behind the counter a tall, sturdy-looking woman, somewhere between forty and fifty, wearing a white sweatshirt and overalls, was using a metal scoop to pour herbs onto a scale. She had a well-scrubbed face with no makeup and long brown and gray hair pulled back in a ponytail. She looked up at me with clear and vibrant blue eyes and smiled warmly. In her smile was a pleasant air of self-confidence and compassion. She had to be Hanna.

"Hi," she said.

"Hi," I said back.

Hanna held the metal scoop loosely in her right hand while she looked me over. Then she tilted her head slightly and her smile disappeared. She put the scoop down on the counter.

"You are very ill," she said in a thick Swiss accent. Her words jolted me and tears welled up in my eyes, but I choked them back. I took a deep breath, exhaled slowly, and nodded.

I said, "Somebody from Natural Selection Health Foods said you might know of a good holistic practitioner in the area. You are Hanna, aren't you?"

She nodded. "Yah."

"I've had some sinus operations that didn't work out too well. Maybe you know someone who can help."

"Mmm," she nodded again. "I have a list in the house. I'll get it."

Hanna walked briskly out and then quickly turned back as if she'd forgotten something. She stuck her head in, pointed at the pot, and said, "Oh, if you'd like some tea, help yourself." And she disappeared again.

"Thank you," I said loudly, but Hanna was already halfway to her house. The tea smelled great, but I was fading and felt like if I didn't get out of there in the next few minutes I'd have to ask Hanna if she had a cot in the back room. Tea and a chat were out.

I looked around the small shop. There were about fifteen oak barrels filled with different teas and grains. Built into one wall was an oak unit of little bins that housed maybe a hundred different kinds of herbs, and off to one side was a low freestanding magazine rack with half a dozen holistic-type magazines. I would have picked one up, but it was too far to reach.

In less than a minute, Hanna came back with the list. She came around the counter and stood next to me, flipped the first page over, and ran her index finger down until she found what she was looking for—Lloyd Kessler, M.D. Hanna tapped the paper twice with her finger and looked at me. "This guy is very good," she said. "He has a big practice in Cambridge. He's a psychiatrist who went into natural healing when his daughter got very sick. I'll write his name down for you."

"Thank you very much," I said, leaning on her counter for support.

Hanna wrote the name and number on a yellow sticky pad, tore it off, and handed it to me. She looked at me again with kind blue eyes and said, "Go home now and rest. And call that man."

"I will." I nodded, smiling the best I could. "Thank you, Hanna."

I walked out the door, jingling the bell as I stepped into the cold. The winter air felt jagged in my lungs and against my skin, and I was a little light-headed as I groaned and slumped behind the wheel.

I drove home carefully, hobbled upstairs, climbed in bed with my clothes on, and slept like a dead person.

I put off calling Dr. Kessler all winter. I guess my grip on life was so tight and so tenuous that I had trouble letting go long enough to give him a chance. Rikki provided gentle care and support, and eventually I was able to return to work, albeit at a greatly reduced schedule. But by March I was once again lower than a snake's ass in a wagon wheel rut, and when I bent down in an airport to get something out of my overnight bag and couldn't get back up, I decided it was time to make the call.

Two weeks later I was at Kessler's office. Hanna was right about the guy having a booming practice. It took up half of one floor in a large modern office complex. He had a staff of more than twenty, including a nutritionist, a physician's assistant, an acupuncturist, nurses, doctors, lab technicians, and people manning the in-house health food store.

When I first saw Dr. Kessler, he was standing behind his large desk in his spacious walnut-paneled office, facing a wall of windows, drinking a glass of something that looked like swamp water. He finished drinking, put down the empty glass, and patted his lips with a white handkerchief. He shook my hand, smiled without warmth, and waved me to one of the three client chairs in front of his desk.

Dr. Kessler was about fifty, tall and thin, with a doughy face and a full head of curly white hair that gave him the appearance of being older. He read the extensive medical history his physician's assistant had pumped from me during the previous hour and asked me some additional questions about my symptoms and my diet. And then to my surprise, without examining me at all, Kessler told me he believed he could help me get well. Just like that. With an angstrom of hope, I said I'd try whatever he suggested.

Lloyd put me on a strict elimination diet for a few weeks and had me take a number of different vitamin supplements, enzymes, immune system boosters, and antitoxins. I took a food allergy test, which showed that I was allergic to more than a hundred different substances, including wheat and all dairy products. Incredibly, it appeared that my sinus infections had all been caused by eating foods I was allergic to.

The dozens of courses of antibiotics Mercer had poured down my throat had weakened my immune system so much that it couldn't have kicked the skin off a rice pudding, let alone knock out a common cold. On top of that, since Mercer had never told me to take acidophilus with the antibiotics, I'd developed a severe case of candidiasis, which, left untreated, could have killed me.

To my total dismay, for a while I felt even sicker than I had when I'd crawled into Kessler's office—like pure poison was coursing through my veins. He'd told me that might happen, but that if I just stuck with it and didn't go jumping off any bridges, I'd feel better before long. So I kept at it, even though I wanted to throttle the guy three or four times a day. Sure enough, after two months, the vultures were finally gone.

For the whole spring and summer I stuck to my new diet and wouldn't have touched a cheese steak sub if you gave me ten bucks. By the fall I was feeling and looking almost lifelike. I resumed working full-time and wasn't getting lost in my hometown anymore. I even managed Buns in Space with Kai again, which made me cry with joy. Rikki wasn't there when that happened or she would've cried, too. She was thrilled to hear about it, though, and hugged me like she wasn't afraid I'd break.

Rikki looked even more vibrant than usual. She stepped lightly and breathed easily, as if it were the last day of school.

She had her man back . . . or so she thought.

FOUR

On a late afternoon in early October, Rikki and I sat side by side in forest-green Adirondack chairs on our large deck. The hues of the autumn foliage reminded me of Trix cereal. Kai was playing at a buddy's house and we were enjoying a rare moment of peace and privacy. The day had been unseasonably warm, but the chill of approaching dusk sent Rikki into the house to get a sweater and a blanket. She closed the sliding glass door behind her as she came out, cozied up on her chair, and draped the blanket over both of us. It was time to tell her.

I took her hand in mine. She saw the look on my face and the peacefulness in hers evaporated. She looked at me intently. "What's wrong?" she asked. I was afraid she meant "What now?" and it made me cringe.

I shook my head. "I don't know exactly," I said, "but something . . . it feels like the inside of my head is very loud. Something in my head . . . in my mind . . . is shifting constantly. I don't know what to make of it. I'm worried."

Rikki turned in her chair to face me fully, still holding my hand. She rested her gaze on me and listened with all of herself while I told her about the bizarre loss of control I'd experienced in the company washroom the previous year and the strange way I'd felt "taken over" when I'd talked to Handwerker on the phone from my sickbed. Her eyes grew more intense when I told her how since I'd regained my health I'd been experiencing the oddest feelings in my head, like things were shifting—aligning and realigning in layers and concentric circles. And then I was through talking and we sat quietly, looking at each other.

Rikki has a degree in psychology and had worked with emotionally disturbed kids for ten years before Kai was born. Once she'd stopped a seven-year-old boy from hanging himself. Another time she'd talked a ten-year-old girl in from the ledge of a three-story building. Rikki knew a sip from a swallow. And she could tell there was something wrong with me that vitamins wouldn't fix.

She squeezed my hand. "Maybe you need to see a therapist," she said with great concern. A gust of wind blew a wisp of her hair across her face and I gently brushed it away with the back of my hand.

I nodded with a sad smile and said, "Maybe I do."

The faint outline of the moon peeked through a veil of ever deepening purple clouds. The first star would soon be out. *I sure could use a wish.*

FIVE

The next day I went looking for a therapist in the local yellow pages under "Psychologists." There were a lot of them, and I didn't have any idea whom to choose so I just picked one, Arly Morelli, Ph.D., because she had a large ad that made her appear very experienced and professional. I dialed her number and left a message on her answering machine.

She called me back later that day. The first thing that struck me was her heavy New York accent; she sounded tough, but her carefully chosen words conveyed warmth and compassion. We chatted for longer than I would have expected. Her questions were penetrating, and I got the feeling she was checking me out as much as I was her; she wanted a match, someone she could relate to, not just a fee. I liked her. We set up an appointment for the next morning.

Her office was on the second floor of an attractive brick building on the main street in the town next to ours. The building, like most in the center of town, had been built in the early part of the century. I walked up a creaky old wooden staircase to the second floor and took a seat at the top of the stairs on an iron bench with oak slats.

On the wall opposite the bench was an antique blue-stained wooden bookcase filled with books on psychology, relationships, family dynamics, divorce, and nutrition. I noticed six little hardcover children's books in the corner, too. Hanging on the wall above the bookcase was a broken sword that had been mounted on a large piece of bright red wood. I was the only patient waiting in the hall. *Good.*

I sat down nervously with ten minutes to kill and looked absently out a wavy double-hung window that must have been there before Harry dropped the big one. Across the street was a classic red-brick firehouse, and in its tiny front yard birds flitted around in a maple tree. My hands were cold even though it was a warm and sunny fall day, and I kept rubbing my right hand against my thigh so when Dr. Morelli shook it I wouldn't give her frostbite.

Before long I heard some voices coming from the office, and then the raised panel door opened and an attractive middle-aged woman, wearing an expensive dark blue business suit, emerged into the hall carrying a huge tan leather purse. For a second I thought she was Dr. Morelli and I got a little blast of fear, but she looked at the floor, carefully avoiding making eye contact, and quickly hurried past me down the stairs and out of the building. My heart didn't slow down, though, because I knew I was up next. I rubbed my hand on my pants a few more times.

About thirty seconds later the real Arly Morelli stepped into the hallway. Her face looked exactly like her voice had sounded on the phone—Mulberry Street. But her eyes were Monte Carlo—sharper than the crease in a gambler's pants. She had a bushel of black hair and a crooked nose. She was medium height, trim, in her early forties, and she wore a long black linen jacket over a white shirt, a bolo tie, and faded blue jeans. There were no shoes on her stockinged feet. I noticed a ring with a big cobalt blue stone on the middle finger of her right hand.

She smiled at me and said, "Hi. I'm Arly Morelli. Are you Cameron West?"

"Cam," I said, smiling tentatively.

She offered me her hand. I took it and it felt warm and strong. I bet mine just felt cold.

Arly's office was small and narrow with a high ceiling, white walls with crown molding, and a big window that looked just like the one at the top of the stairs. The wooden floor was dark from age, mostly covered with an oriental carpet in deep shades of red and gold. On the right wall were two matching light brown chairs separated by a glass-topped table with a ceramic cat and a tall box of Kleenex on it. In the corner stood a hat rack filled with hats from the days of cigarette holders and cars with running boards.

Arly's chair was maroon leather and there was a round leather ottoman in front of it that looked like it was meant to be shared. A tan portfolio lay on her chair and a black Montblanc pen stuck out of the crease in the middle of it.

Arly waved me to the chair opposite hers and scooped up her portfolio. We both sat down. She put her feet on the ottoman. I left mine flat on the floor and squirmed around in my chair trying to get comfortable. There was no chance of that happening no matter how much squirming I did; I was wishing I hadn't called her in the first place.

Arly flipped open the portfolio, pulled out the pen, smiled and said, "I hope you don't mind. I like to take notes."

I nodded. "Go ahead." I felt my emotions surging. *This is a mistake. I'm outta here.*

"Well then, Cam," she said, "tell me why you've sought therapy." *Too late.* She hit a bleeder with the first stab and all of a sudden tears welled up in my eyes. I looked down, trying to blink them back.

I swallowed hard and said, "Something is very wrong with me. I . . . I think I lost my soul." And then my shoulders shook and I began to cry softly. *Damn! I've been here thirty seconds and I'm already crying! My soul. Oh brother.* Arly reached over and offered me a Kleenex. I took it without looking at her.

She leaned back and studied me. "You lost your soul," she repeated, making a note on the yellow pad. I nodded, covering my eyes with my right hand and blotting the tears. I sniffled, took a fresh tissue, and blew my nose.

For the next fifty minutes Arly asked me background questions—about my relationship with Rikki, my job, my illness. Toward the end of the session she asked me if I'd ever been to a therapist before.

"Um . . . actually I saw someone a few times when I was fifteen," I said.

"How come?"

I cleared my throat and nervously picked a piece of lint off my pants. Then our eyes met.

"I tried to kill myself by swallowing a bottle of aspirin."

Arly raised her eyebrows and wrote some more. "Your folks took you to a therapist after the suicide attempt?"

I stretched, yawned, rubbed my neck and looked out the window. "You know," I said, "I used to want to be a psychologist. When I was nine or ten. Wanted to know what happens to the mind—"

"Cam?"

"What?" I looked back at her. "Oh," I said. "No. They didn't take me to see anybody. I took myself to a clinic and talked to someone a few times. They never said another word about it. It was a secret. It didn't happen. Hell, I practically forgot about it till you started poking around."

"A secret," Arly said.

It wasn't a question so I didn't say anything.

She put her pen down and laced her fingers. "Cam," she said, "how much of your childhood do you remember?"

I shifted in my seat and looked out the window some more. Arly waited.

"I got a belt with a big buckle for my tenth birthday."

"Nothing before that?"

A flash of anger jabbed me. "What are you looking for? There's nothing to know."

Arly said nothing. She just looked at me.

"Sorry," I said, embarrassed I'd snapped at a total stranger.

She waved it off. "What do you remember about the houses you lived in?"

"Just a little. The kitchens. TV rooms . . ."

"Anything else? Your bedrooms?"

"No. Don't remember them. The hallways go to nowhere."

"To nowhere," she repeated, picking up her pen and rolling it back and forth between her fingers.

"I don't remember. Are you going to write something or are you just giving your pen a massage? Sorry, this is hard."

"What was your parents' relationship like?"

"They never fought. I suppose she told him what to do and he did it. They were very different. Her father was a banker and his father owned a chicken store."

She started writing again, alternately glancing at me and her notes. "What was he like . . . your dad?"

"I don't know. I never really knew him."

"What about your mother?"

"Christ, my mother. Ask me something else."

"All right. Your brother. What was it like growing up with him?"

"I don't know. Okay, I guess. I don't remember. He looked like my father and I looked like her."

She stopped writing. "What do you mean?"

"I don't know."

"You looked like her."

"I was her favorite. I was a good boy."

I glanced at the clock. It was ten to. Our time was up. Arly asked if I wanted to set up a regular meeting. I hesitated for maybe half a minute before saying yes.

I wrote her a check, said goodbye, and walked into the hallway. Someone was sitting on the bench and I instinctively shifted my gaze to the floor just as the woman in the business suit had. I walked quickly down the stairs and out the door. The air felt chillier and it made me shiver.

Arly and I started off at once a week, but we moved it to twice pretty quickly. And it wasn't because it was fun. The more I went, the worse I felt. She'd ask a question and sit there with her stockinged feet up on that ottoman and write and look up and ask another question and write some more. She never gave her opinion about anything; she just let me stew around, and it pissed me off. But I kept coming back.

The shifting in my mind increased, and faint confusing whispers licked at me like flames up the inside of an old chimney. Sleep became more difficult, too, as the darkness amplified the rumble of a comet hurtling at me from the edge of my universe.

And then, deep one cold and moonless December night, I abruptly awoke from a heavy sleep and my eyes opened wide to the bedroom's pitch blackness. The stillness of the freezing night had been shattered by three words that kept repeating in my head. *Safe not safe . . . safe not safe . . . safe not safe.*

What the hell?

The eerie phrase droned on. *Safe not safe . . . safe not safe.* My heart beat wildly and I was shivering as if I'd fallen through the ice on a skating pond. My fists were clenched tightly and I unballed them and touched the sheets, realizing that they were soaked with cold sweat.

Safe not safe . . . safe not safe . . . safe not safe. The bizarre phrase repeated in my head. *STOPPPP!!!* I looked over at Rikki, who was facing away from me, fast asleep. *Safe not safe . . . safe not safe.* I clapped my hands over my ears, desperately trying to block the chilling phrase. I heard the heater kick on in the basement.

Guided by some strange force, I reached to my left and took a pen and notepad from my nightstand, the wrenching words incessantly marching in my head. In the darkness I began to write, "safe not safe safe not safe," over and over again. The words filled a page. I couldn't stop writing. "Safe not safe safe not safe." I turned the page and Rikki stirred. I was afraid I might wake her.

I got up carefully, the pad in one hand and the pen in the other, my body shivering in the dark from the shock of the cool air on my damp skin. *What's happening to me?*

I went downstairs without dressing, no light but the blue digital clock on the stove as I passed the kitchen, no sound but the whirring of the heater. In a strange otherworldliness, I glided through the living room, across the hallway, and into the blue room at the front of the house where the baby grand piano stood. My bare feet slid across the soft carpet, the words repeating loudly in my head: *safe not safe . . . safe not safe.*

Without turning on the light, I sat down mechanically, slid under the piano, and resumed copying the message in the inky darkness. Time was liquid and my hand cramped from its tight grip on the pen, but I couldn't loosen it, and I couldn't stop writing. "Safe not safe safe not safe safe not safe." Two pages, three, four, five. Then there was a change. "Safe not safe" became "not safe not safe not safe." I continued writing in the blackness under the piano, feeling nothing. I was somewhere else, but where?

safe not safe safe not safe safe not safe
safe not safe safe not safe safe
not safe safe not safe safe not safe
safe not safe safe not safe safe
not safe safe not safe safe not safe
safe not safe safe not safe safe
not safe safe not safe safe not safe
safe not safe safe not safe safe
not safe safe not safe safe not safe
safe not safe safe not safe safe
not safe safe not safe safe not safe
safe not safe safe not safe safe
not safe safe not safe safe not safe
safe not safe safe not safe safe
not safe safe not safe safe not safe
safe not safe, not safe, not safe
not safe not safe not safe not
safe not safe not safe not safe
not safe not safe not safe not safe
not safe, not safe not safe not
safe not safe not safe not safe
not safe, not safe, not safe not
safe not safe not safe not safe
not safe not safe not safe not
safe not safe not safe not safe
not safe not safe not safe not
safe not safe not safe not safe
not safe not safe not safe not safe
not safe not safe not safe not safe
not safe not safe not safe not safe
not safe not safe not safe not safe
not safe not safe not safe not safe

An excerpt from the pages written the night of safe not safe.

After some period of time the words in my head suddenly ceased and my hand stopped writing. I put the pen down. For a brief moment I felt strangely peaceful. Numb. Then I gradually began to feel again, a light tingle like a wind chime echoing in my mind and body. Then it wasn't just a tingle. I winced in pain as I tried to wiggle my fingers. A creeping fear and confusion filled me like a pitcher of something foul. *What the hell just happened?* Naked and cold, I sat in the stillness trying to loosen my aching fingers, wanting and not wanting to understand.

After a few minutes I gave up and crawled out from under the strange safety of the piano and quietly headed back upstairs to bed. I stopped in the bathroom at the top of the stairs and picked up two dry bath towels to place between my body and the sweat-soaked sheets. I climbed into bed, closed my eyes, and fell into a thick and dreamless sleep.

The next morning I awoke early and immediately reached for the yellow pad on my nightstand. *Maybe it didn't happen.* But it had. There were the words repeated over and over: "safe not safe safe not safe." I flipped through six pages until "safe not safe" turned into "not safe not safe," and that rambled on for another four pages. *Not good. Definitely not good.* I woke Rikki up, showed her the pad, and told her what had happened.

"God, what's happening to you?" she said, frightened, her soft face puffy from sleep.

"I don't know," I said, shaking my head. I pulled her to me and we held each other tightly, wanting whatever it was to go away.

It was Sunday. The day passed quietly. Rikki and I played with Kai and read books to him. We watched Bugs Bunny cartoons, which distracted and comforted me and made Kai laugh out loud. Neither Rikki nor I said a word about what had happened; we let it lie. And strange feelings began to seep into my consciousness from very dark places in my mind.

That night, after Kai was asleep and we were in bed, I turned to Rikki. "I think something terrible happened to me . . . but I don't know what."

Rikki pulled me to her and held me close and it occurred to me that she wasn't just holding me; she was holding *on* to me and I was holding on to her. I looked out our bedroom window into the thick night and, without my glasses on, the three-quarter moon looked like a giant cotton ball. For a second I wished it would come down from the sky and swab me like a naked baby in a bassinet. I didn't know then that it would to take a cotton ball a whole lot bigger than the moon to get me clean.

SIX

Snow had fallen during the night, and I arose early in the morning to the wintry sound of a four-wheel-drive snowplow clearing our long, steep driveway—the clank of the plow dropping, the scrape of the blade on the pavement, the whine of the transmission as the jeep backed up to make another pass. Clank scrrraaape whine. Clank scrrraaape whine.

The action inside my head was nowhere near as coordinated or predictable. Normal neurological pathways felt piled high with heavy snow, while driverless microscopic plows forged random routes through my brain.

Pants. I need pants. Gotta get a pair of pants. Shower. Shave. Dress. Forget food. Kiss Kai. Kiss Rikki. Go. Not to work—to get pants.

I started the Benz and did the luge thing down the driveway, swinging around the plow that had just finished clearing the bottom. *Which way? Left, to work? No, right. Where am I going? Pants.*

The Lincoln Common was a snappy-looking outlet mall situated ten minutes from our house just off Route 128. It was designed to look like a New England village, with blue-and-cream fake clapboard siding, cobblestone footpaths, fake gaslights, and carved and gilded wood signs. Plows had already cleared the expansive parking lot, and I pulled in and parked. *What am I doing here? Oh yeah . . . pants.*

My wire-rimmed glasses fogged for a second when I stepped out of the car into the damp cold, and I squinted up at the spotlight of sun behind a thin section of swollen gray clouds. My glasses cleared and I noticed there were only two other cars in the lot. *Pants.*

I walked over to a cobblestone path and started looking in windows until I found pants. The lights were out. I shook the door. Closed. I moved on and tried another store. Then another. All locked. *Shit! They sell pants. Why can't I get pants?* The sky started to spit snow and several flakes fell down my neck. I shivered and huddled deeper into my coat. *What's going on? Why can't I get pants?* Then in an instant of clarity, it occurred to me: *The mall's not open yet.* I pushed back the sleeve of my coat and looked at my watch. *Eight-thirty.* I sat down on the cold, snowy cobblestones and noticed I was only wearing one sock. And then I was gone . . . somewhere.

When I came back, my first thought was that my ass was cold. Then I realized I was sitting on the ground. Where? I looked around. A shopping center? Yeah, Lincoln Common. I'm sitting on the ground in the snow at Lincoln Common. Whoa! What am I doing here? Oh yeah, pants. Pants? I'm getting out of here.

I got up, brushed the snow off the back of my coat, and hurried toward the parking lot. There were maybe fifteen cars there now. *Which car am I driving, silver or blue?*

I spotted the Benz near the entrance, parked perpendicular to the lines that marked the spaces. The driver's door was ajar. As I walked toward the car, I reached into the right pocket of my coat and felt the keys through my black leather gloves. I got in the car and tried the ignition. It roared to life. *Thank God.*

Not knowing where I was going, I pulled onto Route 128 and headed north. I looked up at a green-and-white highway sign. "Lexington one mile," a strange voice said aloud, slowly, carefully pronouncing each syllable. *What the hell?* I glanced at the passenger seat to see if someone was sitting next to me. "Speed limit six five," the voice said as I passed a speed sign.

The voice was coming out of my mouth, but it didn't sound like me; it was tentative and childlike. *Hey! I don't read road signs out loud!*

But this voice did. My heart raced, my neck was stiff, and I felt like my mouth had been shot up with Novocain. My eyes dropped to the speedometer. *Twenty-two miles an hour.* The young voice read another exit sign aloud, slowly and deliberately, "Ant-eye-och Road." *Wait. Antioch Road. Not so busy.*

Get off here. I exited the four-lane highway in slow motion, my left hand cautiously feeding the steering wheel to my right. *Two lanes. No traffic. Better.*

My breath was coming in short gasps and I felt panicked. The voice read another sign off in the distance, in front of a large brick building. "Har-bing-er P-siich . . . . *What? Holy shit! Harbinger Psychiatric Hospital. Maybe they can help me. I've got to pull in there.* But I couldn't. I pulled into a parking lot I thought was the right one, but it didn't connect to the hospital lot and must have been for the building next to it. I could see the hospital up on a hill just a few hundred yards away. *Right there! I can get help right there!*

I pulled out and took a left, but drove past the hospital and pulled into the wrong lot again. *SHIIITITT!* I stopped the car and looked across the parking lot at the psychiatric hospital, this time from the other side of it. I realized I must have been looking at the back of the building, that the entrance had to be somewhere on the other side. I put the car in park and rested my head on the steering wheel, totally exasperated.

Then I looked over at the passenger seat and noticed the cell phone. *Arly.* I couldn't remember the number so I pulled my gloves off and fumbled in my wallet until I found her card. *What did she say I could do in an emergency? Dial the number and let it ring once and hang up, then immediately dial it again.* I picked the phone up off the seat and switched it on. My hands were shaking. *Please be there!* I dialed, heard the phone ring once, and hung up. The second time I dialed, Arly answered after the first ring.

"This is Dr. Morelli," she said.

Sweat dripped down my lip and tasted salty, and my heartbeat sounded like an elephant getting hit with a broom. The words gushed out.

"Arly, it's Cam. I don't know what's happening. I'm in my car. A voice is talking out loud. My voice, but not my voice. Something's wrong. I was sitting in the snow. I tried to buy pants. My car was open. I tried to go to a hospital. That hospital!" I shouted, jabbing my finger at the building in the distance.

"Cam, calm down," Arly said. "Hold on a minute."

"Okay," I said, my breath coming fast. "Okay."

I waited, hunched over the steering wheel, the phone pressed to my right ear, watching huge fluffy snowflakes fall and immediately melt as they landed on the warm windshield. After what seemed like ten minutes, Arly came back on the line.

"I'm in a session," she said, "and I asked the client to step out into the waiting room."

"Oh Jesus, I'm sorry, Arly! I'm sorry."

"It's okay, Cam. It's okay. Where are you calling from?"

"My car."

"Do you know where you are?"

"On Antioch Road somewhere . . . out by Harbinger. I'm looking out the window at it."

"Okay," she said calmly. "Don't worry about the hospital. Are you able to drive yourself home? I need to know." She spoke slowly. "Can . . . you . . . drive . . . yourself . . . home?"

"I think so . . . yes," I said weakly. "I think I can get home."

Then I broke down. "Wh-what's happening to me, Arly?"

"Take it easy, Cam. You're going to be okay," she said confidently. "Right now I want you to drive home very carefully. I'll call you there in about a half hour."

"I'm scared," I whispered and then repeated it louder. "I'm sca—

"Cam," Arly said sharply. "Right now you need to concentrate on getting home." Then in a softer tone, "We'll talk in half an hour."

"Okay, Arly. I'm sorry," I said and sniffled again. "You'll call me?"

"Yes."

"What time is it now?"

"About a quarter to ten. Half an hour, then. Drive safe, Cam. Goodbye."

I laid my head on the steering wheel and looked out at the big flakes dying on the windshield.

"I'm melting," I said to no one.

Rikki was lifting two bags of groceries out of the back of the Volvo when I spun tires up the slick driveway, parked sloppily, and pulled myself out of the car. She set the bags down and eyed me worriedly.

"Where have you been?" she asked, her breath coming out in little bursts of steam. "You just took off and I didn't know where you went. I called the office and Diana said you never showed up. I couldn't reach you on the car phone. What's going on?"

I walked around the car and leaned back against the warm wet hood. Rikki tilted her head and looked at me more closely through the falling snow. She came over to me and felt my forehead and touched my cheek.

"Do you have a fever? What is it? What?"

I grabbed her wrist. "In the house," I said. "Let's go in the house."

We picked up the groceries and walked the forty feet up to the house, the accumulating snow crunching under our feet. We got inside and Rikki put on some water for tea while I put away the food and told her in detail everything that had happened. She leaned against the counter and watched me and listened, her fear and concern growing more audible with my every word.

Arly called me at 10:15 as she said she would, and I took it in the piano room. Rikki stayed in the kitchen while I laid it all out for Arly. Then it was Arly's turn. I wanted an answer. She had one.

After we hung up I walked back into the living room holding the cordless phone. Rikki was standing at the counter sipping a mug of lemon tea. She looked at me expectantly.

"She said I was experiencing dissociation."

"Mmm. I remember reading about it in psych classes."

"A part of my mind was disconnected from the other parts."

"The voice reading the road signs . . ."

"Right, and my hand writing 'safe not safe.' She said to just let it happen and don't worry but . . . Jesus Christ, Rik. Don't worry? What the hell's happening to me? I feel possessed. I'm talking gibberish in the mirror. I'm sitting under the piano in the middle of the night. Somebody else's voice, coming out of my face, is reading road signs out loud . . . and mispronouncing them! What the hell is going on here?! I got disconnected? What is this, some snafu at AT&T?!" I hurled the phone against the stone fireplace, smashing it into pieces.

I covered my face with my hands, and Rikki ran over and threw her arms around me. Confusion boiled in me, and shame. Tears came, and they felt hot and caustic.

"What's happening to me?" I whispered.

Rikki held me tighter. "I don't know, sweetie," she said softly. "I don't know."

SEVEN

A camera flashes. Pop! Squinting, blinded, I trace the slow motion arc of the spent flashbulb through the air and hear the hollow crackle as it bounces and bounces again off the hard floor and rolls away.

I look up . . . see an image . . . white pubic hair, head-high, tiny right hand raised, held by a woman's bony hand, pushing reluctant young fingers into warm, wet vagina. Leaving his thumb out. Strange pungent smell of sweat and . . . something else. Jangling fear, excitement, a tiny hard penis pressed against underwear and pants.

Frozen terror. Sweaty grandma. Bad grandma. Bad bad bad. Then it's over, tension released; she's through. His tiny wrist is freed from the bony grip. Her deep raspy voice whispers "gooood boy" as painted fingernails stroke his left cheek. She washes the little boy's hand, bends down, foul smoky breath close by. Yuchhh. She kisses his tiny hard penis through his pants, then takes him by the hand to the kitchen and gives the good little boy two cookies. Mmm, cookies. Her evil finger touches her painted lips. "Sshhh."

I awoke, startled, drenched in sweat, and shook my head hard. *What just happened? White pubic hair? Vagina? Oh, my God.* My stomach felt like I'd swallowed a dozen riverbed stones. Horrified, my eyes wide open staring blankly at the ceiling, not wanting to close them even to blink, I steeled myself to open the squeaky faucet in my mind just enough to let the terrifying images trickle in. In a millisecond, the trickle became a torrent and the torrent a raging flood. My face flushed and my body started to convulse. I sprang from the bed and, doubled over, stumbled to the bathroom.

I turned on the shower so no one would hear me, dropped to my knees in front of the toilet, and threw up every meal I'd ever eaten. Exhausted, I wiped my mouth with the back of my hand and caught a glimpse of my fingers. The horrible images rushed back in an ugly wave. And right behind it another wave of nausea crashed and I retched again, my empty stomach rippling, nothing coming up but a sour liquid, tearing eyes clamped shut to lock out the disgusting view.

Then it was over and I hung limply, half-kneeling, half-slumped in front of the toilet, my face on the lip of the cold porcelain bowl, until I managed to pull myself to my feet, flush the toilet, and climb into the shower. I adjusted the water to almost scalding and, desperately needing to get clean, scrubbed and scrubbed and scrubbed until all the hot water was gone.

I shut off the faucet and stepped out, ragged and raw, grabbed a towel, and staggered from the steamy bathroom to the bedroom to get dressed. I threw on some clothes and shuffled back into the bathroom to hang up the towel. Some of the steam had dissipated, and as I turned to leave, I caught a glimpse of my reflection in the mirror.

Instantly I froze, my eyes locked on the image. Suddenly, the image forced me back, way back, somewhere in my mind, and as I diminished, someone passed me going the other way . . . someone small. And then I was on a distant hill, a spectator, without any control over my body.

Rikki and Kai were up and had already eaten breakfast, and as my body descended the stairs I was vaguely aware of the smell of bacon lingering in the air. Rikki looked up from the soapy dishes and smiled warmly as I . . . we . . . passed.

"Morning, sweetie," she said brightly. "Thanks for using up all the hot water. It stopped snowing. There's school, but Hank hasn't plowed us out yet. I'm keeping Kylie home. He's in the playroom." I couldn't talk; I just walked mechanically by Rikki and into Kai's playroom. He was on the floor building a castle out of Legos.

Kai looked up from his blocks and said, "Hi, Dad." I sat mutely on my distant hill. My hand grabbed a Mexican blanket, Kai's sketchpad and a box of crayons and markers, and I glided silently into the lighted toy closet and sat down, leaving the door slightly ajar. Kai went back to building, glad to have me nearby, unconcerned that his daddy was sitting in his closet.

My left hand reached into the box, took out a washable red marker, and as I watched from far away, drew a continuous line around my right hand, across the knuckles. Then the marked hand was held in front of my face and rotated slowly, back and forth, while the small person's eyes carefully inspected the crimson line. I watched silently, dispassionately.

Then the hand took a pencil and began to draw a crude picture on the sketchpad. The picture was a front view of a naked woman and a back view of a small child, in front of her and slightly to the right. The woman was holding the child's right hand up to her vagina. No fingers were visible, only the thumb and child's hand. Next to that was a picture of the child holding his right hand up, the fingers separated from the hand. An open scissors was near the hand as if to show that it had been used to cut the fingers off. The word "No!!!" was written in a cartoonist's dialogue balloon that came from the boy's mouth. The word "Sshhh" was drawn the same way at the lady's mouth.

The small person controlling my body drew another picture, this time in pencil and red crayon—the face of a little boy with enormous eyes and huge tears streaming down his cheeks. He held up his right, fingerless hand, blood-red droplets falling from it. The caption read "Sad Davy."

What is this?

I felt the fingernails of my left hand dig into the left side of my face high on the cheek. I was vaguely aware of some pain but couldn't do anything to stop it. And then my body and mind were still. The only sound in the room was Kai's running dialogue as he built his castle.

I heard Rikki come into the room and say, "Where's Dad?"

Kai pointed toward the closet and said, "In there," and went back to playing. Rikki opened the door, saw me, and gasped. It startled me. I felt my body shake and suddenly became aware of the small person passing me and disappearing, allowing me to come forward again. I looked up at Rikki's horrified face. She bent down and took my face in her two hands, turning it to examine where I'd been scratched. My cheek felt raw when she touched it, and I saw blood on her fingers when she pulled her hand away. I looked around. *Where am I? I'm in the closet. Oh, shit, I'm in the closet.* I looked down at the sketchpad in my lap. Three simple child's drawings, stick figures, almost. *Sad Davy?* "What did you do?" Rikki snapped. Then she noticed the pad, picked it up and looked at it, puzzled.

A drawing Davy made in the closet his first day out.

"What . . . what did Daddy do?" Kai said.

"Nothing, honey. It's nothing," she reassured Kai, her eyes still fixed on the crude pictures. That was good enough for him and he resumed his construction.

"I . . . I don't know," I stammered softly, touching my cheek. It felt puffy and hot. Rikki took me by the hand, pulled me to my feet, and walked me to the bathroom. I stood dazed, looking into the mirror at my scratched face while she ran warm water and dabbed at the wound with a damp washcloth. I wasn't cut badly, but the upper part of my left cheek looked as if I'd slid into home plate face first. Weak and shaky, I sat down on the closed toilet seat.

Rikki noticed the red line around my hand and pointed at it. "What's that? I didn't see that."

"I don't know, Rik," I murmured, surprised to hear the sound of my own voice. "I don't know what the hell's going on with me. Something bizarre. Something so bizarre. A dream . . . or a flashback . . . or a memory or something. I don't know. White hair. My grandmother. I . . . I think that . . . maybe . . . my grandmother did something bad to Davy."

Rikki closed the bathroom door part way, knelt down in front of me and whispered, "What are you talking about? Who's Davy?"

I shuddered. "I'm a good boy." I shuddered again and tried to say something, but my voice got caught in my throat. I looked at my hands, too embarrassed and ashamed to meet Rikki's eye.

She took my hands in hers and said, "I'm calling Arly." I nodded and bit my lip.

Rikki rinsed out the washcloth, hung it up, put some first-aid cream on my face, and went to the piano room to make the call. I walked shakily back to Kai's toy room and went into the closet again, this time curling up in a ball under the blanket. Rikki left a message on Arly's machine, came back to the playroom and sat down nervously, placing herself between Kai and me. A gust of wind rattled the storm windows and the heater kicked on.

After a while the phone rang, and Rikki jumped up to answer it.

"Hello?"

"Hi, Rikki. It's Arly Morelli."

"Oh, thank God you called," Rikki gushed.

"What's going on?"

Rikki slumped into the blue-and-white love seat near the piano, tucked her legs under her, and shifted her body so Kai was in full view in the next room. She cradled the receiver in one hand and half-covered the mouthpiece with the other so he wouldn't overhear her.

"Things are not good here, Arly," she said.

"Uh huh."

"Cam is acting so strangely. He went into Kai's playroom closet right after he got up and drew some wild pictures of a woman and a child in a sexual pose. And he drew with a red marker across the knuckles of his right hand."

"He drew on his knuckles?"

"Yes. And he scratched his face."

"With what?"

"His nails. Gouged it. His face was bleeding. Not badly, but it was bleeding. He seems totally out of it, totally regressed. He sort of snapped out of it when I found him in there and that's when he told me about this dream—"

"What dream?"

"He said he'd had a dream that his grandmother did something to someone named Davy."

"Davy? Who's Davy?"

"I don't know. Then he looked funny and said, 'I'm a good boy,' in a weird voice."

Arly was quiet for a few seconds. "Anything else happened since you left the message?"

"No."

"Where is he now?"

"He's curled up in a corner of Kai's playroom closet, just . . . out there. He may be sleeping. He's not talking. I'm really scared." Rikki sighed and a whimper slipped out. "Arly, do you understand what's happening here?"

"Yeah. I think I do," Arly reassured her.

"Have you seen this before?" Rikki said. "I mean I realize you haven't seen him, but do you know what's going on? I mean, I don't know if I can handle this, Arly. I need to know that you know what the hell's going on here. I can't handle this alone. He said something about his grandmother, that she had white hair. I think the picture he drew was of his grandmother. Jesus. You should see his face! And the red line around his hand. Jesus." She combed her fingers nervously through her hair.

Arly said, "On which side?"

"Huh? Which side? Ah, the right side."

"No," Arly said, "on what side of the family, his mother's or his father's?"

"Oh . . . his mother's."

"Mmm. What do you know about her?" Arly asked.

"Nothing," Rikki said, shrugging her shoulders. "I mean, I saw a picture of her. She did have white hair. She died when Cam was pretty young."

"How young?"

Rikki looked over at Kai and shrugged again. "Four? Five? I don't know. He's never really talked about her. All his mother ever said about her was that she really didn't pay much attention to her or the family, but was always very well dressed." Rikki whispered, "Was the dream about him? Could she have sexually abused him?"

"I don't know. No point in jumping to conclusions. It happens. Children get sexually abused." Arly paused and then said, "Cam's acting like this for a reason."

"It's like it's not even Cam," Rikki said. "He's gone and someone else is there. I mean the drawing looks like something Kai would do."

"Has Kai drawn pictures like that?"

"No, of course not!" Rikki snapped, then quickly caught herself. "Sorry," she said. "I didn't mean that. I just meant that the drawings are very childlike." She looked in at Kai playing in the other room. "Arly," she whispered again. "Cam never told me anything about this before. Nothing. Could this be a memory of something that happened to him that he's forgotten about for all these years?"

"I don't know if this is something that actually happened, Rikki. It's possible. Memory isn't exact. It's really a series of impressions." They were quiet for a few seconds. Then Arly continued, "I'm guessing that, whether or not this specific incident happened, something happened that impressed him very deeply . . . so deeply that he wasn't able to deal with it at the time . . . that he had to disassociate himself from it—hence the word 'dissociation.'"

"You mean—"

"That he dissociated in order to protect himself from being overwhelmed at the time. Sorry for interrupting."

"It's all right."

Arly continued. "Some children have an innate ability to dissociate—high hypnotizability."

"And he could forget all about it for all these years?"

"It's possible," Arly said. "Picture this. You have a photograph of some horrible accident—an accident you witnessed or were actually in, one so awful that you couldn't bear to be reminded of it. You keep the photograph, but you bury it under huge piles of other things . . . bury it so well that you are able to forget about it for years and years. At some point though, when you are cleaning out your closets, or moving, or if your house burned and you were sifting through the rubble before you rebuilt, you might come across it. And be as horrified as you were the day the accident happened."

They were both quiet while Arly let that sink in.

Then Rikki said, "Rebuilding . . . Cam was really sick for a long time—"

"I know."

"And he's been getting better. Maybe Cam's getting better is like rebuilding after the fire . . . maybe he's cleaning out the rubble in his mind so he can rebuild."

"Maybe," Arly said.

"What about the red marker?" Rikki said.

"Sounds to me like a very creative way to keep from harming the body," Arly said. "A simulation . . . a mock amputation."

"Oh my God," Rikki gasped. "I used to work with abused kids. I saw them act out all kinds of things that happened to them. Very bad things." Rikki shook her head. "I think you may be right."

"It's conceivable that something happened to Cam when he was young," Arly said. "Something he's never dealt with. Whatever it was—we don't really know and may never know—we have to deal with its effect on him now. He needs your support now, Rikki."

Rikki looked into the toy room again at Kai happily playing. She took a deep breath and let it out gradually. "Arly," she said softly. "Will you help him? Will you help me?"

"Of course," Arly said. "Can you bring him over tomorrow morning at ten? I think I can free up that time."

"Of course. Kai will be at school."

"Okay, good," Arly said. "See you then. Stick with him. Let him know you're there and keep him safe. Call me if you need me, and I'll try to get back to you within an hour. Chin up."

"Okay." Rikki paused for a few seconds and then said, "Arly?"

"Yeah?"

"Thank you."

"You're welcome." And they hung up.

Rikki came back into the playroom and gathered the large throw pillows that were scattered around the room. She arranged them against the wall in the closet next to me and, grabbing a handful of children's books from the bookcase, managed a cheerful sound in her voice and said, "Hey guys, how 'bout a bookfest? Let's cozy up!"

"Yay!" Kai chirped, thrusting a tiny fist in the air. "Read *What Do People Do All Day.*"

"Sure," Rikki said, nestling into the pillows next to me and pulling Kai to her. Holding the book in his lap, she found my hand with her free one and held it gently as she began, with a sad and worried heart, to read us a story.

Nothing bad happened for the rest of the day. My mind remained under a dark canopy in a deep woods. Later that night, from our bedroom, I listened to Rikki read a short story to Kai and then tuck him in and go off to the bathroom to wash up.

Then I heard Kai say the familiar words, "Fluff my pillow down, Daddy." The sound of his little voice cut through the dense forest and my mind temporarily cleared. I got up and walked heavily into his room, fluffed his pillow, and hugged and kissed him goodnight.

On the way back to our bedroom, I noticed the bathroom door was open a crack, spilling a wedge of yellow light into the hallway. I pushed the door open to see if Rikki had gone off to bed and left the light on by mistake. She hadn't. She was sitting on the floor in the far corner, hunched over, rocking back and forth, sobbing silently into a towel in the yellow light. I froze.

Oh my God, what have I done to my best friend . . . to my wife?

I desperately wanted to go to her and hold her in my arms and cry with her and tell her everything would be all right. But I couldn't. I would have shattered like a lightbulb. So I just backed away quietly and climbed into bed.

After a few minutes I heard the water start and stop in the bathroom and the sound of Rikki's footsteps in the hallway. As she slipped under the covers I caught the scent of perfumed soap. I faced away from her, my light off, pretending to be asleep. Rikki shut off her light, turned her back to mine, and lay silently in the dark, alone in the deep recesses of her own private cavern of pain.

EIGHT

I awoke feeling surprisingly chipper and clear, although the left side of my face was raw and sore. Rikki kissed me warmly and then grimaced when she saw the nasty scratches on my cheek. She looked a little haggard, as if she hadn't gotten much sleep.

Soon after Kai left for school, we drove to our appointment with Arly—Rikki at the wheel, the pictures of Davy folded on the seat between us.

My calm state evaporated as we walked up the creaky stairs, and I felt like a thousand tiny soldiers were marching on my skin. Arly must have heard our footsteps in the hall, because when we got to the top of the stairs she was standing in her doorway waiting to usher us in. She took Rikki's hand in both of hers, shook it warmly, and said it was a pleasure to finally meet her in person.

I sank down heavily in the chair opposite Arly's, the incessant thud in my chest making me feel like there was too much blood in my veins. Rikki sat down, nervously clutching her purse in one hand and the pictures in the other. She leaned over and handed the pictures to Arly, who unfolded them and studied them for a minute without saying anything.

I gripped the arms of my chair as if it were plugged in and stared blankly at a spot on the wall to Arly's left. There was sweat on my upper lip. Rikki watched Arly nervously, sensing something big was going to happen, but not knowing what. Arly rested her gaze on me, first on the scratches on my face and then at the red line encircling my right hand.

There was a prickly silence; we were an inch from the sleeping beast. Then Arly stepped on the twig.

"Davy?" Arly said. Suddenly my body shuddered and I was zipped off far away. Shudder, switch, gone. And Davy was there.

Davy's head snapped back, his eyes wide with terror. His left hand grabbed his right wrist and yanked it up in the air above his head as if it were trying to pull him out of the chair, and he let out three piercing screams. "Aaahhh! Aaahhh! Aaahhh!" His right hand tried to twist free of the grip as his left hand pulled up, jabbing the fingers at some invisible target. The right hand pulled back, helpless against the stronger left. "Aaahhh!"

Rikki's jaw dropped and she stared in amazement.

Arly said firmly, "Davy, can you hear me?" Davy panted, tears and sweat streaming down his face. Nothing. "Davy, can . . . you . . . hear . . . me?" Arly asked again. Davy nodded.

"What do you see?" Arly asked, sitting forward in her chair.

"W—white hair. W—wet. Ugh," and he began to gag, the left hand still jerking the right hand up and down. "Let go!" he screamed. Rikki looked on in horror.

"What's happening with your right hand?" Arly urged.

"She's got it," he sobbed. "Yuchhh!"

Arly leaned forward. "Who's she? Who's got your right hand?"

"Grandma!" Davy cried. He screamed again, "Aaahhh!"

"What is Grandma doing with your hand?"

"My . . . fingers . . . in . . . her . . ." he gagged again and rocked back and forth, his eyes focused upward at some object only he could see. Now Rikki was crying softly.

"Where are you, Davy?" Arly said.

"Grandma's house," he said, sniffling.

"Is your grandma saying anything?"

Davy wheezed in and out, shaking his head.

"Davy, listen to me," Arly said. "You're not with your grandma. You're not in her house. You're remembering something that happened a long time ago. It's not happening now. You're okay. You're safe now.

Look around the room. Look around the room. Grandma is not holding your wrist. Let go of your wrist."

Davy's breath was coming fast and his hair was drenched with sweat. His gaze unlocked from the unseen figure in front of him, and he peered slowly around at Arly and Rikki. His left hand let go of his right and it dropped limply into his lap. He pushed at his groin, trying to make his erection go away. And then his shoulders began to shake and he closed in on himself and cried a desperate wounded cry.

Suddenly his look of terror returned and Davy bolted upright again. He raised his right hand, and with the first two fingers of his left hand he made a scissors and, grunting with effort, attempted to cut off the fingers of his right hand.

Rikki gasped, "Oh, my God!"

"Davy!" Arly snapped. "You don't have to cut your fingers off. Look at your hand. It's all right. You don't have to cut your fingers off."

Davy's hands dropped to his sides and he slumped back in the chair, exhausted and whimpering, his breath coming in spasms. He started scratching at the wound on his left cheek.

"Don't scratch yourself, Davy," Arly said firmly. He continued scratching and Arly jumped up, took his left hand, and put it at his side. "No scratching, Davy," she said. "You've been hurt enough." She sat back down. "You're all right, Davy," Arly said soothingly. "No one's going to hurt you. You're safe now. Just relax and take a deep breath."

Arly took a deep breath to show him, and he followed. So did Rikki. After maybe a dozen deep breaths, Davy's breathing became more regular and the spasms became less frequent. Arly spoke again.

"Why were you scratching your cheek, Davy?"

"Fingernails on my cheek," he said softly.

"I don't understand. Your fingernails on your cheek?"

"Grandma's," he said, "like this." Davy crossed his right hand over his face and stroked his left cheek with the back of the fingernails. Arly exchanged a glance with Rikki and turned back to Davy.

"She scratched you?" Arly asked.

"No."

"But you remember the feel of her fingernails on your face? Is that it?"

Davy nodded. "I don't like it," he whispered.

"Do you know where you are, Davy?" Arly asked. He shook his head. "Do you know who I am or who she is?" she said, pointing at Rikki. Davy looked over at Rikki. Her eyes were red and puffy and her mascara had run.

He shook his head again. "No."

"My name is Arly Morelli. I'm a psychologist. I help people with their problems. I'm Cam's psychologist. Do you know who Cam is?"

Davy shook his head again. "How old are you, Davy?"

He held up four fingers. Rikki looked on in stunned silence, beads of sweat covering her upper lip. Arly held up the pictures and pointed to them. "Did you draw these, Davy?"

"Yes," he said in a scared, small voice.

"Look at your right hand, Davy," Arly said. "Do you see that the fingers are still there? Can you wiggle them?"

He wiggled his fingers.

Arly said, "Davy, did someone make you do something with your hand that you didn't like?"

Davy nodded and said softly, "Grandma. Sweaty Grandma. She put my hand in her wee wee."

"She put your fingers in her vagina?" Arly asked. Davy nodded. Rikki cringed.

"Then she took me into the bathroom and kissed my wiener and gave me two cookies."

Arly said softly, "I'm sorry that happened to you, Davy. That shouldn't have happened. And it will never, ever happen again. I promise." Arly looked at Rikki. "Right, Rikki?"

"No," Rikki said, with an aching sadness in her eyes. "That will never happen again . . . Davy."

Arly sat back in her chair and said, "Davy, look down at your body . . . all the way down to your feet. Do you notice anything?"

Davy slowly looked down at his body, his gaze wandering down his shirt to his thighs and his knees. Then he leaned forward and peered over the edge of the chair, down at his feet.

"Wow," he said, incredulous, eyes wide. "I'm big. I'm a giant."

Arly chuckled, "No, you're not a giant, Davy, but your body is all grown up now. You've been inside somewhere for a very long time, and while you were inside, a lot of time went by. Remember when I asked if you knew who Cam was?"

Davy nodded.

"Cam is you, all grown up. And Rikki is his wife." Davy looked at Arly and then over at Rikki.

"I'm not kidding," Arly said. "They have a house and even a little boy of their own named Kai, who's about your age."

Davy leaned forward trying to look past Rikki to see Kai.

Rikki smiled and said, "No, Kai isn't here. He's at school now."

"Oh," Davy said, leaning back in his chair.

"Cam comes here to talk to me, Davy," Arly said, "and you are welcome to come out and talk to me, too . . . anytime. Okay?"

Davy nodded again.

"I want you to know that you are safe now, completely safe. I'm going to ask you to close your eyes now and think of yourself in a very comfortable place, maybe a place with lots of stuffed animals and a blanket, and I'm going to ask for Cam to come back. All right?"

"Okay," Davy said gently, closing his eyes.

Arly took a deep breath and said, "Cam?" She waited. "Cam? I want you to come back." And then . . . shudder, switch, and I was back.

I opened my eyes and the room came into focus. I shook my head hard, trying to clear my mind. I looked at Arly and over at Rikki, and then a wave of emotion flooded me and I burst into tears.

Rikki sprang off her chair and knelt by my side, throwing her arms around me, holding me as if I was going off to war. And we cried. For Davy.

After a couple of minutes Arly said, "We're getting a little tight on time." Rikki and I let go of each other, and she sat back down on her chair and reached for a Kleenex. We both looked at Arly expectantly.

Arly leveled her gaze at me and said, "How much of what just happened do you remember?"

I spoke slowly, piecing together what had taken place. "We came into your office . . . I sat here, where I'm sitting now." I tried to clear my throat a couple of times; it felt hoarse and raw. "You looked at the pictures and asked for Davy, and I kind of disappeared in a swirl . . . somewhere. I was barely aware of what was happening. My body felt tight and there were screams and . . ."

Arly nodded.

I looked out the window. "This is embarrassing," I said.

"It's okay," Arly said soothingly.

"I had tight pockets. Still do, sort of. Then I heard my name called, and I kind of swooped down into my body, like a bird diving after its prey . . . and then I was back."

Arly sat silently for a moment with her hands clasped together, her index fingers making a steeple against her lips. She put her hands in her lap. "Do you know about Davy?"

I shook my head. "Not really. Just the pictures, and my face got scratched . . . and something weird happened here, I can tell. I'm sweaty, my throat hurts, I've been crying, and you're eyeing me like I'm a bug under a glass." I was sweating and my pants were sticking to me. I shifted in my seat to try to get comfortable, but it didn't work.

Arly said, "Davy is a part of you, Cam. It looks to me like your grandmother might have sexually abused you, if what Davy said is accurate. At any rate, Davy just abreacted, or relived, an experience of being forced to masturbate a woman with his right hand, specifically with the four fingers of his right hand. Do you have any memory of that having happened to you?"

"No. I never knew my grandmother," I said. "She died when I was about four and a half." I had a big knot in my stomach. "I don't remember being sexually abused ever . . . by anybody."

"Well," Arly said, "Davy does."

I looked over at Rikki and she nodded.

I bit my lower lip and tears welled up in my eyes. "Well, this isn't too good, now, is it? This isn't too good at all." Rikki leaned over and grabbed my hand and held it tightly. I looked at Arly. "What does this mean?"

"Davy is a dissociated part of you," she said. "You, when you were probably around four years old. But not entirely you. Just the you who experienced some trauma at the hands of this woman. Davy split off and went inside your mind somewhere in order to protect you from knowing what had occurred. For whatever reason, he's surfaced now."

We were all quiet for a moment.

"Cam," Arly continued, "Davy didn't know who you were, who I am, or that you're married to Rikki and have a son."

"Well, did you tell him?" I asked. "Does he know now? Jesus, what am I talking about?"

"Yeah. I told him." We were quiet some more and then Arly spoke again. "Have you ever heard voices talking in your head—not like a conscience—but commenting on your actions?"

"Well, yeah. I hear voices. Doesn't everybody? They're not outside my head. Nobody's telling me the CIA is after me. I'm not schizophrenic, if that's what you're looking for."

"Do you ever experience feeling separate from your body, the way you described leaving when Davy came out?"

I nodded. "Sometimes. Sometimes it feels like I'm there but then I'm not there. Like I'll be in a store or somewhere, and I'll just start to feel very distant, like I'm looking down at myself, watching myself glide down the aisle or talk to a clerk or whatever. Or I'll be tying my shoes and then just forget how to tie them and have to figure it out." Rikki looked at me with surprise. I shrugged.

"Do you keep a journal?" Arly asked.

"No."

"Go out and get one. I think you should start keeping one."

"Okay," I said.

"Write in it every day and just let whatever happens happen. Don't try to stop it."

"Arly," I said carefully, "was I sexually abused as a child?"

"What do you think?" she asked. Rikki squeezed my hand. I looked at her and back at Arly.

"I don't know what to think. Davy? What the hell is all this? What the—"

"From what I saw here today," Arly said calmly, "I have no trouble believing that you experienced sexual abuse."

I shuddered. "Well I do. You're talking about me here, about something that might have happened to me, except I don't know anything about it . . . don't remember anything. But we've got Davy here, and he knows all about it, and oh yeah, he's scratching me up and trying to cut my fingers off, and . . ." I squirmed in my seat, "getting a stiff one talking about my grandmother." I let out a big sigh. "Sorry."

"Denial is the first reaction people have to this kind of thing," Arly said.

"Well, at least I'm doing it in the right order."

Rikki said, "You've seen this kind of thing before?"

Arly nodded. "Yeah, I have."

"Then you know what to do?"

Arly nodded again. "Mm hmm."

"Thank God," Rikki said.

"So what now?" I said.

"You get that journal and start writing in it, and we keep working together. Oh," she added, "and get Davy his own teddy bear. If he comes out, make him feel comfortable and safe."

Rikki and I nodded tentatively. I sat back in my chair, still holding Rikki's hand, looking out the window. Down below, a group of maybe fifteen young children flanked by two women watched while a fireman, in full dress, pointed out the features of a fire engine. The kids looked like Christmas candies in their colorful winter coats, hats, and mittens. My mind flashed on Davy. *Good enough to eat.* I looked at the red mark on my right hand and shook my head in disbelief.

"I never even knew my grandmother," I said softly.

NINE

After we left Arly's, Rikki drove us over to a Barnes and Noble bookstore, where we picked out a small, sky-blue journal with lined, light-blue pages. From there, she took me to Toys 'R' Us.

I'd been to Toys 'R' Us dozens of times before, but this was the first time I'd ever been there to buy something for me. *A bear? For me?* Feeling like a fifteen-year-old in a pharmacy shopping for condoms, I walked down the stuffed animal aisle trying to look totally nonchalant, hoping nobody would notice me. Of course nobody cared. Why would they? Rikki sensed my hesitation and just walked right over to the bears and started squeezing them.

"I'm going to get one for myself, too," she announced. "I need my own bear."

That did it. That made it all right. *Screw it. I'm getting a bear.*

My eyes and hands started wandering over all the brown-and-white stuffed dogs and bears, pink bunnies, and *Sesame Street* characters, and for a minute I actually felt happy. *I'm in the teddy bear aisle. The Isle of Teddy Bears. What a lovely place to be!*

I was poking and squeezing and rubbing the good ones against my face, checking them for softness, no longer caring what anyone might think, when I felt a powerful push from inside propel me toward a big fluffy blue bear, one I wouldn't have looked twice at. *This one! This is the bear!* Shudder, switch, and I was gone, and Davy was there holding that bear.

"Toby," he said.

Rikki walked over holding a white polar bear she'd picked out for herself. She knew it wasn't me, but she wasn't worried, or at least she didn't look it. I watched from some distant place.

She smiled and said sweetly, "You found a bear?"

"Toby," Davy said, holding the bear toward her.

"Toby," she repeated. "He's a nice one. Look," she said, showing him her bear, "I picked one out, too. I'm gonna call him Puff." Rikki was the best.

She paid for the bears and drove the four of us home.

That night Rikki and I lay in bed, face up, shoulders touching, holding our bears. Kai was fast sleep in the other room, and we both stared silently out the window at the full moon that rested on the leafless branches of the big trees in the yard. The bedroom lights were out and the moon's glow washed a ghostlike chiaroscuro over everything in the room. The wintry stillness was broken only by the sound of two squirrels scurrying across the snow-crusted roof.

"I can't believe this is happening," I said. "My grandmother."

"What do you know about her?" Rikki asked.

"Nothing. You know what I know. She came from a large family. She married my grandfather when she was really young, She wasn't very good at taking care of the kids."

"What do you mean?" Rikki said. "Oh, yeah, your mother always said *she* had to take care of your uncle from when she was just a kid; her mother couldn't do anything for herself. That's all she ever said." She sighed. "I don't know. Your grandfather, your uncles, your mother. Whew. Remember what your grandfather said when your dad died? 'Get over it'? I couldn't believe that. Your dad's dead a week and he's telling you to get over it. And your mother. She's about the most narcissistic person I've ever known. Everything has to revolve around her. She has to control every little thing. This is so screwed up," she said, spitting the words out like bad milk.

"I can't ask my mother about this," I said. "I've felt so weird around her lately."

Rikki and I were quiet for a while, watching the big moon out in the yard.

"Maybe I should call my mother's cousin Abbey," I said, "and ask her about my grandmother's family. She ought to know something." I propped myself up on my elbow and looked at Rikki. Her hair looked silky in the moonlight. "Didn't my mother say she and Abbey grew up on the same street?"

"I don't know," she said. "I think so. What do you think she'll tell you?"

I lay back down. "I don't know," I said. "She was there. She must know something."

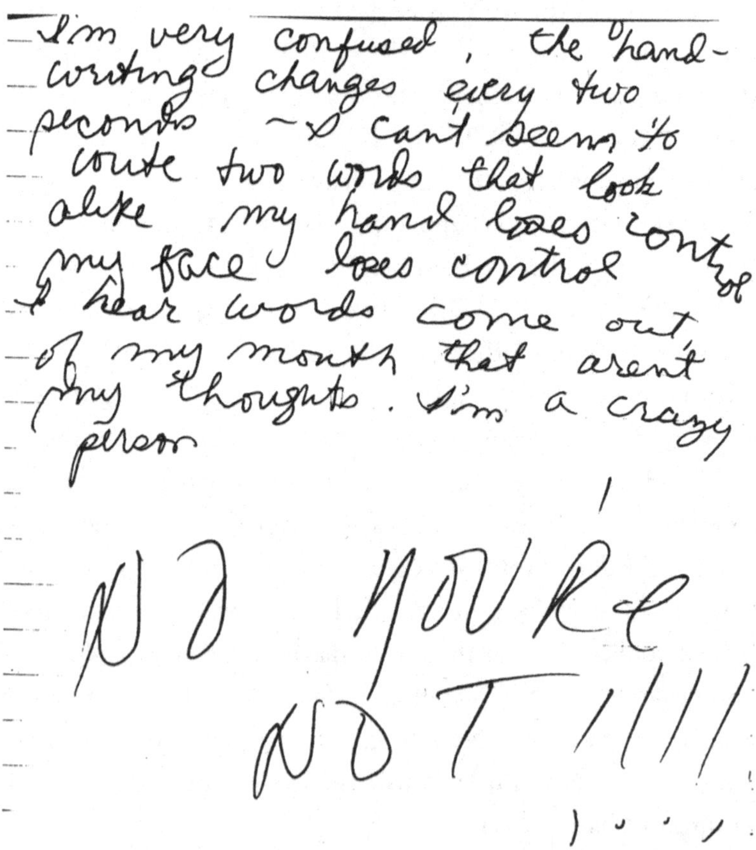

I'm very confused, the hand-writing changes every two seconds — I can't seem to write two words that look alike my hand loses control my face loses control I hear words come out of my mouth that aren't my thoughts. I'm a crazy person

NO YOU'RE NOT!!!!

A very early journal excerpt.

In the next room we heard Kai cry out, "Get away from my tank, you meany." Rikki and I looked at each other and laughed.

"He's dreaming," she said and turned back to look out at the stillness and the yellow, hanging moon.

I let out a deep sigh. "Maybe I am, too. Maybe I'm just making this whole thing up." Rikki turned back to me and propped herself up on her elbow. I could feel her penetrating gaze along my spine.

"That's denial talking," she said, shaking her head slowly, her voice quavering a little. "In Arly's office . . . Davy . . . the hand reaching up . . . the screams. Cam, there's no way that wasn't real."

I rubbed my temples. "I don't know what's real. I'm losing it. My past . . . my life . . . my brain is getting pried apart. I don't know what happened. And I don't know what's going to happen."

Rikki sniffled and shook her head again and I saw a silvery tear hit the pillow next to me. I reached up and wiped her cheek with the back of my hand and pulled her down to me.

She rested her head on my shoulder and said softly, "What's going to happen to our family?" and then she started to cry. I closed my eyes and held her, and the room swirled gently like white and dark chocolate intertwining in a warm pan.

TEN

The next morning, I awoke determined to make the call to Abbey. Taking the pen and pad of yellow paper I kept on my nightstand, I went downstairs to the piano room, sat down on the thick blue carpet, and went over in my head what I knew about her. *Widowed, lives alone in Detroit, two kids about my age, artist, diabetic.* I'd spoken with her maybe three times in the last thirty years.

I punched the number for local directory assistance and asked for the area code for Detroit. I got it, hit the flash button, and dialed Detroit information. They had a listing for Abbey, and I wrote it down on the yellow pad. *Act calm. Don't lead her at all. Just find out what you can about your grandmother's family and get off the phone.* I punched the numbers into the phone, took a deep breath, and waited. Abbey answered on the third ring.

"Hello?" Her voice sounded like she was surprised to get a call.

"Hi Abbey, it's Cam West." Two seconds of silence, then recognition.

"Ca—am!" She sang my name like a two-note song, high-low. "What a surprise! How are you?"

"Oh, I'm gr—"

"So, how are Rikki and Kai?"

"We're all great, Abbey," I lied. "Kai's getting big. We moved to Massachusetts, you know . . . two years ago."

"You did?"

"Yup."

"Well, are you happy there?" she said.

"Oh, yeah. Everything's going great. How're you feeling?"

"Pretty good," she said. "I've got diabetes, you know."

"I know," I said.

She didn't say anything. That was it for the small talk.

After an uncomfortable silence, Abbey said, "So . . . what's on your mind?"

Don't screw this up. Sound calm.

"Well, Abbey," I said hesitantly. "Uh, lately I've been wondering what my grandmother's family was like. My mother really never told me anything about her life when she was growing up, and . . . well, you lived on the same street when you were kids."

"Yeah, across the street and two houses down," Abbey said.

My stomach was churning, and a drop of cold sweat trickled down my side.

"So," I said, "what was my grandmother's family like?"

Silence. *Wait. Don't say shit.* I looked nervously out the window, listening to the hum of the long-distance line. A squirrel scampered up a tree. After maybe a full ten seconds, Abbey spoke.

"There was no incest that I know of," she said flatly, and her words hung in the air like the smell of lightning.

A shot of adrenaline flashed through my body, and my face felt red hot.

What??!! What the hell?!

With my pen gripped too tightly in my hand, I copied her words down verbatim. "There was no incest that I know of." Next to that I wrote, "First words out of her mouth. Unsolicited." My heart felt like it was trying to punch its way out of my chest. I felt light-headed. This was definitely not a response one would expect to that question. This was something . . . tangible.

I shook my head hard to rid my mind of all the messy thoughts. *Say something, asshole!*

I swallowed hard. "What do you mean, Abbey?" I asked. Silence.

More phone hum. I wondered for a second if she'd hung up on me, then decided she hadn't. I waited her out. After about fifteen seconds Abbey started talking. I wrote it all down.

There were lots of brothers and sisters in my grandmother's family. After they grew up, the siblings remained in the same neighborhood, but the sisters shopped at different grocery stores, sometimes traveling far to avoid bumping into each other. None of the women wanted their sisters to see what food they'd purchased. Abbey's mother and aunts, including my grandmother, binged and purged by forcing toothbrushes down their throats; Abbey knew this because the cousins talked about it. When the children took craps they weren't allowed to flush the toilet, but had to show them to their mothers or they'd be given enemas. *Jesus!*

"My mother, too?" I prodded. Both my armpits were soaked now and my stomach felt like a hundred crickets were floating in it.

"Your mother? Oh yeah, sure," she continued. "I told her she could get out of getting an enema by saying she'd shit and flushed by accident." Abbey sounded proud when she told me that. She was on a roll now, and I didn't have to prod her too much. I just kept writing.

According to Abbey, everyone in the neighborhood knew that my grandmother's family was crazy. She remembered watching one of her aunts beat her young son mercilessly on the head, for no apparent reason. He'd tried to run away but had gotten his foot stuck between two fence posts. When his mother caught him, she continued the beating.

Abbey said my grandmother was an extremely frightened woman, terrified her husband would leave her.

Like a stranger on a bus, Abbey kept talking, mostly to herself, remembering her childhood. Except the more she talked, the more she remembered things she didn't want to remember. And the more uneasy she sounded.

Then she stopped talking, and there was a deadly silence for what seemed like a full minute.

"Abbey?" I asked, checking.

"You really opened a can of worms here, kid," she said angrily. "You really opened a can of worms."

"I'm sorry, Ab—"

"I wish you hadn't called," she spat. "Don't call me anymore, okay? Just don't call me."

And she hung up on me.

For a few seconds I sat frozen with the phone to my ear. Then bile rose in my throat. I squinched my face and choked it back and quickly put the receiver down. Then I wiped my phone ear with my shoulder and rubbed my hand on my pants. I got up too quickly and became dizzy, stumbling against the piano.

I went into the bathroom and turned on the water in the sink until it ran hot, worked the bar of soap into a lather, and scrubbed my face and hands hard.

I toweled off and leaned over the sink, examining my reflection in the mirror.

Abbey's words sloshed in my head like brown water in the bottom of a rusty wheelbarrow. I tried to focus. *Bad grandma. Davy is good. Uh oh. Shudder, half-switch, fight it, gone . . . back . . . back . . . stay back . . . there. Clear. I'm clear. Go lie down.*

Groggy, I went upstairs, leaving the yellow pad on the floor in the piano room. I climbed into bed, closed my eyes, and descended the cold stone steps into the dungeon of sleep.

"Cam? Cam? Honey?"

Mmm, honey . . . brassy and shiny and thick and slow.

"Cam? Cam?"

A tunnel. The end of a long black tunnel . . . Rikki in the white hole at the end of a long, black tunnel . . . or is it the muzzle of a gun? Am I inside the barrel of a gun looking out . . . No, that's James Bond.

"Cam? Cameron?"

Rikki . . . Rikki calling me . . . Mmm, I love the sound of her voice.

"Cam!"

Huh? Bright light . . . open eyes . . . focus.

"Cam!"

The room . . . Rikki in the room, calling me.

"I can hear your voice," I said thickly.

"Wake up, honey," Rikki said worriedly. "You've been sleeping for six hours."

I cleared my throat. "Okay," I said. "I'm coming back now . . . I'm coming back." I blinked hard maybe six times and she started to come into focus. *White sweater. Blue jeans. Sweet face. My Rikki.*

Rikki sat down on the edge of the bed and put her hand on my chest. "Are you there?" she asked.

My eyes focused on her. I was back.

"Mm hmm," I said. My mouth felt numb. "Yeah, I'm back."

"Good," she said, patting my chest. "I was getting worried."

"Sorry. What time is it?"

"A little past three."

"In the afternoon?" I asked.

"Yeah."

I wiggled my fingers and toes and scrunched up my face a couple of times, feeling more and more like I was back in my body. After a minute, I sat up.

I looked up at Rikki. "I spoke to Abbey," I said.

"I know. I found this," she said, wagging the yellow pad with the notes on it. Rikki pointed at the page, clearly upset. "She said this? 'There was no incest that I know of'? She actually said this?"

I nodded. "Yeah," I said. "And all that other stuff, too."

Rikki shook her head. "Jesus," she said. "She actually said there was no incest that she knew of? What did she say that in response to?"

I shrugged. "I just asked her what my grandmother's family was like, that's all."

"And she said that? Jesus!" Rikki massaged one of her temples. "I can't believe this."

"She doesn't want me to call her ever again. Ever."

"What do you mean?"

"I mean the more she told me, the more upset she got. Finally she said she never wanted to hear from me again and hung up."

"Whoa," Rikki looked at the notepad, shaking her head. "No wonder your mother never talked about her family."

"Yeah." I said, sitting up a little straighter. "I'm going to call her brother, Dennis. I need more."

Rikki wagged the yellow pad. "This isn't enough?"

"No," I said. "It's not enough."

Rikki gave me a leery look. "What's he going to tell you?"

"I don't know," I said. "Maybe nothing. But he was there, and he's four or five years older than my mother. He's got to know more than Abbey, right?" I took a deep breath and let it out. "I know he was in therapy for a long time," I said. "And his wife's a psychologist. She knew my grandmother, I'm sure. She and Dennis have been married for a long time."

Rikki pursed her lips, considering that for a moment. Then she shrugged. "Okay."

She placed the pen and yellow pad on the bed next to me and got up to leave. At the door, she turned around and said, "I'll be downstairs." As she walked out, I heard her mutter again, "Jesus."

I took the brown leather address book from the drawer in my nightstand and thumbed through it until I found Dennis and Sandy's phone number in Michigan.

Sitting cross-legged on the bed, I put the phone in my lap and glanced out the window at the big oak trees in the front yard. The gray afternoon light made them look sad. I cradled the receiver between my shoulder and left ear, picked up the pen and yellow pad, and dialed the number. *This isn't happening.*

Before the first ring, I made up my mind to tell them straight out that I'd remembered something important about my grandmother, then just wait to see how they responded. I couldn't tell them it was Davy who'd had the memory; that was way too crazy. Who the hell would believe that? I didn't even believe it.

I was about to hang up after the third ring when Sandy answered the phone. I felt a little jolt of adrenaline at the sound of her voice. I said it was me, and she sounded surprised and pleased, not having heard from me in years. We went through the usual small talk before I blurted out, "Sandy, the reason I called is because I've been having strange thoughts that maybe I was sexually abused by my grandmother."

"Grandma Lynn?" she gasped.

"Yes."

After an uncomfortable pause, she said matter-of-factly, "That very well could be. She liked to fondle the children."

Fondle the children?!

For a moment neither of us spoke, then Sandy said curtly, "Hold on a minute, I'm going to get Dennis."

Her hand muffled the conversation on the other end of the phone. Then Dennis got on the line, and he didn't sound anywhere near as pleased to talk to me as Sandy had. Instead, he accosted me right off. "What's this about my mother?" he barked.

My sphincter felt like a bolt cutter and my hands got clammy.

I'm talking about this guy's mother. It hadn't even occurred to me that he might be outraged that I was making this awful accusation about his mother.

I took a deep breath and repeated what I'd told Sandy. "I've been having weird dreams and thoughts that your mother sexually abused me."

I nervously tapped the pen on the yellow pad, listening to the interstate phone buzz. After what seemed like five minutes, Dennis said stiffly, "She used to bathe your uncle Alan . . . way past when he was able to bathe himself."

What?

Dennis paused. I scribbled.

"Once, from the hallway," Dennis said, "I saw her washing him, but doing something she shouldn't have been doing. She shouldn't have done that!" he snapped. "That really pissed me off!"

An icy wind blew through my mind as I watched my hand robotically transcribe Dennis's words. My face felt numb and my head ached like my brain was being jabbed with a knitting needle. *The woman Davy said had abused him had been seen abusing another child.*

I shook my head to try and clear it. "Did she ever do anything sexual to you?" I asked tentatively.

He barked at me, "That's none of your business!"

I winced and clenched my teeth and almost dropped the phone. *I wish Rikki were here.* I took a breath and decided to keep going.

"Do you know if she ever did anything sexual to my mother?"

"Ask her!"

There was another painful silence.

I said flatly, "I think there's more, Dennis. There's something you're not—"

"Ask your mother."

"Dennis, what are you—"

"What the hell do you want from me, kid?! You come busting into my life from out of nowhere dragging up this crap about my crazy goddamn family! I've got my own pain!"

The long distance line hummed like fluorescent lights while I waited.

Then in a low, penetrating voice Dennis said, "The apple doesn't fall far from the tree, kid."

"What? What do you mean, Dennis? What are you—"

"You figure it out," he snapped.

My stomach tightened and I thought I might have to put down the phone and throw up. "Dennis, I—"

"I'm hanging up on you," he said.

"Den—"

"That's *it!*" he said, biting the word off like he was champing steel.

And I knew that was, indeed, it.

"Okay," I said, stunned. "Goodbye." And I hung up the phone.

I sat motionless on the edge of my bed in the fading light, Dennis's words creeping over me like black spiders. *The apple doesn't fall far from the tree.*

Something was not right. Something was very not right. I looked down at my hands; they were shaking. And inside—way inside—a sticky black substance oozed down the corridors toward the very center of me.

I went downstairs to the living room feeling very wavy, and lay down on the floor next to Kai, who was building some sort of vehicle out of Legos. Rikki looked up from the book she was reading and raised her eyebrows. I nodded toward the piano room.

Without taking her eyes off me, Rikki said, "Kylie, Daddy and I are going into the piano room for a minute to talk."

He said, "Okay," and rolled his new vehicle back and forth, making a sound like a truck engine. I followed Rikki into the piano room, and we sat down next to each other on one of the love seats.

"So what happened?" she said, looking at me intently.

I told her everything. After I finished, Rikki covered my hand with hers and squeezed it. I saw fear in her eyes.

"I don't know what's happening here," I said. "It's all burning up behind me. I'm trying to get a handle on this but it's burning up behind me. This isn't happening."

Rikki said, "I don't understand. Dennis was saying your *mother* is an abuser? How would he know that?"

"This isn't happening."

Rikki and I sat quietly for a few minutes holding hands, while Kai vroom-vroomed in the other room.

Then I said, "The voices . . ."

Rikki snapped out of her thoughts and tilted her head at me. "Huh?"

"The voices."

"What?"

"This stuff with Davy . . . it won't leave me alone."

"What? What voices?" she said, searching my eyes. "What won't leave you alone?"

"Rik, Davy's not the only one."

Rikki raised her eyebrows. "You're saying there are more? More . . . people?"

I nodded.

She let go of my hand and ran hers over her hair. From the other room Kai's little voice called, "Mom, Dad, are you comin' back in?"

Rikki answered. "Just a minute, honey. Okay?"

"I'm hungry for chicken nuggets."

"Okay," she called back. "We'll be right in."

"Dad, you there?" Kai called.

I cleared my throat. "Sure I'm here, Kai. We'll be there in a minute, okay?"

"Okay."

Rikki rested her gaze on me. "Like who?" she said. "Who else is there?"

I screwed up my courage. "Well," I said, hesitantly. "There's an older guy who sits at a draftsman's desk. He wears Ben Franklin type glasses. His name's Per."

Rikki's jaw dropped. "You're kidding," she said. "Like in, 'I ate a pear'?"

"Right," I said. "Per. But it's spelled P - E - R."

She looked bewildered. "How do you know this?"

I spread my hands and clasped them together in my lap. "I don't know," I said. "I just . . . know it."

Rikki leaned back, perched her feet up on the ottoman, and thought for a minute. Then she looked at me and said, "If I ask to speak to him . . . to Per . . . do you think he'll talk to me?"

"I don't know," I said. "I've never even spoken to him. You could try. You could just ask for him to come out, I guess. I don't believe this."

Rikki took a deep breath and let it out slowly. Then she put her feet on the floor, slapped her knees, and stood up. "Okay," she said, "this is what we're gonna do. We're going to have something to eat, we're going to put the little guy to bed, and then I'm gonna talk to Per." She put her hands on her hips. "So, what do you want for dinner?"

ELEVEN

Knowing what we were going to do after Kai went to bed kept Rikki and me pretty quiet during dinner, but it didn't bother Kai; he just munched and spilled stuff and chirped away as if the world was a good place. After we finished eating, I took him upstairs for his bubble bath and read him *Ernie Gets Lost* while he splashed around in the tub having a grand time. I read the simple story and watched Kai play and secretly wished I could be enveloped by his innocent joy, could peel off my cloak of fear and misery and float carefree among the glorious bubbles for just a minute, knowing I was safe, that everything was all right. But it was just a dying wish into an empty well; that cloak was on me good, and it was going to be three long years before even one button came undone.

Before long, Ernie got found, Rikki finished in the kitchen, and Kai got rinsed, dried, and tucked in, the way a kid ought to be. Inside of three minutes he was asleep, twitching like Elvis and dreaming about two-foot candy bars. Lucky him.

Rikki and I turned out the hall light and went nervously downstairs, not really knowing what to expect. We made some tea and sat down in the living room by the huge stone fireplace. The heater was humming pleasantly, and the pottery table lamps cast a glow like sunset around the room, giving it the cheery feel of a ski chalet. If we didn't know about all the bizarre things that had been going on lately, we might have figured Sven the ski instructor was going to come knocking on the door any minute to tell us the Warren Miller movies were starting. Well, Sven wasn't coming. And there weren't any movies. There was just Rikki and me . . . and maybe Per.

Rikki looked deeply into my eyes. "Per?" she said tentatively. "Can I speak with Per?"

Instantly, shudder, switch, and I was gone and Per was there. A strange warm calm filled my body as I felt him assume control.

Per looked at Rikki and smiled pleasantly. "Hello," he said. Per's soothing voice sounded curiously familiar in the room. It was the first time I'd heard it outside of my head.

Rikki studied him. "Hello," she said cautiously. "Are you Per?"

"I am," he said in a velvety tone.

"Do you know who I am?"

He smiled at her. "Are you Rikki?"

"Yes," she said, eyeing him closely.

"This is Cam's house and you are his wife," Per said.

"That's right," she nodded, puzzled. This was not her husband. And this clearly wasn't Davy. This was someone else. Someone totally calm and clear-headed. Someone different.

"I'm nervous," Rikki admitted. "I . . . I don't know what to say to you." She thought for a second. "Ah . . . how long have you been there?"

Per rubbed his chin, thinking, and the corner of his mouth curled into an introspective smile. "Hmm," he said, "I'm not sure. A long time, I think."

"How old are you?" She asked, somehow comforted by his gentle and pleasing tone.

"Older than Cam," he said.

"Cam said you have Ben Franklin glasses and sit at a desk."

Per reached up and touched the rim of my glasses. "I wear these," he said.

Rikki took a sip of her tea. "Do you know Davy?" she asked.

Per frowned. "I know who Davy is," he said heavily, shaking his head. "It's very sad."

Rikki turned her whole body toward Per and looked at him closely, concentrating. A little groove formed between her eyebrows. "Who *are* you?"

Per remained relaxed. "I . . . don't . . . know, exactly," he said. "I know I'm in this body. I know this is Cam's body. I know there are others." His gaze slowly arced around the room, finally resting on Rikki.

"It's strange to be out here," Per said, gesturing loosely at the room with his right hand. He tapped his chest. "I'm used to being in here."

Rikki focused on him intensely, chewing a little on her lower lip, a dozen questions jockeying for position. She opened her mouth to speak, but nothing came out. She put her tea down and leaned forward, resting her elbows on her knees, massaging her temples, agitated, wondering where to start.

"I need to know some things, Per, like what do you do in there? And why are you here? And where did you come from?" Per sat placidly, hands folded in his lap, his eyes soft, his face alert.

"I don't blame you for being upset," he said, looking at her kindly. "I don't know where I came from. I watch over things, Rikki . . . over Cam and the others. I watch over the little ones."

Rikki snapped, "What little ones?" then caught herself. "Sorry. What little ones?" she repeated more softly.

"Bad things have happened, Rikki," Per said seriously.

"What bad things? You mean like Davy and what happened to him with his grandmother?"

"Yes. Very bad things. But we shouldn't speak of that now, with sleep and dreams approaching."

"I don't understand, Per," Rikki said.

"You will, Rikki," Per said. "You'll meet the others. They'll come out to see you. The door has been opened. It's safe to speak. I'll go now . . . you can call for me anytime. Be brave, Rikki. He needs you more than ever now. They all need you."

And with that, I felt myself pulled to the front of my mind, Per and I passing like two travelers moving in opposite directions on an automated walkway. I shook my head to clear it and looked at Rikki, who was staring at me with her mouth open, her head shaking slowly.

"Unbelievable," she whispered hoarsely. "Do you have any idea what just happened? Did you hear any of that?"

"Sort of," I said, rubbing my neck. "Like eavesdropping on a conversation two booths down in a diner." I looked into Rikki's deep blue eyes and saw the confusion there. A ripple of anxiety shuddered through me. *What if Rikki thinks I'm nuts. What if she bails on me. I'll die without her. I can't do this alone.*

Rikki clasped her hands together tightly in her lap. "Per told me there were others," she said. "Other little ones. He said that bad things happened. Did you hear that? Do you know what he means by that?"

"I don't know for sure," I said. "It's the voices—and I see vague images of others. No names. Just outlines of shadows—just faces. I don't know, honey." I leaned back on the sofa, covering my eyes with my arm. "I'm so tired, Rik. My mind hurts."

Rikki touched me lightly on the arm.

"Let's go to bed," she said. "That's enough for one night." She gently pulled my arm away from my eyes and touched my cheek. I felt myself begin to disappear into her fingertips. She stood, took my hand, and helped me to my feet. She wrapped my arm around her shoulders and put her arm around my waist. Leaning heavily on each other, we trudged wearily up the stairs to bed.

TWELVE

Rrriinngg. Rrriinngg. Rikki answered the phone. "Hello?"

"Rikki, it's Arly. Something significant happened with Cam in our session tonight. A new part came out and abreacted a memory with full feeling, and Cam's in no shape to drive home."

Rikki winced, as much at having to bundle Kai up and take him out just before his bedtime as at the news that I'd abreacted some new horror.

"What about the car?" she said. "What'll we do with the other car? Can we leave it on the street there?"

"It'll be safe overnight," Arly said. "You can come and get it tomorrow."

"Okay," Rikki said, "I'll be right over."

She scooped Kai from his bed, mumbling something to him about having to go get Dad. She threw on her coat, wrapped Kai in a woolen blanket, and plunged into the wintry night.

Rikki was huffing from carrying forty pounds of sleeping kid up the flight of stairs to Arly's office. She said a cautious hello to Arly, eased carefully into the extra chair so as not to wake Kai, and looked over at me worriedly.

I mustered a dead stare—that was all I had—although inside I felt a mixture of relief and confusion at seeing her. *What's happening? Didn't I drive myself here tonight? Why's Rikki here?* From a far-off place I noticed Kai was drooling on her collar.

Arly began softly, trying not to wake Kai.

"Someone named Clay came out during the session," she said, "and graphically relived a scene of abuse that apparently occurred in a hotel room in Ohio when the family was moving. Cam and his mother had flown ahead while his brother and father drove." Arly paused. "It seems the abuser was Cam's mother."

Rikki gasped. "Oh, my God."

"Clay is eight. He's had a tough night." She turned to me. "Are you there, Clay?"

Shudder, switch, gone. I felt my body tense like the cable in a suspension bridge.

"Y-yeah," Clay stuttered. His eyes were fixed on the lamp next to Arly's chair.

"I'd like you to meet Rikki. She's over on the chair to your left. Can you look over at her?"

Clay's head turned slowly, like a nut being loosened from a rusted bolt. He glanced at Rikki, and from my island, I saw the look on Rikki's face. Pity and fear.

"Rikki is Cam's wife," Arly said. "And the little boy she's holding is their son, Kai."

Clay said nothing, looking back to the floor.

"I want to remind you, Clay, that you're not in a hotel room in Ohio. That was a long time ago." Arly let that sink in for a moment, and then said slowly, emphasizing each word, "Nothing bad can happen to you now, Clay. You're safe here."

"I-I'm a g-good boy," Clay stuttered again.

Tears welled up in Rikki's eyes and trailed down her cheeks. "Yes," she said softly, speaking to Clay for the first time, "you're a good boy."

Arly offered Rikki the box of tissues; she took two and dabbed her eyes. Kai stirred and made a dreaming sound. Rikki stroked his soft hair and said, "Shhh." He settled back to peaceful sleep, his sweet breath warm against Rikki's neck.

Arly said gently, "Clay, you need to rest now. I'd like to ask you to take a couple of deep breaths, feel the air fill your lungs, and let it out slowly."

Clay did as she instructed.

"As you continue to breathe deeply, Clay," Arly said in a soothing voice, "feel your muscles begin to relax . . . first in your toes and feet . . . and now your legs . . . and your belly. Now relax your chest . . . and your arms and hands. Now feel your neck muscles begin to loosen . . . and your forehead . . . and let the tension in your eyes drift away."

Rikki watched with fascination as Clay's body responded to Arly's suggestions.

Arly's tone changed slightly as she sensed that Clay had entered a more relaxed, trance-like state. "I'd like to ask anyone inside who can hear me, to gather around Clay and comfort him, to bring him to a comfortable place inside, and watch over him." Then she said, "Cam, can you hear me?"

I replied in a gelatinous monotone, "I can hear you, Arly." My head hung limply, my eyes semi-focused on the fabric of my blue jeans. "Is Rikki here?" I mumbled. "Rikki?"

"I'm right here, honey," she answered with a strained smile, wiping away a stray tear with the back of her hand.

I turned my head slightly. "Arly, are you there?"

"Right here, Cam," she said, knowing my mind was completely overloaded. "For now, I just want you to relax. I'm going to talk with Rikki for a minute, and after that she'll take you home." With Arly's permission I mentally unplugged, lying back in my chair in a semi-catatonic state, watching Arly and Rikki as if through fog.

Arly turned to Rikki. "As you know by now, Rikki, Cam is highly dissociative. We've already met two dissociated parts of him—Davy and Per."

Rikki nodded.

Arly shifted in her chair. "The dissociative disorders exist on a broad spectrum, and up till now I've hesitated to use a diagnostic label, but it's the appropriate time, so you and Cam can get a grip on what he's experiencing."

Rikki nodded again, listening intently.

Arly continued. "I believe Cam has Dissociative Identity Disorder."

Rikki's eyebrows raised. Arly said, "It used to be called Multiple Personality Disorder."

Rikki gasped and recoiled.

"Here it is," Arly said, hitching up the sleeves of her sweater. "Everybody dissociates. You're driving down the highway and you space out for a while and suddenly you realize you're at your exit. That's normal dissociation. All people do that to some degree."

"Uh huh."

"DID is dissociation taken to the extreme. Picture this: a child is sexually abused by his mother for the first time—the same mother who feeds him, clothes him, and reads him bedtime stories. The child has no capacity to understand or accept this behavior, which is horrifying, maybe even painful, but also sexually stimulating. How does he deal with this? His conscious mind essentially removes itself from the present while another part of his mind comes forward to hold the memory or the pain or the feelings about the abuse. That way he isn't crushed under the weight of what happened to him and can actually go about his life, go to school, go out to play."

"When the abuse is repeated," Arly continued, "the dissociative defense is used again. Either the same part comes out or a new one is created. Over time, these parts develop characteristics that are unique to them and separate from the child's. They become alter personalities."

Rikki's eyes were fixed rigidly on Arly.

"Now," Arly went on, "about Clay—"

"Wait a minute," Rikki interrupted. "What exactly are you talking about here, Arly? You mean like Sybil?"

Arly nodded. "In a way, yes," she said, "although in Sybil's case her personalities were so separate she would black out completely whenever they came out. I don't think Cam experiences that. His alters take over to greater or lesser degrees at different times. He's aware of them when they're out, and they seem to be aware of each other. That's called co-consciousness."

Rikki nodded, taking it in. "That's what happens in his journal when they talk to each other. That's why he can sort of hear me if I'm talking to one of them." She shifted her gaze to me. "He can hear us now, even though he's not really *here.*"

"Right."

Rikki shook her head, trying to clear her thoughts. "Isn't this really rare?"

"Nowhere near as rare as people think. Sexual abuse happens all the time. Granted, not everyone who is sexually abused as a child becomes dissociative." She paused. "Only some children have the ability to compartmentalize themselves so completely. The ones who develop multiple personalities generally experience repeated abuse from a very early age. In any case, child sexual abuse usually has a profound impact on the adult psyche. Most people don't come away from it unscathed. Obviously," Arly said gesturing at me with her hand, "from what we've both seen, Cam hasn't come away unscathed."

They sat silent for a moment. Rikki looked over at me. "Why now?" she asked, looking back at Arly. "Why is this happening now?"

"Hard to say," Arly replied. "DID usually gets diagnosed in adulthood. Something happens that triggers the alters to come out. When Cam's father died and he came in to help his brother run the family business, he was in close contact with his mother again. Maybe it was seeing Kai around the same age when some of the abuse happened. Cam was sick for a long time and finally got better. Maybe he wasn't strong enough until now to handle this. It's probably a combination of things. But it sure looks like some of the abuse Cam experienced involved his mother. And sexual abuse by the mother is considered to be one of the most traumatic forms of abuse. In some ways it's the ultimate betrayal."

"So what's the prognosis?" Rikki said, raising her eyebrows slightly. "What's going to happen?"

Arly folded her hands. "It's a long haul," she said, "but people do recover from this. In some cases, eventually there's a full integration of all of the personalities into one, and in other cases, where the personalities prefer to stay separate, they can work toward achieving cooperation so the whole system can function relatively smoothly in the world. Either way, like I said, it's a long haul."

Arly got up and walked over to a bookcase at the right of the door. She plucked a red book from the shelf and placed it on the table next to Rikki.

"This is a good book," she said. "Take it."

Rikki glanced at the title: Multiple Personality Disorder: Diagnosis, Clinical Features, and Treatment by Colin A. Ross, M.D.

Kai stirred and Rikki stroked his head. She said, "What exactly happened here tonight . . . to Clay?"

Arly took a deep breath. "Cam's body tensed up all of a sudden and he started writhing in the chair. He fell out of the chair onto the floor and started groaning and making sexual motions with his hips and pushing his nose into one of the throw pillows. I asked who was out, and he stuttered, 'Clay.' I asked him to describe what was happening to him and he told me. He was with his mother in a hotel in Ohio when the family was moving, as I said, and he evidently had oral sex and perhaps intercourse with her."

Rikki gasped again.

"I asked him his age and he said, 'eight.' When I was able to calm him down, he gave me some of the details. For Clay, whatever happened was very, very real. He literally crawled to my bathroom and vomited. After that, I called you. I was able to get Cam back briefly. He was barely aware of what had happened and claimed to have no memory at all of what happened in Ohio. I believe him."

Rikki sat dumbfounded, holding our sleeping boy. She looked at the floor and sighed deeply, shaking her head in amazement.

"Rikki," Arly said, folding her hands in her lap, "Clay is a part of Cam who's going to need particular care. When he emerged tonight, he thought he was in that hotel room, that it was the 1960s. Although I explained to him who you are, I'm sure he'll need to be reminded of that."

Rikki shook her head slowly. "This is unbelievable."

"I know. But denying it isn't going to help—you or him." She nodded at me. "Especially him."

Arly leaned forward. "This is a very big pill to swallow. I'm not just talking about the diagnosis. Accepting that your past isn't what you thought it was, that someone you trusted did you grievous harm, is an enormous obstacle for most people with DID. Denial can be a very, very powerful foe."

Rikki blotted away fresh tears. She glanced over at me, the mannequin with a heartbeat, and back at Arly. "I'm counting on you, Arly," she stated, her eyes deadly serious. "This is my husband. This is my life. And I . . . am . . . terrified."

Arly nodded. "I know."

THIRTEEN

The next morning, I heard the sound of leather soles on solid rock as Rikki climbed the four semicircular fieldstone steps at the front of our little stone house on her way back from walking Kai down to the school bus. An icy wind blew in as she opened the heavy oak door and stepped into the living room. She looked over at me huddled on the couch, clutching one of the pillows to my chest, and a look of concern clouded her face. She took a deep breath and let it out slowly.

"Are you all right?" Rikki asked, moving quickly over to the couch and sitting down beside me.

I gritted my teeth and gripped the pillow tighter, trying to stay composed so she wouldn't worry. But as our eyes met, tears welled up and I began to tremble.

I shook my head and whispered, "I don't think so."

Rikki's composure crumbled, and she burst into tears and threw her arms around me. "Oh, Cam," she cried. She held me tightly as I clutched the pillow, her soft face next to mine, her warm tears running down my neck as she cried with me. Rikki hadn't taken off her olive-green leather jacket, and the collar felt cold against my chin. She held me tighter, and the sound of the jacket stretching made me think of cowboys and horses. "Shhh," she whispered, rocking me gently back and forth. "Shhh."

Even though January's brutal chill penetrated the cracks and seams of our old stone house, the room was still very warm, and I was sweating.

With her coat on, Rikki was getting warm, too, and as we rocked, I felt the heat from her body escaping from under her collar.

When the surge of tears was over, she held me in silence, the soft whirring of the heater the only sound in the room. Inside me a tiny earthquake hit—shudder, switch, gone—and Clay was there.

"W-will y-you read me a b-book?" Clay stuttered.

Rikki let go of me, leaned back, and studied Clay a moment. Clay looked down at the floor.

"Clay?" she asked, checking.

He nodded.

Rikki patted him gently on the shoulder and said, "Clay, I need to talk to Cam for a minute, okay?"

"Okay."

"Cam?" she called to me. "I need to talk to Cam." Shudder, switch, back.

"Yeah," I said weakly. My eyes were focused on the pattern of blue stripes on the couch. I shook my head twice, trying to come back. My stomach felt ripply and heavy, like I'd swallowed a bag of sand, and my jaw felt like it needed oiling. Very slowly and deliberately I said, "I don't think I'm doing too well."

Rikki placed her slender hand on my shoulder, and I could feel her gaze. "I'm going to call the office and tell your brother you can't come in," she said. "Then I'll get a book and read to Clay; he asked me if I'd read him a book."

"Okay," I replied flatly, my gaze still focused on the lines on the couch.

Rikki got up quickly and walked to the wall phone in the kitchen. She picked up the receiver and punched the speed-dial button for my office.

"Hi Diana, it's Rikki. Oh, okay. Is Tom in yet? Yeah, please. Thanks."

A few seconds went by while she waited for my brother to pick up, then she turned toward me, leaned against the white Formica kitchen counter, and spoke into the phone in a clipped tone.

"Hi, Tom . . . Not so good. Look, we need to talk. Cam's having a really hard time here, and I don't know when he's going to be able to come back to work." Rikki wormed her finger through the telephone cord and sighed. "The truth is," she said, "I don't know if he'll be able to come back . . . ever, or at least for a long time." Rikki picked a pencil up from the counter and began fidgeting with it. "Tom," she said gravely, "you know all this stuff that's been happening with Cam? Well he's really sick. He's been diagnosed with Dissociative Identity Disorder. It's Multiple Personality Disorder with a new name . . . I know. It's incredible. I can't believe it either . . . Yeah, just like Sybil. Well, sort of. You always said he seemed like two different people."

Rikki absently tapped the pencil on the counter. "Uh huh . . . Yeah, Dr. Morelli seems to know exactly what she's doing, thank God . . . Yeah, we've got some money . . . I think so, if we cut back . . . I thought I could come to the office to help out some . . . As soon as I can, but I can't leave Cam today. He's not doing well at all today." Rikki looked over at me and frowned, a small gully forming between her eyebrows. "There's a lot more I need to tell you about, Tom, some things that happened last night . . . well, I can't now. I should really get back to Cam . . . Thanks . . . Yeah, I'll call you later . . . Sure I will. Bye." Rikki replaced the receiver.

She took a deep breath, pursed her lips and blew out. Then she turned on her heels, walked over to the staircase, and went quickly upstairs. In a moment she came back down with a pile of books in one hand and Kai's light green down comforter and pillow tucked under her other arm.

Goody, books. Thank God. Thank God for Rikki.

I laid my head down on Kai's pillow, and Rikki covered me up with his comforter. She sat down by my head and placed all the books but one next to the blue ceramic lamp on the old oak end table. She shifted her body to get comfortable, put her feet up on the ottoman, and began to read *Mickey's Flying Lesson* aloud. My head sank into the fluffy pillow, and I tucked the warm comforter under my chin. A tiny smile crossed my lips . . . and my heart.

I faded into the distance while Clay listened to Rikki's soothing voice as she read *Mickey* and the books that followed. Every so often I'd become aware of her voice, and when I did I'd wonder where I'd been. *Winnie the Pooh? I thought she was reading Mickey.* I turned my head and looked up at the dust motes pirouetting in the sunlight. They didn't care that time was slipping.

At 11:30 Rikki asked if anyone was hungry. "I'm r-real hungry," Clay said, although *I* didn't feel hungry at all.

Rikki put the book down and said, "Would you like a peanut butter and jelly sandwich and some juice?"

"Mm hmm. I have to g-go to the b-bathroom."

"Sure," she said. "It's right around the corner there."

Clay nodded. Rikki got up and went into the kitchen, and Clay stood up to go to the bathroom with me in tow.

"I'm w-way up high," he said, amazed, looking down the length of my adult-sized body.

"What do you mean?"

"Big. I'm b-big."

"Ohhh," Rikki said, remembering what Arly had told her about alters having to get used to being in a different body. "Yes, you are big."

When Clay finished washing his hands, he glanced in the mirror over the sink, and from somewhere inside, I peered out through his eyes at the reflection. He'd caught sight of my face in the mirror, and I felt his muscles tighten and heard a guttural sound in his throat. He quickly looked away, confused. I felt nothing but the faint registering of a bizarre fact: *The person looking in the mirror isn't me.* Clay toweled off and returned to the living room.

Rikki was at the kitchen counter making sandwiches. "Chips?" she asked. "Would you like some chips with your sandwich?"

"Y-yes, please."

"Would you like orange juice or water?"

"J-juice."

"Okay. Come and sit down at the table."

Clay and Rikki ate in silence, and from a distance, I could vaguely hear the chewing sounds Clay made as he ate. It was like lying out in the grass at midnight, looking up at the starry night and not being able to tell where you end and the rest of the universe begins.

Clay mostly gazed down at the red maple kitchen table while he ate, but sometimes he'd look up and take in the room, noticing for the first time things I was familiar with: Rikki's dried-flower wreaths—one hanging on the kitchen wall, the other over the fieldstone fireplace—the framed pictures of Kai on the rough-hewn log mantle, the bumpy nap of the white Berber carpet, the Mission-style oak chair and writing table.

Rikki studied his face.

"You look sad, Clay," she said.

"I am," he nodded, without looking up at her. "I'm tired and sad."

Rikki got up and walked around the table to him and gently stroked his back. "Can you tell me why you're sad?" she said sweetly.

A jolt of electricity shot through Clay's body. His hands gripped his thighs and his upper arms pressed tightly against his chest. A low groan emitted from his throat and he began to rock back and forth.

Rikki pulled back, shocked. "What's the matter?" She had the impulse to call for me to come back, but she resisted it. If I came back, Clay would still be in agony. She stuck with him.

Clay groaned, "I s-saw in the m-mirror." He continued to rock as Rikki's mind raced to understand what he was talking about.

"I s-saw in the mirror," he moaned again.

Then a thought clicked in Rikki's mind. *The bathroom.* Before lunch, in the stillness of the house, she'd thought she heard him make a similar guttural sound. She put her hand gently on Clay's back and spoke cautiously. "You looked in the mirror when you were in the bathroom, didn't you."

"Y-yeeaah," he groaned, his whole body tight as a high wire.

"It's okay, Clay," Rikki comforted, bending down close to him. "It's okay. Try to relax your body and take a deep breath, like at Arly's. It's okay." Clay inhaled deeply and slowly let it out.

"Gooood. Now again." Rikki said, rubbing his back gently. Clay took another deep breath. He was still rocking back and forth, but she could feel his body begin to relax.

"One more time," she said.

Clay took another breath and let it out.

"Ver-ry good," Rikki said, pulling a chair next to Clay. She wondered what Arly would say next.

"Clay," she began carefully. "The person you saw in the mirror is Cam. He's you, all grown up. When bad things happened to you—remember what you told Arly about?"

Clay stopped rocking and nodded.

"After bad things happened, you went inside, inside Cam's mind. And while you were inside a lot of time went by. Cam grew up. He married me. He even has a son. Kai is Cam's son." She paused again. "Clay," she repeated, "Cam is you all grown up. That's why you were so surprised when you looked in the mirror. You thought you'd see a kid in the mirror, right? You."

Clay nodded sadly. "Y-yeah," he whispered, and a single tear trickled down his cheek. Rikki caught it with her knuckle.

"Yeah," she said softly, her hand on his shoulder. "Would it be all right if I gave you a hug?"

Clay nodded, and as he did, his shoulders shook and the tears came more freely. Rikki leaned over and gently pulled his face against her shoulder. She softly caressed his hair, and Clay let go and sobbed the tears of a lost child.

After a few minutes he began to calm down. Rikki handed him a paper napkin and he blew his nose. Then she stood up, held out her hand, and, looking down at him with a gentle smile, said brightly, "Come on. We'll go look in the mirror together." Clay timidly took Rikki's hand and she led him up the stairs toward the master bedroom, where a full-length mirror hung on the door. They paused at the top of the stairs to look out the large double windows facing the ridge behind the house. Not more than twenty feet away, a doe and two fawns were nibbling at a scrawny bush. They looked up, startled by the movement. Sensing no danger, the fawns went back to nibbling, but the doe pawed the ground twice to keep them alert.

Then Clay pointed and said excitedly, "There's d-deer." The fawns jerked their heads up, and the three deer bolted effortlessly up the hill and out of sight.

"D-deer," Clay said.

"We have lots of 'em here," Rikki said, smiling. She gave his hand a slight tug and they turned and walked down the short hall past Kai's room toward hers.

They entered the big bedroom and she made a sweep with her hand and said, "This is where Cam and I sleep, Clay." She paused and added, "And it's your room, too."

Clay looked around nervously and nodded. Rikki closed the bedroom door and, taking him by the shoulders from behind, gently guided Clay in front of the full-length mirror. She could feel his body tense immediately and she softly said, "It's okay. Take a deep breath and just let it out slowly." She did it with him. "Now one more." His body relaxed a little.

"See, Clay?" she said, pointing at their reflection in the mirror. "This is what you look like now." They stood silently while he took it in. *Tall—bigger than Rikki.* A *grown-up.* Then a thought occurred to him.

"W-where's my m-mom?"

Rikki puzzled over the question for a moment, searching for the right words. Clay had his hands clasped tightly together and was rocking back and forth slightly.

Rikki looked at him in the mirror, gently touched his hand said, "While you were inside . . . somewhere . . . Cam grew up. A lot of years went by. Now he lives here with Kai and me. He doesn't live with his mom anymore. She doesn't live here, Clay, but you do . . . and nothing bad is going to happen to you."

Clay glanced at his reflection and said, "Oh. N-nothing b-bad?"

Rikki shook her head and smiled. "Nope. Nothing bad is going to happen to you. Like Arly said. Remember Arly?"

"Um hmm."

"It might seem like bad things just happened to you, but really they happened a long, long time ago. Nothing bad is going to happen here. Ever." She patted him on the shoulder. "You're safe here."

They stood in silence, Rikki's hands softly touching Clay's shoulders, while the strange concepts trickled over Clay's eight-year-old mind.

Rikki said, "It'll take some time for you to get used to this, but it's gonna be okay, Clay. You're welcome here."

Clay stared into the mirror for a moment. Then, with his head tilted slightly to one side, he nodded almost imperceptibly.

"I'm w-welcome here."

FOURTEEN

In the belly of night, where secrets lurk and whisper, the dream came. A hydraulic claw, the kind that loggers use, viciously ripped my spine from my body while I screamed hopelessly, silently, arms outstretched, fingers pleading for help that wouldn't come. Over and over and over, an endless loop of pain and despair. And it repeated night after night. The first half dozen or so times the dream came, it got what it wanted—the cornered prey, the pool of sweat, the thundering heartbeat. Then, after a week or so I acclimated to it—expected it. The terror diminished, the night sweats stopped. It took its toll, though. The constant roiling left me walking gingerly through the weeds of madness, looking for purchase on angry ground. I stopped grooming myself as the raggedness inside spilled over. My features took on the wild expression of people in the shadows, as the fault lines in my mind growled and buckled, disgorging toxic fumes.

Per wasn't kidding when he said there were others. Alters began to emerge and communicate, and my blue journal became the town square, filled with the noise and confusion of strangers meeting. Watching my hand write someone else's words quickly became familiar. *Who are you? What's going on here?*

Gone were the quiet happy moments, the family laughs, Buns in Space. But for Kai everything was somehow still okay. Having one sane and attentive parent seemed to quell any fleeting fears he might have experienced. Rikki covered for me. My face got scratched on some branches. I wasn't feeling so well and needed some rest. He was used to that; I'd been sick for most of his life. Rikki made it clear that alters weren't to talk to Kai. No way. No alters from Mars were going to invade his six-year-old galaxy. So the zombie in the closet was just Dad. Kai wasn't meeting any alters. That was the law. Hell, they looked like me. As long as they didn't talk to him maybe we could slip it by him that Dad was a nut.

Shaving was iffy. My hair started to do this Beethoven thing. Working was definitely out. Rikki began going to the office in my place, doing her part to help Tom manage the operation. She put Kai in an after-school program so I wouldn't have to take care of him till she got home.

Driving was a little shaky for a while. Rikki made a verbal agreement with us that I was the only one allowed to drive. That didn't always work out, though, and more than once she got a phone call from someone who was lost or had gotten behind the wheel while the car was parked and didn't know what to do. *Cell phone . . . press memory 11 . . . ask for Rikki . . . Rikki will call for Cam.* Shudder, switch, back. Drive home safely. No worries, mate.

In therapy, Arly decided to probe the source of my recurring dream. She simply asked if any part of me knew where the dream was coming from.

Shudder, switch, gone, and Bart came out. I'd seen his writing in my journal, but didn't know who he was. Bart—twenty-eight, bold and easy—told Arly he was behind the dream. Why? Because that was his job—to scare the shit out of anyone who wanted to tell. To keep them quiet. What would they tell? About the bad things. Bart had been around since Davy and Grandma. Kid wants to tell? Scare the kid. Crazy? No. It was a form of protection.

When Bart first came out he described himself as wearing a witch's costume. When anyone got the urge to tell the secrets, he'd spring from the bushes somewhere in my mind and frighten the kid. Arly explained to Bart that a long time had passed, that there wasn't any danger anymore, that nothing bad would happen if secrets were told, that his job was obsolete. As soon as Bart heard that he didn't have to keep anybody quiet anymore he dropped the witch's getup. He was a black-leather kind of guy anyway, he said. Arly gave him a new job, too, to help Per watch over the little ones, and to comfort anybody who was having trouble. She asked Bart to stop playing the bone-ripping dream, and he did. It was that simple.

Over a couple of months Arly, Rikki, and I met a parade of others. They arrived as strangers, guests in my sad hotel, moving their luggage into the already cramped quarters of my mind. Some came for a brief stay, then faded back. Others took up permanent residence. My guys.

Leif was smart and steely, tough as a nickel steak. He was my age and had been exerting his force on me for years without actually taking over completely. He'd make things happen, whatever needed to get done, whatever was too tough. He'd just push right through without worrying at all about who got trampled in the rush. I'd just be swept up and dragged by the collar, not knowing what was making me so frantic or why I couldn't stop. His armor would surround me, and he'd torpedo me through any task, alienating people who knew me, sometimes even Rikki. Leif was the guy who had closed the spoons deal.

Stroll was the sexual one. About my age, Stroll was heavy-lidded and serpentine, a female pleasure source. For years he'd moved through the world just behind me, overtaking me when he perceived even the most furtive sexual glance from a woman. More than once he acted out with strangers, leaving me confused and embarrassed, an unwitting traitor to the woman I adored. Stroll despised himself, convinced he was nothing more than a whore. In his first meetings with Arly, which were at night, he refused to let her even look at him, insisting that she look away or turn down her office lights. When Stroll came out I felt like a panther. Arly also redirected Stroll's energies to help Per watch over me and the others.

Dusty was a shy, sweet, twelve-year-old girl. She liked girl things: taking care of babies, grocery shopping, watching boys. Dusty described to Arly in detail an experience of anal rape by an adult male—someone she didn't know or wasn't willing to expose. She knew she'd been created to deal with this particular incident of abuse, which astonished me, because I had no memory of experiencing any abuse at all. None.

Switch was an angry eight-year-old boy whose voice I'd been hearing in my head since I was a kid, tormenting me, telling me hateful things. His anger was directed both at me and at all females. I'd hear his voice say, "Girls are lucky, just 'cause they're girls. And ladies can do what they want, whenever they want." Rikki had felt Switch's wrath at times, when his bitter remarks spilled out of my mind and off my tongue. She used to think it was some strange sexist side of me she just didn't understand, inconsistent with the man who loved women, the man she fell for. Hell, I didn't understand it either. Women were by far my favorite sex. Sensitive, considerate, caring, and they had soft parts with no bones, too. So where did Switch come from? Why was he so angry at women? Because of something bad. What? We'd know soon.

Anna and Trudi were four-year-old girls with completely contrary personalities. Anna was happy and light-hearted, with an ever-present ear-to-ear smile that made my face hurt whenever she came out. Anna told Arly she'd been orally raped in her house by a man with hairy hands wearing a brown leather belt. After he was through with her he wiped her face with his handkerchief, warned her never to tell, and told her to go outside to play. It had happened in the fall, Anna told Arly, when the dead leaves were "crunchy under your feet." Anna wasn't angry about having been abused; she had no feeling about it at all except she was glad she had been a good girl. She didn't feel the pain.

Trudi felt the pain. She'd been present for the same experience with the man with the hairy hands. She held the horror, the shame, the guilt, the sadness. Pensive and withdrawn, Trudi never talks. But in Arly's office she screamed and gagged and spit and gagged some more, her jaw aching from being forced open by the large penis, her little stomach heaving from the thick, salty liquid in her mouth. And after it was over, when Anna went outside to play, Trudi went somewhere deep inside, to a dark place, a place of mute misery, a place of anguish. Trudi *is* pain. Anna and Trudi: the happy little girl who didn't mind, and the haunted little girl who did. Like Dusty, Anna and Trudi were created as girls, because some things just aren't supposed to happen to boys.

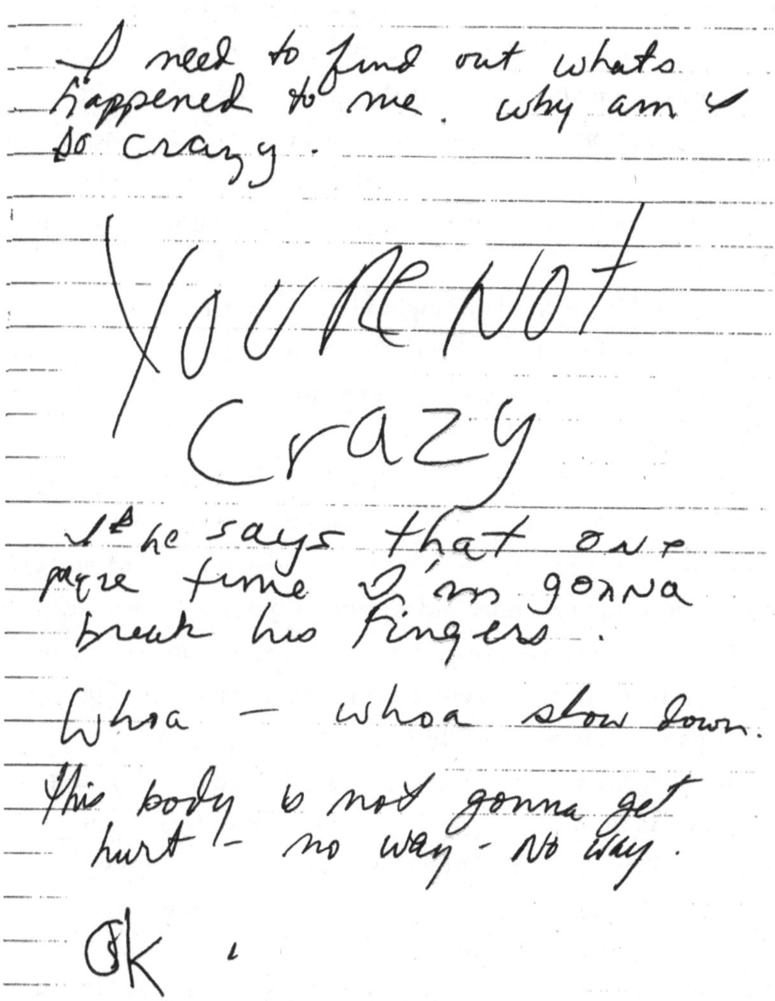

I need to find out whats happened to me. why am I so crazy.

YOU'RE NOT CRAZY

She says that one more time I'm gonna break his fingers.

Whoa — whoa slow down.

This body is not gonna get hurt — no way - No way.

Ok.

Early stages of denial. Switch foreshadows self-harm.

There were others, too—a group I called "The Boys." Kit, Tracy, Toy, Nicky, Lake, and Casey came out in rapid succession early on, each about ten years old, each with his own thoughts, memories, and mannerisms, each one briefly touching the blue of the flame and then quickly dripping back down the candle of my consciousness to the deep pools where dreams conspire. I never got to know them well. The Boys disappeared too soon.

There was Bart's buddy Kai—his straight man. After a while he somehow blended with Bart until they were completely merged.

Sky was about thirty. He was the gatekeeper—a guy with no feelings, just two strong hands on one big wheel that controlled the flow of all the pain and memories. He could tighten it down when a flood was coming, or open it up when it got too dry. That was Sky. The man at the wheel.

Keith was fifteen, kind of gangly, kind of shy, and glad as hell to have a beard to shave. He got me through some of high school, and when he infrequently comes out now, he's always surprised to have money in his pocket and no homework to do.

Sharky was primitive. When he first came out he bit everything: tree bark, plates, Kleenex boxes, our kitchen table. He ate bugs. His head would sweep back and forth like a prison searchlight and he'd grunt. But he learned to talk some, and we taught him how to eat with a fork and spoon. Why was he like that, such a primitive oral being? Because Sharky was there when we were forced to have oral sex with the mother. A silent partner, Sharky was there.

Soul was gentle, serene, ageless. He lived in a damp cave deep in my mind, covered in moss and dust, a precious antiquity hidden, perhaps, since my mind first divided. When Soul would come out his words glided like mist over a meadow, calming us all, even Per. Soul rarely presents, though, unless he's called upon.

Along with Per, Davy and Clay, and Mozart, Wyatt, and Gail, whom we'd meet later, these were my alters, twenty-four in all, the people who lived in my mind and took over my body. I wasn't me anymore. I was us.

FIFTEEN

Rikki sat stiffly in a corner booth at The Border, a small, earthy restaurant with a lot of big windows that overlooked Little Lake a few miles from our house. She was wearing old blue jeans, a gray sweatshirt, and hiking boots. She hadn't bothered to comb her hair or put on makeup. The restaurant was about half-filled with a boisterous crowd of people, drinking beer and margaritas and eating from big plates of Mexican food.

Across from Rikki, her friend Tanya was nursing a margarita on the rocks and looking placidly out the window at the frozen lake. The moon was almost full, and its light made the ice look like polished black onyx.

Tanya was pretty, with long thick dark hair, large brown smiling eyes, and a coppery complexion that showed her Latin heritage. She was wearing black silk pants, a black cotton T-shirt, and a red Toreador jacket. Tanya and her husband Eddie had lived next door to us before we moved to the stone house. Kai had been best friends with their daughter Jessie for a while, and Tanya and Rikki were comfortable with each other from two years of chatting together over coffee while watching the kids play. Tanya was safe.

Rikki had phoned her and asked to meet, saying only that she was in the middle of a crisis and needed to talk. Tanya could tell that Rikki was struggling with something dark; since they'd arrived at the restaurant, other than deciding what to order, Rikki hadn't said two words. It was time.

Tanya took a sip of her margarita. "You called me," she said, looking at Rikki over the lip of her glass, "and I'm here."

"Thanks," Rikki said, meeting Tanya's gaze for a second and then looking away. "You could probably tell I really needed to get out."

Tanya nodded, taking another sip. "Yeah. The part about the crisis—that's what tipped me off."

The waiter, a good-looking kid with a lot of earrings and platinum blond hair pulled back in a ponytail, came over and set an enormous plate of food on the table.

Tanya's eyes got big and she straightened up the way people do when their order arrives. "*This* isn't about crisis, Rik," Tanya said, smiling. "This," she spread her hands gesturing at the food, "is about nachos."

Rikki was sipping her margarita when Tanya said that, and she burst out laughing and started to choke. She put the drink down without spilling it, and Tanya quickly reached over and slapped her on the back a few times. Some people looked their way and Blondie made a move toward the table, but Tanya signaled him that it was okay and he went away. Rikki got her breath under control.

"Smooth, huh," she said, coughing and wiping her mouth with her napkin.

"It wasn't that funny," Tanya joked. "You all right?"

Rikki nodded, patting her chest and taking a deep breath. "Shit, that's the first time I've laughed in I don't know how long," she said. "Thanks."

"Sure," Tanya said, grinning. "Later I'll push ya down the stairs."

Rikki smiled, picked up a huge nacho piled high with refried beans, chicken, green chilies, and cheese, and took a bite. So did Tanya.

"Mmm," Tanya said with her mouth full, "eezer gray."

Rikki raised her eyebrows and nodded in agreement. They ate noisily for a few minutes without talking. Tanya signaled Blondie for two more drinks and he brought them over and cleared the empty glasses.

"Nobody finishes those," he said, gesturing with his chin at the half-eaten plate of nachos. "Well . . . the bowlers do."

"Leave 'em for now," Tanya said without looking up. "Oh, and could you bring us a couple more napkins?"

"Sure," Blondie said and went to get them. He came right back, set the napkins down near Tanya, and moved off to another table.

Tanya's eyes followed him. "Nice ass," she said, but Rikki wasn't paying attention. She was poking nervously at the ice in her drink.

"So," Tanya said brightly, "how'd you get out tonight?"

Without looking up from her glass Rikki said, "Kai's sleeping . . . and for the moment, all's quiet on the western front."

"What do you mean, 'for the moment'?"

Rikki didn't answer. She shifted her gaze out the window. Across the lake a light popped on, and then another and another in a small cluster.

"Someone's home," she said to no one.

"Huh?"

"Someone across the lake just came home and turned their lights on."

Tanya turned to have a look and then turned back. "Mmm," she said. "What do you mean 'all's quiet on the western front'?" Rikki hesitated, aware that she and Tanya had rarely had a conversation that didn't center around their children. Rikki was an extremely private person and never really opened up to anyone. This was hard. She rotated her glass slowly, staring into it.

"*Talk* to me, will ya?" Tanya prodded.

Rikki pushed her glass away. "All right," she said. "It's about Cam. He's been having problems. Serious problems." Tanya folded her hands, waiting. Rikki shifted in her seat.

"Mental problems," she said. Tanya raised her eyebrows. "He's been seeing a psychologist for a few months, and some bizarre things have been going on."

Tanya gazed at her intently. "Bizarre things?"

"Tanya," Rikki said, "Cam's been diagnosed with Dissociative Identity Disorder. DID. It's the new name for Multiple Personality Disorder."

"What? Oh, my God," she said, placing her hand on her chest. "Are you kidding me?" She searched Rikki's eyes. "You're not kidding me."

Rikki shook her head slowly.

Tanya looked around the room as if everyone in the restaurant had heard. She leaned in and said in a loud whisper, "You mean like Sybil?"

"Yeah."

"I . . . I don't . . . know what to say." She smoothed her hair. "Jesus. Cam?"

"Yeah, my Cam," Rikki said, staring out the window. "I've known him for fifteen years, we've been married for thirteen." She shifted her gaze back to Tanya. "And the whole time he always seemed so stable . . . so together."

Tanya nodded.

"Not one time," Rikki said, raising a finger, "did he ever raise his voice to me. Or treat me with disrespect. We've never even had a fight. He's always been so gentle and sweet . . . the best dad and my best pal." Rikki looked absently out at the lake. "You know, he did have this weird side of him, though, that would come out whenever he had to do something difficult . . . anything. He'd just change into somebody totally intense, I mean totally driven. He was . . ." she searched for the word, "fierce. His brother used to call him 'Killer.'"

Tanya thought about that. "You know, I think I saw him like that once . . . when I stopped by his office. It was kind of scary."

"It didn't scare me," Rikki said, "but it was weird. And the second he was done with whatever it was . . . building something, moving something, making a big deal go down . . . whatever," she snapped her fingers, "he was back to the same lovable, easygoing Cam, and everything was okay again."

Rikki took a small sip of her drink and set the glass down. "Another thing I never really understood was that Cam said, more than once, that if people *really* knew him, they'd have him locked up. 'I'm right on the edge,' he'd say. I'm a crazy person.' That always seemed odd to me . . . didn't make sense. And he couldn't really explain what he meant. It was just a feeling he had."

Tanya leaned forward, placing her elbows on the table, and rested her chin on her hands. "Rik, you're talking about him like he's gone."

"Oh my God," Rikki said, her voice full of emotion. "But, you know, it's like he is gone. And there are all these other people in his place."

"You mean they look different? Do they dress different? What?"

"No, they don't dress differently. And of course they look like him. But not really. Their mannerisms are different. The way they talk. They're all different ages. There are girls."

"Girls? Whoa. Back up, okay? You're talking to somebody who had one semester of intro psychology." Tanya leaned in and rested her chin on her fist. "Exactly what is Dissociative Identity Disorder?"

Rikki took a deep breath and let it out gradually. Then she told Tanya the tale. When she got to the part about my mother Tanya gasped, "His mother!" She made a face like she'd just tasted an old penny. "Ugh," she said, "that's sick." She hunched her shoulders up and shivered.

"Yeah."

They both sat silently for a moment.

"So exactly where did the personalities come from?" Tanya asked. "And don't forget about the girls."

"They were created during different episodes of the abuse." Rikki thought for a bit. "It's like this," she said, picking up a fresh napkin and holding it in front of her. "When Cam was abused as a child, his mind couldn't accept it, couldn't register it. He wasn't capable of reconciling how someone who took care of him could also do something so terrible."

"Who could?"

"So," Rikki tore a thin strip halfway down the left side of the napkin, "a piece of his mind split off like this, taking with it the memories of the abuse and the feelings about it. That way, Cam didn't have to remember what had happened—he could go on being a little kid. This protected him from the horror of the abuse."

"You mean he knew he was doing this?" Tanya said.

Rikki shook her head. "No. It was an unconscious strategy—a defense mechanism. Pretty creative, if you think about it."

Tanya raised her eyebrows. "I guess."

Rikki continued. "The next time something terrible happened, either that same part came out again to deal with it," Rikki wagged the torn section, "or another one was created." She ripped another strip halfway down the napkin. "And the next time, and the next time." She ripped two more strips. The separated pieces of napkin draped loosely over her hand. "The way I understand it, when certain parts were called on a lot, they started to develop a sense of themselves as being separate from Cam."

"And Cam didn't know about any of them?"

"No. Not until recently. He had no memory at all of having been abused. Then all of a sudden, these personalities just started coming out, and *they* relived the abuse—like flashbacks—right in front of me." Rikki was talking excitedly now. She grabbed one of the loose strips of napkin. "This one got it from the grandmother." She grabbed another. "This one got it from some strange man." She grabbed a third. "This one got it from his mother. It was amazing." She took a deep breath to try to calm herself down and wiped some sweat from her forehead with the back of her hand.

Tanya looked at her, astonished. "And the girls . . ."

"Cam's mind couldn't cope with being abused by a male. That could only happen to a girl."

"Right," Tanya nodded. "So, what are the personalities like? Do they have names? Do they know who you are? Who Kai is? What does he know about this?"

Rikki started to explain, but was interrupted when Blondie came over and asked if they wanted more drinks. Rikki shook her head no at Tanya.

Tanya looked up at Blondie and said, "No thanks. And you can take the nachos." She looked at Rikki to double-check. Rikki nodded. Blondie cleared the plate.

"Not bowlers, huh?" he said.

"Not bowlers," Tanya repeated impatiently. When he was gone, she sat forward and said, "Continue."

Rikki told Tanya about each alter, the memories they had, and how they communicated with each other and with her. She explained that we'd managed to shelter Kai from most of what was happening, but that he was just now beginning to be aware that something was wrong.

"Is this going to go away, or what?" Tanya asked. "I mean, if these guys are going to be sticking around you're going to have to tell Kai something, right? I know he's a peanut, but kids aren't stupid. It's going to come up."

"I know that!" Rikki snapped. "Sorry. It's just that . . . kids aren't supposed to have to deal with this stuff. He's little. He thinks he can touch the moon if you hold him up high enough. How's he going to deal with this? A little at a time, that's all. I'll tell him a little at a time."

"As much as you think he can handle."

"Right."

"What about the mother?"

"Her," Rikki grunted. "She's not coming to my house again. She's not seeing Kai again. No way."

"What'll he think of that?"

"I don't think he'll care, except for the presents. She always brings him something. Too much. Buying his affection. Goddamn her!"

"What about Cam's father? Oh, right, he's dead. Where the hell was he while all this was happening?"

"Cam said he kept to himself. His therapist said in abusive families there's usually a triangle. The perpetrator, the victim, and the one who denies it. Cam's father was the one who denied it. I guess he was looking the other way."

Rikki slumped against the back of the booth and took a sip of her drink, which by then was mostly melted ice. She put her hand on her chest. Her heart was racing. A delicate thread was dangling off the spool of her tightly wrapped emotions.

"Does the mother know about this?" Tanya said. "I mean, of course she knows about this—oh, shit, I don't know what I mean."

Rikki's breathing got heavier and her face turned scarlet, the tension mounting inside her.

Tanya drilled on. "What about Kai? If she abused Cam, could she have—"

Rikki exploded. "Goddammit, Tanya! I don't fucking know!"

Everyone in the restaurant stopped what they were doing and looked over.

Tanya was shocked. "Shit," she said, taken aback. "I'm sorry. I'm really sorry."

"No, Jesus, I'm sorry," Rikki apologized, embarrassed that she'd blown up at Tanya and caused a scene. The spool of emotion stopped for a second. "I'm a total wreck about this," she said. "She spent some weekends with Kai. Arly, Cam's therapist, said if Kai shows any signs, any weirdness, to take him to somebody . . . not to go hunting for something that may not be there, but . . . oh God, I'm really sorry I yelled."

Tanya put her hand up. "Stop," she said. "It's okay." She looked down at the torn napkin still in Rikki's hand. She gingerly took it and ran her fingers over the ragged strips.

"Poor Cam," she said shaking her head. "Do you think he's going to be all right?" She glanced up at Rikki and saw tears welling up in her eyes.

The thread started unraveling again and nothing could stop it now.

Rikki bit her lower lip. "I don't know," she said softly, putting her face in her hands. Her shoulders started to shake and she began to weep uncontrollably. Tears pooled in her hands and ran down her wrists, turning the cuffs of her gray sweatshirt black. "What about me?" she cried. "What about Kai and me?"

Several people glanced over curiously from the next booth. Tanya gave them the eye and they quickly looked away. Blondie was talking with the bartender, who was pointing at Rikki. Blondie made a move toward her, but Tanya spotted him and shook him off.

Tanya stood up, slid into the booth next to Rikki and put her arm around her. Rikki buried her face in her friend's shoulder and for the first time let the pain, the fear, and the anger cascade out of her. Tanya covered Rikki's hand with hers and Rikki gripped it tightly and wept.

She gasped for air several times, her shoulders shaking from the torrent of emotion. Tanya gazed silently at the lights across the lake, not knowing what to say.

After a few minutes Rikki's sobbing died down, her chest stopped heaving, and her breathing became more regular. She lifted her head from Tanya's shoulder, sniffling, her hair matted against her tear-stained face.

"I'm sorry I soaked your jacket," she said, smoothing out the soggy lapel. She took a deep breath, composing herself.

"Rikki?" Tanya said, smiling.

Rikki sniffled. "Yeah?"

"Can I have my hand back?" Rikki let go, embarrassed. Tanya held her hand up. "The claw," she said, and they both burst out laughing, relieving the tension.

Tanya got up and slid back into her side of the booth.

Rikki grabbed her purse. "I'm gonna go clean up," she said and headed for the ladies' room.

While she was gone, Tanya had Blondie bring two glasses of water and some more napkins. In a few minutes Rikki returned with her hair combed and a little makeup on. Her face was still red and her eyes looked puffy. She slid into the booth and took a sip of water.

For a moment Rikki and Tanya sat in uncomfortable silence, avoiding each other's eyes, no longer in that protected lane where it's safe to take your hands off the wheel.

Then their gaze met and Tanya spoke.

"Cam's a good guy, Rik," she said. "No matter what happened to him . . . no matter what he's like now. Don't you give up on him."

Rikki felt the tears coming again, but forced them back. She picked up the torn napkin, carefully fitting the ragged strips back together, and shook her head slowly. She looked Tanya in the eye.

"I won't," she said.

Rikki signaled for the check and Blondie quickly brought it over. He handed it to Rikki, but Tanya snatched it and insisted on paying. She gave Blondie some cash and told him to keep the change. The two women put on their coats and walked out, stopping in the parking lot to hug each other and say goodbye.

"Thank you," Rikki said softly.

Tanya smiled at her warmly. "No charge," she said and walked off toward her car.

Rikki climbed into the Volvo, turned the key, and sat for a moment with the motor idling. She reached for the shift to put the car in drive, stopped herself, and placed her gloved hand back on the wheel. Startled by her hesitation, she sat back and stared pensively across the lake at the darkened houses, imagining all the husbands and wives asleep in bed, feet touching, their struggles suspended for the night. She sighed deeply, slipped the car into gear, and eased out onto the road toward home.

"For better or for worse," she thought.

SIXTEEN

A warm fire crackled in the stone fireplace, the smell of burning oak mixing happily with the sweet scent of hot apple cider and cinnamon that wafted from a pot on the stove. Rikki had just popped a tray of corn muffins into the oven and soon the entire downstairs would smell like a Whittier poem.

Rikki jostled the logs with the poker, picked up a pen and a brown leather portfolio from the oak desk, and sat down on the couch. Propping her feet up on the ottoman, she flipped to a blank page on the yellow pad and began drafting a letter to my mother. The letter would describe the occurrences of the past months, including the memories of abuse that involved my mother and grandmother. It would be a painfully controlled letter, each prickly word carefully chosen for its precision and weight.

The density and closeness of Rikki's emotion frightened her, but she knew that writing the letter and dealing with the confrontation that might follow fell directly on her shoulders. My mother was going to want to see Kai before long, and she could not be allowed to. Not after what Rikki had seen Clay go through. Not after what Uncle Dennis had implied. And not after what we'd learned about Switch.

Over the course of several grueling sessions with Arly, Switch had revealed that his first memory was in my mother's bedroom looking back at a very young, very sad Cam standing in the hall just outside the door. My mother was in her bed with the unmistakable look of predatory desire.

Cam should not see this. Cam should not do this. No. I'll do this. Go away, boy. Close the door. Wave goodbye and close the door. And I did. I'd waved goodbye to Switch and pulled the bedroom door closed, and Switch had been abused. Switch had done what my mother had wanted. And when she was finished and said, "Good boy, Cam," it was Switch who'd hated her. He'd chuckled silently to himself that she didn't even know his name. Oh, yeah, he'd been a good boy, though. Switch had been a very good boy.

Rikki wrote the letter, and the words came rapidly in snarling bursts, pouring out of her heart onto the pages. The oven timer went off, snapping her out of her intense concentration, and she put the pen down, realizing her hand was cramped from gripping it so tightly, from pressing so hard.

Rikki got up and turned off the oven, pulled the muffin tin out, and placed it on a towel on the counter. The sweet, moist aroma penetrated the brittle cage of her thoughts and she inhaled deeply through her nose, letting it seep in.

Just then, Kai and his friend Adam came zipping through the living room wearing capes and masks and waving flexible plastic swords. They stopped in the kitchen.

"Mommy, that smells great!" Kai said. "What is it, cake?"

"Corn muffins. Want one?"

"Itchy, you want one?" Kai said to Adam—he'd nicknamed Adam "Itchy the Great" after a tiny rubber toy figure.

"Yeah!" Itchy shouted, like he'd just seen a grand slam in the bottom of the ninth.

Kai shouted, "Yeah!"

"Okay, go wash up," Rikki said. "They're going to take a minute to cool down. Do you want orange juice or cider?"

Itchy said, "Orange juice, please," and Kai looked at him and said, "Yeah!" and they gave each other a high five and ran off toward the bathroom.

A half hour later I got back from Arly's. Rikki was back on the couch still working on the letter when I walked in the front door. She looked up and smiled at me.

"Hi!" she said. "I'm glad you're home."

I sniffed. "Mmm, this place smells so good."

"Corn muffins and hot apple cider."

"Great," I said, putting my journal on the table. I took off my jacket and hung it in the closet. I wiped my feet, walked over to Rikki, kissed her, and went into the kitchen. I poured myself a cup of cider, put a muffin on a plate, and sat down in a big oak chair by the fireplace.

"How was Arly's?" Rikki asked.

"Hoo boy," I said, looking into my cup. I blew on the cider and took a sip. "Mmm, this is good." I looked over at Rikki, still watching me, waiting to hear. "It went all right," I said. "Not dead yet."

Rikki frowned.

I took a bite of the muffin and sat back in my chair munching. It was good to be home. Rikki went back to writing.

"What're you doing?" I asked.

"I'm writing a letter to your mother."

Instantly, shudder, switch, gone, and Bart was out. "Hey, Rikki," he said, crossing his legs casually.

"Who's there?" Rikki said, looking up from the letter, realizing there'd been a switch. She recognized Bart's mischievous grin. "Oh, hey Bart. Cam got upset when I mentioned his mother, huh?"

"Christ. He's so sensitive." He eyed my sneakers and muttered, "I should be wearing Beatle boots."

"Huh?"

"Nothin'. So, a letter?"

"To his mother. To tell her about what's happened, and about what people remembered. What do you think of that?"

"Beat her over the head with it," Bart said, popping the rest of my muffin in his mouth. He mumbled, "Probably break on her hair." Rikki watched him wash the muffin down with some cider.

"She can't be allowed to see Kai," Rikki said. "I don't think there's any choice here."

"No," he said casually. "Definitely not."

"I know this is upsetting to Cam," she said, "and if he's listening now, I want him to know that it's going to be all right."

Bart shuddered a little and said, "Uh oh, I think I gotta go. Love your muffins." He shuddered again, and we switched and I was back. I shook my head a couple of times to clear it.

"Whoa," I said.

"Did you hear?" Rikki said.

It took a second for Bart to fill me in. "My mother and Kai," I said. "She shouldn't see him."

"Right," Rikki said. "There's no choice here. We can't let her be alone with him, and we have to tell her why."

"I know," I said weakly. "It's just . . . what if . . . this didn't happen. This isn't happening. How am I supposed to . . ." I heard Rikki growl with annoyance as my head began to throb and I felt myself falling into the dark zone, the swirling place where angry mustangs bucked and kicked, their eyes blazing, teeth bared . . . at me. Then whispers came from inside—*dead man, dead man, dead man*—louder and louder—*dead man, YOU'RE . . . A . . . DEAD . . . MAN!!!*

I sprang from the chair and screamed, "STOPPP ITT!!" clamping my hands over my ears in a futile attempt to block the deafening sounds within. Rikki scrambled from the couch, dropping her notepad and pen, and rushed over to me.

"Cam! Cam!" she shouted, frantically grabbing me by the shoulders and shaking me.

Kai ran into the room crying, "Mommy, what's wrong with Daddy?" with panic in his little voice. "Daddy?" he called, grasping my hand. Instantly the sounds vanished, and my gaze locked on Kai's huge pleading eyes.

"Oh, my God," I said breathlessly. "Kylie, I'm sorry." I pulled him to me, and Rikki hugged us both tightly. "I'm so sorry I scared you."

"What's wrong, Daddy?" he pleaded.

Rikki dropped to one knee. "It's okay, sweetie," she said. "Daddy just had some thoughts in his head that made him really upset."

"I thought he was yelling at you."

"I would never yell at Mommy like that," I said.

Rikki said, "Kylie, we need to talk about something. I'm going to set Itchy up in your room with a movie. Be right back." And she headed out of the room.

Kai and I sat down on the floor and waited. Rikki came back in a minute and sat down cross-legged with us. She took a deep breath.

"You know how Daddy's been acting kind of different lately? Sitting in your closet and not answering right away when you call him and stuff?"

"Yeah."

"Well, that's because he remembered some really bad things that happened to him when he was very little. Things that upset him a lot. Things his mom did to him."

"Grandma?" Kai said. "What kind of things?"

"Remember what they taught you in school about good touches and bad touches?"

"Nobody's s'posed to touch ya here," he said, pointing at his crotch. "Or push ya."

"Right. Well, Grandma didn't push Daddy, but she touched him on his penis."

"That's baaad," Kai said, and inside my head started to glow red, and I heard an echo of "that's baaad."

The echo continued as Rikki told him more, and I got far away and only heard her words every now and then pinging off the walls of my mind. "She wasn't supposed to . . . said not to tell so she wouldn't get in trouble . . . it hurt his mind very badly . . . pushed it out of his mind so he wouldn't have to think about it . . . he gets far away . . . sometimes like a child . . . can't help it . . . did she ever touch you like that . . . you would tell me if she had, right . . . yeah . . . we're not going to be seeing Grandma anymore."

"Good," Kai said, and the word whooshed like a slamming door. I was back.

Kai cupped my face in his hands. "You all right, Dad?"

"Yeah. I'm all right."

"Don't yell 'stop it' anymore, okay?"

"Okay."

The worry melted from his face and a smile replaced it. He stood up, looked at us both and said, "I'm gonna go play with Itchy now." And he took off.

Rikki and I were quiet for a minute. A log crackled and hissed and Rikki glanced over at it. "Well, now he knows," she said. "A little."

Rikki picked her portfolio up off the floor and looked for the pen. She found it sticking out from under an end table, grabbed it, sat back down on the couch, and flipped open to the letter.

I slumped wearily into my chair, noticing the empty plate on the end table.

"Did I finish my muffin?" I asked.

"Bart did," Rikki said flatly, her focus back on the letter.

I bit my lip. "I hope he picked up the check."

Rikki was draining spaghetti in the brass colander while I sliced up a loaf of Italian bread at the table, not all the way through, but like they do in restaurants so you can break off a slice or two. Itchy had gone home and Kai was upstairs singing "I've Got You Under My Skin" with Frank Sinatra. He thought his name was Franksin Atra and called him Franksin. Rikki and I loved that.

"What's it like?" Rikki said over her shoulder.

I knew what she meant. I cut the last two slices, picked up the loaf, and held it up with an end in each hand.

"It's like this," I said. "All these separate pieces, but connected at the bottom. And the information travels along there so everyone sort of knows what's happening if they're paying attention." I flexed the loaf so it yawned and different pieces moved to the apex. "Constantly shifting, back and forth, so one minute I know what's happening and the next minute Kennedy's the president." Anger and frustration jabbed at me as I showed her. I raised the bread over my head with one hand, about to throw it, but stopped myself and dropped it into the basket. I pulled a chair back, slumped into it, and put my face in my hands. Rikki turned around still holding the colander.

I babbled, "What if I'm just nuts? What if nothing happened? What if I'm making all this—"

"Enough," Rikki shouted, slamming the colander down on the counter. It startled me, and I looked up at her. She was still facing the sink.

"Cam, there's no way. Goddamn that denial! You think Davy made that stuff up about your grandmother? Clay? Switch? Are they making it all up? Did you make *them* up? That's impossible." She slapped her hand against her forehead. "I can't believe this," she said, half to herself. "You're mind's a floppy loaf of bread and you think you made it all up."

Rikki turned around to face me and leaned against the counter.

"You haven't seen them like I have. Nobody could make that up. And even if they could, why the hell would they?" She shook her head. "This is real, Cam. You better believe it."

SEVENTEEN

The next day, Rikki was sitting at the desk in Cam's office when his mother walked in.

"Hello, Rikki," she said.

Rikki looked up, startled, and a tiny burst of fear jabbed her stomach. The letter was in her purse, ready to be mailed. She hadn't expected this. She swallowed hard.

"Eleanor," she said coolly. "What are you doing here?"

Eleanor posed in the doorway, wearing an elegant cobalt blue suit, Gucci floral print scarf, coral suede pumps with matching purse, pearl stud earrings, and a Patek Philippe watch. She was five feet seven, with perfectly coifed, dyed-blond shoulder-length hair, an angular stay-pressed face, rebuilt nose, and Firestone Ccups.

"I stopped off to see Tom, but he's in Boston for the day. Where's Cam?"

Rikki ignored the question. Eleanor's look-at-me pose stirred her anger and disgust, and her momentary fear dissipated.

Eleanor said, "So how's my little Kai? I haven't seen him for a while. I'd like to see him." She quickly unsnapped her purse and pulled out a small appointment book. Flipping through it, she said casually, "I'm pretty free after the twenty-third. I could pick him up about three on the twenty-fourth." She glanced up from her book. "Is that okay?"

Rikki felt the anger gnawing viciously, creeping up fast. "Ele—"

"I saw the cutest little robe and slippers—"

"Eleanor!" Rikki barked, springing out of her chair, and the genie was out of the bottle.

Eleanor took a step back, shocked. "What?"

"I can't let you see Kai."

"What?" she cried. "What are you talking about?"

Rikki pulled the letter out of her purse and threw it down on the desk. She looked at Eleanor accusingly.

"Cam knows what you did to him when he was little! He told me you sexually abused him!" She spat the words out like bits of rancid meat, jabbing her finger at the letter. "It's all in there. You . . . your mother . . . and God knows who else. Do you have any idea what you've done to him?"

Eleanor's jaw dropped, and for a few heartbeats it was as if time was suspended, as in a western when the sheriff fires his gun into the air and all the commotion stops. An arid silence hung in the room.

Rikki's eyes locked on Eleanor's. Without a word, Eleanor clamped her mouth shut, spun on her heels, and stormed out.

Rikki scrambled around the desk and followed her toward the front door, trying to catch up. Eleanor slapped the front door open, slamming it back against the stopper. It rebounded as Rikki was coming through, but she caught it before it hit her. She took two quick steps outside, grabbed Eleanor by the shoulder, and spun her around.

"You did it, didn't you?" Rikki shouted. "You fucking did it!"

"Get your hand off me!" Eleanor screeched, pulling away. She glowered at Rikki and hissed, "You don't know anything about me." She tore away from Rikki's grip, turned abruptly, and stormed over toward her car.

Furious, Rikki ran after her, grabbed her hard by the arm and spun her around again.

"Let go of me!" Eleanor shouted, jerking her arm free.

"You killed my husband!" Rikki screamed at her. Tears of rage pooled in her eyes and spilled down her cheeks. "You killed him!" she screamed again. "How could you do it?"

Eleanor took a faltering step backward as if she'd been shoved, and without another word turned away and got in her car.

Rikki stood alone in the parking lot, chest heaving, her breath coming in short gasps, and watched Eleanor drive off.

"I hate you," she whispered.

Rikki walked slowly back to the building, her mind swirling in a sick vacuum. People studiously avoided looking at her as she passed by on her way to my office. She grabbed the letter off the desk and stuffed it carelessly into her purse.

As she turned to leave, a thick, sour fluid rose in her throat and she sprinted for the restroom, burst into a stall, and threw up violently, continuing to retch long after anything was coming up. After her stomach stopped rolling, she pulled herself to her feet, walked unsteadily to the sink, and turned on the cold water. With her hands supporting her on either side of the sink, she leaned forward and peered in the mirror.

"Ashes, ashes, we all . . . fall . . . down," she sang, and the words mixed with the splashing water.

She rinsed her mouth out and patted her face dry with some paper towels. Stepping into the hall, she opened her purse and took out the letter, and as she passed Diana's desk on the way to the front door, she dropped it in the outbound mail tray. Diana looked up from her computer screen, the phone to her ear, and nodded at Rikki. Rikki nodded back and walked out of the building into the sunshine.

She drove home slowly with the radio off, mulling over what had just taken place. As she pulled into the driveway she noticed how gray and barren everything looked, and right then Rikki made up her mind. She parked the car and sat with the motor idling for a full minute. Then she turned off the ignition and said out loud, "We're outta here."

A week later a letter came from my mother denying having ever sexually abused me. Along with the letter was my birth certificate.

EIGHTEEN

"What would you think about moving to California?" Rikki asked without looking up from the electric potter's wheel she was working at in our glassed-in sunroom.

She was wearing a long work apron, a faded red sweatshirt with the sleeves pushed up to her elbows, blue jeans with a big rip in the knee, and old sneakers. Her hair was in a ponytail that stuck out through the vent in the back of her white baseball hat.

Her right foot pressed lightly on the control pedal, spinning the wheel counterclockwise, hypnotically. Thumbs locked for stability, she reached to the bottom of the pot, applied pressure and pulled steadily upward, a ring of soft clay rising like a hula hoop as the pot grew. A slick, milky gray mixture of buff clay and water coated her hands and dripped off her right wrist onto the slowly rotating wheel.

I was sitting eight feet from Rikki on the redwood steps of our Jacuzzi, my open journal resting on my knees, having a written conversation with Bart, Per, and Dusty about what had just transpired between Rikki and my mother. "Who said California?" I wrote. "Not me," Dusty wrote back. "California?" Bart wrote. I looked up from the journal, eyeing Rikki quizzically.

The midmorning sun shone through the wall of windows behind me, giving everything a slightly washed-out honey glow. A perfect photograph: "Artist at the Wheel." Rikki would've laughed at the artist part, since she'd only thrown about a dozen pots in her life, but still it would have been a good picture.

Rikki pressed her heel down on the pedal and the wheel came to a stop. She glanced over at me, wondering if I'd heard her question, but the symmetry of the pot she'd just made tugged at her attention and she shifted her gaze back to it.

"Hey, not so bad, huh? Looks sorta kinda like an actual real pot, almost . . . maybe." She giggled, swiveling on the stool, leaning out of the way so I could get a look. "At least it's not from Pisa."

"It looks really good. Probably answered an ad that read 'Be a professional pot, or just look like one.'" Rikki chuckled.

Shudder, switch, gone.

"I love it!" Anna shouted, an ear-to-ear grin on her face.

Rikki turned to face Anna. "Who's that?" Rikki asked. "Is that Anna?"

Anna nodded bashfully.

"Well, thank you, Anna," Rikki said sweetly. "How are you today?"

"Good." Every time you ask a kid how they're doing they say the same thing, "Good." And when they grow up they change it to, "Fine, thanks," and you don't know any more than you did before you asked the question.

"Anna, can I talk to Cam for a minute?"

Anna nodded.

"Cam?" Rikki called. A couple of seconds passed while I switched back.

My eyes narrowed, refocusing. "Yeah?" Rikki repeated her question.

"What would you think of moving to California? I've been thinking that maybe it's time for us to go . . . to get away from here. Away from these rotten winters . . . and everything. We've been threatening for years to get out of here."

Inside my head was the familiar clatter of alters expressing their opinions. Not just Per, Bart, and Dusty. Almost everybody had been listening. I tried to ignore it. A few seconds passed. "What about the business?"

"I talked to Tom. He said he'd buy us out." She picked up a little piece of clay and balled it with her fingers. I watched her. "We talked for a while," she said. "You know what he told me? That he doesn't think he was abused because he looked like your dad. He didn't look like you and your mother."

I felt a jab of pain in my head. "He said that?"

She nodded. "That's what he said. And that your mother never loved him—that you were the one she loved."

I swallowed hard. "I don't feel so good."

She said, "Neither do I."

I watched her roll the ball of clay into a little worm while we sat silently for a minute.

"So what do you think," Rikki said. "About moving."

I smiled tentatively. "Okay." More clatter.

"We could make a new start."

"Yeah," I said, nodding. The idea sounded good to me. "You know I hate the winters here."

"Exactly," she said, turning to rinse her hands in the water bowl, wiping them on a rag. She shook her hands to air-dry them, turned back, and rested her elbows on her knees. "And Kai's still a midget, so it won't impact him too heavily. If we're going to make a move, now is a good time for him before he really gets settled in with friends. He'd be starting at a new school next year anyway."

"But what about Arly?" I said. Now it was getting loud inside.

Rikki raised her eyebrows, took a deep breath, and exhaled slowly.

"That's a major concern," she said. "How you and all your guys would deal with leaving Arly. You know I don't take that lightly. She's our main support, and we'd need to know for sure that it was okay with everyone to leave her. If anybody else is around I'd like to hear what they think."

Shudder, switch, Bart.

"Hey, Rikki," he said, grinning. "Wow, you're a mess. Nice pot."

"Thanks. Did you hear what I was just talking about with Cam? About maybe moving?"

"To California, right?" he said. "Yeah. I think it's a great idea!

Sunshine, here we come! Course we need to discuss it as a group, though. I mean, right now everybody's making a racket. Like lunch time at Zabar's. We definitely need Per at the wheel on this one."

"Absolutely," Rikki said, and then she looked puzzled. "You've been to Manhattan?" Bart shrugged.

She shook her head. "Anyway, moving would mean leaving Arly, and—"

"Ahh, don't worry about her," Bart said, making a get-out-ofhere gesture. "She doesn't need us."

"You've got it backwards."

"Huh? Oh, right. You mean us getting along without her. What's the big deal?" Huge racket inside now. "Wait, she's great," he said, backpedaling. "I'm not dumping on Arly." He flicked a speck of something off my shirt.

Rikki looked frustrated. "This is important," she said.

"Sorry." He put his hand up, embarrassed. "You're definitely right. I'll talk it over with these guys," he said, gesturing with his thumb over his right shoulder.

"Good," Rikki said and turned back to the wheel.

She reached for the bat—a plastic disc with two holes that fits precisely over two flat-topped bolt heads on the wheel so when you finish a pot you just lift off the bat with the wet pot on it, place a new bat on the wheel, and throw a new ball of clay down in the center. That's what Rikki did. Then she dipped her hands in the water bowl, stepped on the pedal, and started in on a new pot. Bart picked up the conversation in the journal.

Having conversations in the journal is like watching a color printer print a page with every few lines changing color. There's only one print mechanism moving back and forth, but there are brief pauses as the different colors in the cartridge alternate. With us it's very similar. My hand holds the pen and the flow of writing is fairly continuous, but there are slight interruptions as different alters exert control. I feel different alters grip the pen differently, and I see the writing style and grammatical expression change, sometimes dramatically, sometimes almost imperceptibly. Usually I hear the words in my head as they're being written, much as I do when I'm writing alone, although when there's a running conversation, I'm aware that the voices belong to others who live in the lazy Susan of my mind. After a long conversation in the journal I'm always tired. This one was a long one.

Rikki worked silently on the new pot for a few minutes, but it ended up crashing. She shut the wheel off, threw the crashed pot in the scrap bucket, sponged off the bat and the wheel, and went to wash up. She came back into the room just as we were finishing our internal chat.

"Hi," she said, sitting down next to me Indian-style. "Doing a lot of writing, huh?"

I heaved a sigh. "I'm beat." I looked up from the journal and looked at Rikki. "Oh, you done throwing?" I said, noticing she'd changed clothes.

"Yeah," Rikki chuckled. "About fifteen minutes ago."

She'd let her hair down, applied makeup, and changed into a plum turtleneck, denim jumper, cream-colored tights, and fluffy scrunched-down socks that matched her shirt. She looked fresh and vibrant and beautiful.

"I love you," I said and leaned over to kiss her. As I did I felt a sharp twinge of pain in my mid-back.

"Oooh!" I moaned, grimacing, reaching around to massage it. "I shouldn't have sat like this for so long."

"Here, let me get it," Rikki said, feeling for the spot. "That's it!"

I winced. "Oooh!"

"Lie down," she said, scooching over.

I stretched out on the floor next to the hot tub and she knelt next to me, kneading the spot. Soon the knot began to loosen and the pain melted into pleasure.

"That better?" she said.

"Oh, yeah. Thanks." I was hesitant to ask her to continue,

although I wanted her to. I felt like she was doing so much just by being there for me—for us—that it wasn't right to ask for anything more. A massage was way above the call. I guess Rikki didn't see it that way. Without stopping, she moved her hands to my shoulders and continued the massage.

"So," she said, "was everyone talking about maybe moving?"

"Yeah. Lot of talk. It's a big deal. I think it's a great idea, though, except it scares the shit out of me to think of leaving Arly."

"Yeah," Rikki nodded. "It is scary."

Her touch felt wonderful. The rhythmic kneading of my shoulders relaxed me and my mind began to drift hypnotically. "Well," she said, working the muscles in my neck, "it's still winter and we wouldn't want to leave until Kai gets out of school. We could put the house on the market and hopefully sell it by June. In the meantime, you and your guys could be working on things with Arly so you're all prepared for the move."

I was in a distant place now, skipping through poppies.

"So if you agree, then we'll do it," she continued, still rubbing. "I'll call Hillie Randall about the house. He could sell boots to a fish."

My voice said, "So could he."

"He?" Rikki said. "He who?"

"Him," the voice said. "Cam."

Rikki pulled her hands back like she'd touched something hot. "Bart?"

"Mm hmm."

Startled, she slid back a foot and shifted from her knees to a sitting position. Giving me a massage was one thing. Giving one to Bart was another.

Bart rolled over, propping his head on his hand. He could see she was upset.

"What's up?" he said.

"Bart, we've gotta get something straight," Rikki said, annoyed. "I need to know when someone other than Cam is out. I don't . . . like . . . surprises. Now let me talk to Per, please."

"Okay, sure," he said, a little hurt and embarrassed. He paused a moment. Rikki waited for the switch. Nothing happened. "What am I supposed to do?" Bart said with a splash of bitters. "Run into a phone booth?"

Rikki raised an eyebrow. "Aw, don't worry," he said. "I'm just kidding. I know what to do. We do this all the time at Arly's. I'll just close my eyes and fade back and let Per come out." He closed his eyes for a couple of seconds and reopened them, looking at Rikki. "It's just that sometimes I'm just . . . here . . . and don't want to leave. Like I'd be glad to move over and let somebody else be here, but I don't want to leave." He pointed at his chest with his thumb.

"That makes sense," Rikki said sympathetically. "I can understand that. Well . . . it's good for you to stick around. That's co-consciousness, right?"

"Yeah."

"So all you need to do is just sort of go inside a bit and let Per . . . or whomever . . . come out. What does Arly tell you all to do?"

"She either calls somebody out by name or says that the person who's out should just relax. Usually there's a lot going on and people just come out whenever they have something to say. It's pretty wild."

Rikki looked deeply into Bart's eyes. "Well, I don't want 'wild' here," she said seriously. "I want things as normal as possible. And having you come out and not say anything while I'm giving Cam a massage falls into the 'wild' category for me. So please don't do that anymore, okay?"

"Okay. I'm sorry."

"It's all right. Now I'd like to talk with Per for a minute. Just relax a little and let Per come out."

"Okay, see ya," Bart said, closing his eyes and taking a long, slow breath. In a couple of seconds he gave a little shudder, and Per opened his eyes and blinked the way people do when they first wake up.

"Per?"

"Mm hmm. Hello Rikki. How are you?"

"Oh, pretty good, thanks. And you?"

He looked down at himself. "I guess I'm lying on the floor."

"Yeah. I was giving Cam a massage and—"

"Oh, that's nice," he said warmly.

"And Bart came out without announcing himself. It sort of startled me, and we just talked about it. I told him I want people to announce themselves whenever they come out."

Per nodded, a pleasant smile on his face.

"I don't expect the young ones to do it; frankly I can recognize them pretty much right away. I guess it's just with the adults."

"It makes good sense, Rikki. I think doing that will increase your sense of stability. This must be very difficult for you."

Rikki nodded, relieved to have some support. "Yes," she said. "It can get pretty confusing."

"And upsetting."

She nodded again. "And upsetting."

Rikki paused a moment, closed her eyes and leaned back, her face bathed in late February's low sunlight. The warmth was soothing.

She opened her eyes and rested her gaze on Per.

"So," she said, "what did people have to say about maybe moving and leaving Arly?"

"Well . . . some of the young ones were upset. Clay and Anna in particular. Dusty's upset, too."

"I can understand that."

"We'd definitely have to make a priority of finding someone to replace Arly," Per said. He looked deeply into her soft blue eyes. "Is moving to California something you really want to do?"

Rikki nodded. "Yes. I think it would be good for us to get away from here. Not only would we be distancing ourselves from Cam's mother, but it would be sunny and warm a lot of the time. And that'd be good. No more freezing, snowy winters and hot, sticky summers." She tilted her head back and ran her fingers through her hair. "I was thinking about the San Francisco area. An old high school friend of Cam's lives out there, been there for years. He loves it."

"I'm sure it's very nice."

"I'm sure. And there are probably some very good therapists and maybe even some support groups. San Francisco is a pretty liberal place,

I think. Hell, Cam found Arly here," Rikki gestured with her hands, "in Butt Lips, Mass."

"That's true," Per said.

"We should take a trip out there and look around, ya think?"

"It sounds like a good idea to me. Give us a little time, though, if you would, so we can work on this a bit with Arly and by ourselves."

Per made it sound easy. It wasn't.

NINETEEN

The recipe for leaving Arly was simple: Take one barrel, add one man (be careful not to bruise), place mixture at top of Niagara Falls, let go.

Inside it went something like this: I wanna go, you wanna go? Yeah, I wanna go. What about them? Well, I don't want to go. I like Arly. So do I. Leaving Arly doesn't mean we don't like her. Who'd look after us? Bart, Per, Dusty, Rikki. But who out there? Who, like Arly? I don't know. Well? We could find someone. I'd miss Arly. So would I. Why, where's Arly going? Arly's not going anywhere. We're talking about moving to California. How come? To get away. From what, bad guys? No, don't worry. There are no bad guys here. So why do we have to go? Well, it seems like we should go. It would be nice there all the time. Do they have ice cream there? Yes, they have ice cream—lots of flavors. Would Rikki go with us? Yes, Rikki would go with us. Would Arly go with us? No. Arly would stay here. Could we come and see her? I don't know. Maybe. Who gives a shit about Arly? Hey, hey, hey! She's been good to us. Sorry. Don't chew him out. Okay, I'm sorry for saying hey, hey, hey. I'd miss her a lot. Me, too. Yeah, me too. Me three. We'd all miss Arly, or most of us would. Would we be safe? I hope so. What do you mean you hope so? Well, we'd have to be very careful and pay close attention to everybody. We could do that, right? Well for sure. Nothin's easy.

One night I dreamt I was an injured Sambar deer, alone near the bank of a narrow river, my parched throat and seeping wounds having drawn me toward the cool water away from the safety of the herd up on the plateau. Along the opposite shore the crocs watched me with their ancient, lifeless eyes and rows of anxious teeth, waiting for my hoof to break the surface, my head to drop, my tongue to dip into the quenching liquid. Unconsciously I weighed the risk. I could see the danger. But the far greater danger were the crocs I couldn't see, the ones lurking just below the surface, also silently waiting to lunge and drag me under for a death roll at the muddy bottom.

Suddenly behind me I caught the musky scent of a Siberian tiger, followed by the faint sound of rustling in the high grass nearby as it stealthily inched closer, also thirsting, not for water, but for the taste of my blood. There was danger all around. Hmm. To leave the plateau . . . to risk a drink . . . to soothe my stinging wounds . . . possibly to die. Hmm.

It didn't take Sam Spade to figure out what the dream was about. Arly and I talked it over and we agreed that moving was tough, even for regular people, and that going to California would be risky, would tax my system to the limit, maybe past it, even though it might be the best thing for us. She had faith in Rikki, though, and knew my guys and I wouldn't be totally unprotected at the bank of the river. She encouraged us to go.

On the way home I wondered if California would be far enough. It wouldn't. The truth is, wherever you go, your crocs go, too.

TWENTY

In early April, Rikki organized a week-long family vacation/reconnaissance mission. She called my old friend Joe Gearhart, with whom we'd had very little contact over the years, but still had a nice connection. Joe told her everything he knew about the Bay area and suggested we check out Leona as a possible place to relocate to, describing it as a lovely town about thirty miles east of the city, with good schools and easy access to everything.

Rikki explained to Joe that I was very different from the way he might have remembered me from high school; that I had recently been diagnosed with a serious psychiatric condition stemming from child abuse. Joe was shocked and saddened to hear that. He was also a little concerned about how to act with me, but Rikki assured him I'd be okay, that he had nothing to worry about. Joe said he'd accept me any way I was and generously offered to take us around and show us the area when we came out.

And then we were off like a bride's nightie. The thought of being three thousand miles away from Arly for a week gnawed at me the whole way over, and at one point I had to get up in a hurry and have a conversation with the airplane's toilet bowl about it.

I felt a little better after that. Rikki patted my hand, reminded me that she'd packed Toby in one of the carry-on bags, and said she'd go for him if I thought that would help out. We opted to leave Toby stowed, but I admit it was a comfort just knowing he was there.

Rikki was smiling her thousand-watt smile again, which I hadn't seen in a long time, and it helped draw me out of my dark cave. Per was exerting his calming influence, too, having agreed with Arly to stick close and watch over the tribe.

Bart was hoping for beer and peanuts and flight attendant cleavage. *Beer? Hah! Good thinking, Bart! Let's get shitfaced and unwind. Let the crazy man scare all the nice passengers. Right.* No, beer was definitely out. And our flight attendant's name was Rocco. Rocco brought Bart the peanuts, and he took them grudgingly, thinking, *"There but for the grace of God goes cleavage."*

Bart turned his attention to Kai, reading him some books, pretending to be me. While he did that I went inside somewhere and rested, conserving my mental energy for our arrival. It worked, and when we got to San Francisco International Airport I was feeling pretty good. I even drove the rental car out to Leona while Rikki navigated. She'd booked us a cozy suite at a hotel off Santa Rita Road, and it was clean and homey with a nice kitchen, and looked a little like the tiny apartment we'd rented in Boston when we first got married.

The first thing I did was spring Toby and prop him up between the pillows on the king-size bed. *Toby's out. That's good. We're doing all right.* We provisioned ourselves at the Safeway around the corner from the hotel, called Joe to let him know we'd arrived, and made a plan to meet for a tour the following morning. Then we spent the rest of the day at the pool.

The next day we got up early and drove around Leona. Everything Joe had said about it was true. The town was clean, bright, pretty, and well laid out. It was surrounded by beautiful rolling hills and had a nice view of Mount Diablo, a four-thousand-foot peak only ten miles away. The elementary schools looked well tended, and the large park in the center of town was beautifully landscaped. The houses were close together as Joe told us they'd be, and each one had a nice-looking mini-front yard and a fenced-in patch in back. It occurred to me that if we moved here, Kai and I would actually have to use the toilet to take a leak.

Although Rikki and I hadn't seen him in nearly ten years, Joe was the same warm, caring, funny person we remembered. And Kai thought he was the oyster's ice skates. As he'd promised, Joe spent that day and the next proudly showing us all around Berkeley and San Francisco. Rikki and I were impressed with the variety of culture and landscape in both. We liked the close European feel of the neighborhoods in the Berkeley hills and the odd mixture of college kids, old and new hippies, and derelicts along Telegraph Avenue.

Golden Gate Park seemed like a huge, lush playground, delicately veined with a myriad of bicycle and Rollerblade paths. You could pop off to visit the museum, the aquarium, or the Japanese tea garden, and pop back on to head down to the ocean or just around the corner to the zoo. The rest of the city was as throaty and vibrant as Toulouse-Lautrec's Paris. The splendor and the pulse were intoxicating. One could definitely live here. No question. Well, one question. Could I live anywhere?

We had no privacy from Kai so there wasn't a lot of switching during the day. The adults did come out from time to time while we were walking around, leaning over to quietly announce their presence to Rikki, as she'd requested. The only time we had a problem was at the Ghirardelli chocolate shop over by Fisherman's Wharf, when Clay came out. We were poking around, sniffing and looking, and Clay just liked what he saw and popped out before anyone inside could stop him. *Hey, chocolate.* Kai saw that switch and it scared him, and Joe quickly distracted him while Rikki stepped in and called me back. Probably scared Joe, too. At night, after Kai had gone to sleep, my guys were free to come out and talk with Rikki about their thoughts and impressions. Rikki read Kai's books to the young ones and even bought them Tigger bubble bath, which was a wonderful surprise.

We spent the rest of the week getting a feel for Leona, taking Kai to the park and relaxing by the pool. While Rikki and I were driving around one day, shortly before we went home, we discovered Diablo Regional Wilderness, a park on the edge of Leona. It was spectacular. We couldn't believe it. Lush, green hills for miles—we didn't know they'd turn brown for the summer—hawks and cows and lizards, trails, and quiet, like our woods in Massachusetts. So what if we moved into a house on a sixteenth of an acre. We could go to Diablo.

The real clincher, though, was El Balazo, a Mexican place that served by far the best burritos Rikki or I had ever eaten. Monsters with black beans, saffron rice, charbroiled chicken, guacamole, salsa, and sour cream. Mmm. Kai didn't give a damn about El Balazo. What he cared about was Chicken McNuggets, and, of course, Leona had those, too. So he was sold on the move.

What Leona didn't have was bugs. Or rain from May to October. Or snowy, icy winters. Or my mother. Or Arly. Except for the Arly part, it looked good. If we could find someone out here to replace her, we'd be okay. Maybe.

When we got back to Massachusetts we worked the business thing out with Tom, and Rikki called Hillie Randall about the house. Hillie was a tall, wiry guy in his late forties with curly hair, large tortoise-shell glasses and a scraggly poet's beard that made me want to put him in a full Nelson and let Vinnie the barber give him a shave. He was only too delighted to sell our house again—he'd not only sold it to us, but to the people we'd bought it from and the people they'd bought it from. For Hillie, selling our house was a hobby.

When he came over to sign the papers, Hillie was shocked to see me looking so wild and disheveled. I hadn't been to a barber in over six months and my hair looked like it belonged on one of those weird little rubber troll dolls that are supposed to look cute.

Hillie was already aware that I was oatmeal north of the eyebrows. He, his wife Anne, and their two little kids had come over for a visit a while back—the first company we'd had since I'd gone 'round the twist—and it hadn't turned out so well. Dusty had come out and didn't know who Hillie and Anne were, and asked Rikki right in front of them, which startled them to say the least. A few minutes later Clay came out and walked into Kai's playroom, sat down on the floor and started playing with toys and talking to himself. Luckily the kids were all upstairs watching a movie.

Within an hour of their arrival, the Randalls were backing down our long slick driveway in their Cadillac, rolling the road up behind them. We hadn't heard from them since. But this was different. This wasn't social. It was business. And Hillie wasn't going to turn away money.

It took three months for the house to sell. Taking the cover off the pool finally did it, I guess. That and the fact that the gardens were in bloom and the leaves were back so you couldn't see any houses in the distance. Nothing but nature. Complete privacy. The Stone House, we'd called it. That's how all our mail was addressed.

Even the package from my mother containing all my baby pictures that arrived just before Kai's birthday.

TWENTY-ONE

Denial is a pointy rake that slices a jagged music staff into your naked back and plays its screeching, crimson, melody over and over and over until you die. I'm bad for telling. It's all my fault. How could I do this to my mother? I'm not multiple, I'm just a crazy person! I made all this up. Go awaaaay! What do you mean you're not multiple—where do you think we came from, asshole? Try to get rid of me and I'll fuckin' kill you! Did I think that, or did that really happen? Steady, stay steady. I'm losing it! Who's losing it? Who're you? Huh? crazy crazy crazy CRAAAZZZYY!!

Thanks to my mother's letter with the birth certificate, and then the baby pictures, we not only had to terminate with Arly, we had to deal with Denial's Rake. That goddamn rake. It was a revolving door every session at Arly's, alters coming out in rapid succession, each with his or her own pain, fear, or confusion. Arly was like the guy with the spinning plates on Ed Sullivan, except nobody clapped at the end.

During my five minutes of each session—it often felt like that's all I got—Arly chipped away at my denial. She did it gently. With a bat.

"Maybe nothing happened," she said. "But if so, then what about Davy? Or Clay? Or Dusty? Or Switch? What about your mother's reaction to what Rikki said? Is that how you'd react if someone in *your* family accused you of child abuse? Say nothing and walk away? Do you think Davy was abused by his grandmother? What about the calls to Abbey and Dennis? Okay, so you believe it happened to Davy. Do you believe

March 9

I'm not Really
Multiple I'm just cra
they're all wrong
They are all wrong
I'm Not multiple
I made It All up
Because I'm Flawed;
Fundamentally Flawed Should
Be Killed

NO Don

Do It

Denial.

You stop
him
I Dont
want
any one
hurt

Clay? So you believe Clay. Dusty? Mm hmm. Switch? Right. Well, if you can believe that they were abused, then you need to remember that they are parts of you. They . . . are . . . parts . . . of . . . you. If they were abused, *you* were abused."

Goddamn, she pissed me off.

"If your mother walked in here and said she did it," Arly said, "would that help?"

"Of course it would help! That would be the smoking gun!"

Arly leaned back and chuckled. "R-i-i-ght. The smoking gun."

The smile dropped off her face. "Well it's never going to happen. I've been doing this for a long time and I've never seen it happen. It could be that your mother doesn't even remember having abused you, although I seriously doubt it. She's certainly got her own denial. Huge denial. Your mother's not going to deliver the smoking gun."

Her words made my teeth hurt.

"So here's the fix. On one hand," she said, draping her right hand palm up over the arm of her chair, "you're aware of the irrefutable evidence that you are in fact multiple. You've seen the writing in your journal. You hear your alters when they're talking to me. You hear them talking to you . . . or Rikki. Time slips for you when they're out. And on the other hand," Arly draped her left hand over the other arm of the chair, "you've got a damn good reason to think you're just nuts. Because if you're nuts . . . if there is some neurobiological basis to your condition . . . everyone is off the hook. Nobody hurt you. Your past is intact."

Arly leaned forward. "Cam," she said, "you . . . are the smoking gun."

As we got closer to leaving, Arly did what she called "the roundup"—the review of the skills she'd helped us develop over the previous eight months: cooperation among alters, self-soothing, self-acceptance, staying safe. Everything critical to my remaining stable during and after the move. Arly suggested I create a room in my mind where everyone could go to be safe, to relax, get some comfort. I did.

We called it the Comfort Room. It's a large and beautiful high-ceilinged room with thick white carpeting, oversized plush couches, and huge windows that overlook a peaceful sandy beach and the ocean. When we gather, we gather there. When somebody has troubles, he or she goes to the Comfort Room—never alone—always with someone to help ease the pain.

Arly was confident we'd be able to find someone in the Bay area who was knowledgeable about DID. Toward that end she gave me the number of the Sidran Foundation, an international organization that disseminates information about the dissociative disorders.

I called Sidran, and a kind woman gave me information about the International Society for the Study of Dissociation (ISSD), which had a listing of members by states, many of them therapists who, if nothing else, had at least heard of Dissociative Identity Disorder. She also gave me the telephone number for Del Amo Hospital in Torrance, California, which had a unit that specialized in treating people with dissociative disorders.

To my astonishment I was also told about the existence of a self-run group for multiples in Oakland at a place called Sedona House. Oakland was only twenty minutes from Leona. *Other people like me. Support.* Arly strongly urged me to try this group.

"Being with other people with your condition will help you overcome your denial," she said. "Very important."

Our final session was tearful. Per handed Arly a drawing we'd made filled with crying faces, goodbye waves, thank yous, I'll miss yous, and I love yous. Everyone said goodbye to Arly in his or her own way—hugging her, shaking hands with her, or just nodding to her from the client chair.

And then the session was over, and we walked out the door and into the future. Dr. Arly Morelli was no longer our therapist.

Driving slowly home, I wondered who would hold the gossamer thread.

PART TWO

CIRCLING THE DRAIN

TWENTY-TWO

Rikki, Kai, and I moved into our new home on Blackhawk Court with nothing but three suitcases and a half-eaten bag of tortilla chips. The house was an airy, two-story, California design with large comfortable rooms and vaulted ceilings. No stone walls, no deer, no hot tub, no pool, no runs, no hits, no errors (we hoped).

The first day in Leona we met Linda and Peter Withington and their two children Jack and Taylor, Australian neighbors two doors down. Jack was Kai's age, and the two of them went together like good teeth. Linda loaned us some sheets and pillows and things to use until the truck arrived five days later with all of our stuff and our cars. In the meantime, we got Kai set up in the second grade at Canyon Elementary School, right around the corner.

Rikki and I cautiously tooled around town in our rented Buick, trying to look as if we belonged in California. I cut my hair so I wouldn't scare the neighbors. We got California drivers' licenses and read the California newspapers and bought California food from the California Safeway.

On our third night there I ventured out to Oakland for the multiples' support group meeting. Cameron West . . . the wild West . . . out in the Wild West. On the way to Sedona House I developed an incredible thirst and began looking for a convenience store. Driving through San Leandro on Route 580, I spotted one by an exit and ducked off the highway. The jangling clutter inside my head was overwhelming—the anxiety of being in a new place, of venturing out on my own, at night, to a meeting where I didn't know anybody, a crazy people's meeting. I was in a highly dissociated state—everyone and no one at the same time. Not good.

I drove half a block through a rundown neighborhood and pulled into a tiny parking lot in front of a shabby store with a bunch of neon beer signs in the window. I walked in and stopped about five feet from the counter. I couldn't remember what I'd come in for.

I gazed blankly at the clerk, a heavily muscled, mean-looking kid in his early twenties, wearing a skintight T-shirt with the words I'M READY on it in big letters. He was chewing on a plastic coffee stir. We were the only people in the store.

He fiddled with some things behind the counter, waiting for me to pick up some Chiclets or ask him a question. I said nothing; just gave him the blank stare of a mentally ill person.

The stir bobbed in his mouth as Mr. Ready worked on it, sizing me up. Was I there to rob him? I certainly didn't look like the kind of person who'd hold up a convenience store. I made him nervous, though, because after a few darting glances and some more fiddling he stood up straight, narrowed his eyes, and gave me the hard stare—the "bigger dick" stare he probably used in bars.

"What're *you* looking at?" he snarled through yellow teeth, jabbing his chin at me.

His threatening tone triggered Leif, who instantly came out to protect us, and my vacant, dissociated stare quickly changed to a penetrating fiery gaze.

"What did you say?" Leif said icily, and inside I felt my body and my mind harden.

Mr. Ready shifted his stance, screwing down his mean look. His lip curled. "I said, 'What're you looking at?'"

Working the night shift in that neighborhood, Mr. Ready probably saw a lot of weirdos, and he was used to scaring them off with the muscles and the vicious look. Probably liked it, too. Probably practiced in the mirror. He didn't know Leif would just as soon chew on his larynx as buy him a toy.

Leif grinned at Mr. Ready the way a panther would if panthers could grin, and the muscles in his jaw flexed and relaxed. Leif said softly, dangerously, "Ask me nicely if you can help me find something . . . son."

The veiled ferocity in Leif's look and voice jarred Mr. Ready, and he didn't like it. He looked confused for a moment and glanced toward the door, hoping for replacements.

Leif's gaze clamped down harder on Mr. Ready. Outside, the heavy night drooped uncaring over the buzzing freeway, but inside, in that bristling moment, it was high noon. Leif repeated, "Ask me nicely if you can help me find something." *Back down or draw.*

In an instant Mr. Ready's hard stare melted; he'd sensed something in Leif much more powerful than himself. Mr. Ready's face flushed and he looked like he wished he had a lap to jump into.

"Can I . . . uh . . . help you . . . uh . . . find somethin'?" he said carefully. Leif relaxed—we all relaxed. *No more danger.*

After a long pause Leif said, "Club soda."

With a puzzled look on his ugly face, Mr. Ready nervously pointed a thick finger at the cold case. "It's over there."

Leif walked to the case, picked out the drink, returned to the counter, and handed a dollar to Mr. Ready, eyeing him steadily. Mr. Ready took the money and handed him the change without looking up. From the bleachers I noticed he had dirt under his fingernails.

Leif stopped in the parking lot and said inside, "Where's the car? Where are we?" Immediately I switched back out, and he stepped into the background. I walked shakily to the rental car and climbed in.

The internal conversation began. "What the hell was that?" Bart said.

"Nothin'," Leif replied. "The kid was being nasty and Cam was in outer space somewhere."

"That's not n-nice," Clay said.

"I'm sorry. I meant Cam was . . . I don't know. He just needed a hand is all. So I stepped in."

"Okay," Per said. "We're all under some pressure here and we need to relax. Let's drink this water—"

"Club soda," Switch corrected him.

"Let's drink this club soda and take some deep breaths," Per said. "That'll help calm us all down."

"Thank you, Leif, for helping out," Dusty said.

"You're welcome."

Bart said, "Okay . . . deep breaths."

We breathed deeply and began to relax just slightly. I opened the can and took a drink. The cold, bubbly soda tickled my throat and helped me focus on my surroundings. We did some more deep breathing, talking back and forth amongst ourselves while we drank the club soda. Once I looked up and saw Mr. Ready peek out of the storefront window at me, then quickly look away when our eyes met. It was time to get out of there and down to the meeting.

Luckily, Sedona House wasn't hard to find, and I arrived with about ten minutes to spare before the eight o'clock meeting. It was on a steep side street just off Lake Shore Avenue in Oakland. I nosed the car into a spot, careful to turn the wheels hard into the curb like I'd seen other people do on steep streets, just in case my rental car decided to make a break for it. Hell, I wanted to make a break for it. *Just go in. There'll be people like us. I wonder what they look like? You mean kids who are tall? Be brave, Cam. Okay, don't leave me.*

Sedona House wasn't what I'd expected; I'd pictured a community center with fluorescent lights and Pepsi machines, not a regular two-story house from the fifties. I walked across the street, nervously fingering the keys in my pocket. There were some other people walking purposefully toward the building, and I wondered if they were multiples, too. The lights were on all over the house, and I could see a group of ten or fifteen people standing around in what must have been the living room at one time.

I climbed the stairs at the left side of the house, passing several people smoking and chatting casually on a large covered porch. The door was open and I walked in feeling very scared and alone. Inside looked like what it was, a community center in a house. I fell in behind a few people who were lined up in front of a sign-in sheet on a small desk against the right wall of the entrance hall.

To my right by the front door stood a round table with a stack of in-out trays full of notices printed on paper of different colors. There was a stack of Sedona House information packets next to it, and I picked one up and thumbed through it while I waited in line. I flipped open the first page and saw the list of all the different meetings held there: Survivors of Incest, Love and Sex Addiction, Multiple Personalities United, Partners of Survivors, Partners of Multiples, and maybe half a dozen more.

It was my turn to sign in. I looked at the sheet. People before me had written their first names and which meeting they were attending and checked a box if it was their first time. I scanned the sheet for MPU and saw nine other names, eight female and one male. I picked up the pen to sign in and noticed my hand was shaking. I put the pen down, turned to walk out, and practically ran right into a dark-haired woman who weighed maybe two hundred pounds, wearing a huge purple and orange cape.

"Oh jeez, I'm sorry," I said.

She smiled warmly at me and said, "It's all right. I cut a wide swath." She stuck her hand out. "I'm Sally. You are . . . ?"

I took her hand and shook it. "Cam."

"Welcome, Cam."

"Thank you, Sally." I was having a little trouble breathing and wanted to get outside to some air. Inside I heard Bart say, *"Cool out, Cam."*

"First time here?" Sally asked. "I don't think I've seen you before."

"Yes," I said, noticing her deep green eyes. *Something about them.* "I just moved here from Massachusetts a few days ago with my wife and son."

"Wow!" she said. "You must be nervous." Sally was still searching my face for something, sizing me up.

"Yeah, I am," I said, scanning the room. I brought my gaze back to hers. "Really nervous."

She smiled again. "It can be a little overwhelming the first time. Which meeting are you here for?"

"I was thinking about going to the multiples' meeting." I was embarrassed to say it aloud.

"I had a feeling that's why you were here."

"You did?"

"Yeah."

"How could you tell?"

"I've been running that meeting for two years. Have you ever met another multiple, Cam?"

I shook my head.

She nodded. "Just diagnosed?"

"Less than a year ago."

"Well," she said, smiling warmly. "The meeting's about to start. You're welcome to join us if you'd like."

Sally made a move for the stairs and I stepped out of her way. I stood in the lobby for half a minute watching her make a slow and labored ascent to the second floor, my hand in my pocket fingering the car keys again. *Don't run.* I stopped fiddling with the keys, signed the sheet, and followed Sally up the stairs.

At the top, we turned left into what must have been the master bedroom back when people lived there. It was a large and airy room with two single-paned crank windows facing the side of the house I'd come in. Directly across from the entrance were two French doors that led to what seemed to be a small study facing the street. The doors to that room were closed and three empty folding chairs sat in front of them. Throw pillows were scattered around the room on the large worn Oriental rug, and there were two old lime green vinyl-covered chairs to the left, separated by an end table with a box of Kleenex on it. To the right was a dark brown corduroy couch. There were several standing lamps in corners of the room and track lighting along the borders of the ceiling.

A cardboard box filled with stuffed animals sat on the floor in the middle of the room, with a smaller box of coloring books and colored paper next to it. A wicker basket filled with crayons, markers, and colored pencils was next to that.

The nine people whose names I'd seen on the sign-in sheet were spread about, some chatting with each other, some quietly standing alone. A plump woman with rings on all her fingers and both thumbs was on her hands and knees, picking crayons out of the basket.

I crossed the room and sat down on one of the chairs against the French doors. Other people picked their spots and sat down, too. Sally lowered herself with difficulty into one of the green chairs and opened the binder. She glanced over at me and smiled before beginning to read.

"This is a self-run meeting for multiples. It is not monitored by a therapist. Each person here must be considerate of every other person's feelings. There will be no cross-talk when people are speaking unless it is asked for. No one may describe incidents of abuse in graphic detail. Alters are welcome here, but child alters cannot come out and act out in any way. No self-harm of any kind will be accepted here. There is a meeting for child alters on the third Thursday of every month. Try to keep your sharing to no more than five minutes so everyone can have a chance. Once everyone who wants to has shared, then people are welcome to share again."

I looked slowly around the room at the other people: a tall, thin girl with dark brown eyes and broken wire-rimmed glasses; a masculine-looking woman with short, choppy hair, an army jacket and jump boots; Sally; a blond middle-aged guy with piercing eyes holding a ratty-looking bunny; a woman wearing a beret with a lot of pins on it; a hollow-eyed woman with long frizzy black hair and three stuffed animals sticking out of a large backpack; a young woman wearing baggy overalls and a black watch cap furiously drawing on a big sketch pad; a wild-looking woman with freshly bandaged arms and a nervous twitch; and the plump woman with all the rings stretched out on the floor drawing in a *Sesame Street* coloring book. Clay had his eye on that book.

The woman with the rings spoke without looking up or stopping coloring.

"I'm Sarah," she said in a child's voice. "We're having a bad, bad day so we're just gonna color for a while. Our cat died today and we had to take him to the vet and we didn't have the money but the man took him anyway. I'm out cause I'm not gonna cry, but everyone else wants to cry, especially Margie."

A heartbeat later Sarah's face went blank, lifted toward the ceiling, and then contorted with the kind of anguish you see in *Life* war photos of women holding their dead children. She dropped her crayon, sat upright, hugged her knees, and began to rock from side to side and sob pathetically.

"Sssaaaaaammm! You left meeee!" she moaned. "You left meeee!!" She gasped for air. "He was dead he was dead he was dead," she repeated hypnotically, eyes staring straight ahead, tears streaming down her face. And then, click, the channel changed and she was gone and Sarah was back. She wiped her face on her sleeve, laid down on the floor, picked up the crayon, and started coloring Elmo.

"See?" she said nonchalantly. "I told ya Margie was upset." And then she fell silent.

Outside a car accelerated up the hill, and in the room no one spoke; there was only the sound of colored charcoal being dragged across a page by the woman with the baggy overalls. I couldn't believe what I'd just seen. This woman Sarah . . . or Margie . . . switched. Just like us.

After a minute the woman with the bandaged arms raised her hand and said, "I'll go." Everyone looked at her. "I'm Cinnamon," she said, fingering her lower lip.

Everyone said, "Hi, Cinnamon."

Cinnamon took her finger from her lip and pointed it at me. "We want to know who that man is over there."

Pow! Adrenaline shot through my body; I involuntarily jerked, and everyone in the room jumped. I sprang out of my chair, my heart thumping wildly. *Go!*

Startled, Cinnamon said, "I'm sorry. Oh, God, I'm sorry. Please don't go," she pleaded, reaching out toward me with her bandaged arms. "I didn't mean to scare anybody." She smiled at me sweetly. "I just wanted to know who you were."

Sally said, "Cam, please don't leave. It's my fault. I forgot we always announce it when we have someone new in the group."

Her eyes swept the faces in the room. "Everybody, this is Cam. He just moved here from Massachusetts."

Everyone said, "Hi, Cam." Hesitantly, I sat down again. "Sorry to interrupt you, Cinnamon," Sally apologized.

Cinnamon covered her face with her hands like a bashful child. "I didn't mean any harm," she mumbled.

"It's okay," Sally said. She looked over at me. "Is it okay, Cam?"

I nodded, not feeling okay at all. Everyone looked back at Cinnamon peeking out through her fingers.

Cinnamon mumbled, "That's all I had to say. I just wanted to ask that question. I'm done."

Now everyone looked at me expectantly. My skin felt too tight. I wanted to stay. I wanted to speak. I wanted to hide. I wanted to jump out the window. I wanted Rikki. I wanted Arly. Clay wanted to color.

I looked over at Sally for support and opened my mouth to speak, but nothing came out. Tears welled up in my eyes, and I forced them back. My gaze arced slowly around the room, and a rogue tear meandered down my cheek.

I tried to speak again, and this time words came out.

"I-I've never met another multiple. I want to talk here, but I'm afraid I'll switch out and won't be able to come back because I'm so nervous."

My hands were freezing, and I clasped them together between my thighs and rubbed them against each other trying to contain, trying not to run. I hung my head. My nose began to run and it leaked onto my leg. The woman with the wounded glasses passed me the box of tissues and I took a few, wiped my nose, and nodded to her. I looked down at my hands.

"I want to stay. I don't want to run. We don't have a therapist. We don't know anyone . . . I'm so scared."

The tears were scratching like dogs at the door. They wanted out. *Back! Get back!* Too late. I leaned forward, put my face in my hands, and let them out.

No one spoke while I cried. The woman with the glasses passed me the tissues again and I restocked, dabbed my eyes, and blew my nose. After a minute or so I stopped crying and was able to speak again.

"I'm sorry."

Sally said, "It's okay."

Sarah said, "You don't have to be sorry." Shudder, switch, gone, and Clay was out.

"W-what are y-you coloring?" he asked Sarah.

"This," she said, turning the coloring book around to show him. "Who're you?"

"C-clay."

"Hi, Clay."

Other people in the room said, "Hi, Clay."

Then he was silent, aware that everyone was watching him. Sally said, "Clay, do you know where you are?"

"N-no."

"This is a group for people with multiple personalities. People with other people inside."

Clay didn't say anything.

"It's Cam's turn to talk," Sally said. Clay looked at her quizzically.

Sally said, "Do you know who Cam is?"

Clay nodded, pointing his right thumb over his shoulder, indicating me somewhere behind him.

"Well, here we don't just have conversations where everybody talks," she said. "People speak one at a time, okay?"

"Okay."

"Do you want to talk or do you want Cam or someone else to come back?"

Clay didn't say anything.

Sally said, "Okay, I'm going to ask Cam to come back. Is that all right, Clay?"

He nodded.

"Cam?" Sally said. "We need Cam to come out."

Shudder, switch, and I was back. All eyes were on me, and I looked around the room, scrambling inside to figure out what had happened. *Switched . . . Clay . . . coloring book . . . meeting . . . California.* I covered my face, mortified that I'd been seen, and the dogs were back at the door.

The woman with the glasses got up and patted me on the shoulder. "It's okay," she said.

"Yeah, it's okay," Sarah repeated. But it wasn't.

TWENTY-THREE

Kai liked his teacher and had his best buddy, Jack, Rikki had made our new house a home, the sun was shining, and it was beautiful outside. But inside . . .

The bone-ripping dreams returned, though Bart swore he wasn't causing them this time. Along with the dream came the night sweats, the closet, the cum, the pussies, Grandma's rasping cackle, and Mommy's deadly "ssshhhh." *Oh no. Where's the ground? Where's the ground? This shouldn't be happening! Things are good things are good things are good things are bad things are bad things are baaaaddd! Bad things are baaaaddd! Aaaaahhhhh!!!*

The switching was rapid and out of control as my mind's noisy tin barrel rolled and bounced down the hill and over the edge. Rikki couldn't stop it; Arly wasn't there. Once more I was freefalling into the angry engine of madness. And then Switch found the X-Acto knife and slash, slash, slash, made three deep gashes in my right arm, and just like that, we were the next contestants on *The Slice is Right*.

Rikki rushed me to the hospital and my arm got stitched up and the nurses looked worried and the doctor kept silent and Rikki called Arly and Arly called Del Amo and, bang, two days later Rikki dropped Kai at school and flew with me to L.A. to check me into the rubber Ramada. All of a sudden, Cameron West and Company were in the Dissociative Disorders Unit. L.A., baby. Minks and money and Myrna Loy. And my dear, sweet Rikki was back in Leona before Kai got out of school.

A psychiatrist with a bright gold watch and bushy eyebrows evaluated me in a small room on the ward and sent me over to the lock-down unit for twenty-four hours to make sure I wouldn't harm myself again. *Can't fix your head if your body's dead.* The psychiatrist on duty gave me Risperidone to slow down the switching, Serax to diminish the anxiety, and Ambien to induce sleep at night. All three helped.

The next day the sun felt warm on my face as the attendant, a pleasant Latin guy named Angel, walked me back across the enclosed courtyard to the DDU carrying the black nylon bag Rikki had packed for me. Two women, one rail thin and the other of Titanic proportions, were sitting on patio furniture smoking while an attendant stood by. They all eyed me closely as we walked past them into the building. The thin one's right arm was wrapped in gauze. So was mine, but it was covered by my sleeve.

The duty nurse, a handsome middle-aged woman with long auburn hair, freckles, and big hands, was standing by the door holding a clipboard. She introduced herself as Sue and welcomed me by name, which surprised me because I didn't recall having met her before. She said she'd be down in a few minutes to orient me. *Fat chance, Red.* Angel took me lightly by my left elbow and walked me down the hall.

We passed a large room on the left with couches, chairs, and throw pillows. Across the hall was a smaller room. Five women of assorted ages and body types were in there sitting at a table drawing and making things out of colored paper. They looked up to check me out. The new kids in town.

Next to that room was another small room that looked vaguely familiar; it was where I'd been evaluated the day before. Angel and I took a left at the nurses' station and headed down the hall toward my room. We passed another room on the left with a television, exercise bike, and stacks of games and children's books. Just before we got to my room I caught a whiff of Spaghettios behind me. Lunch was being wheeled in.

"Number seven," Angel said. "Lucky seven. You got your own room, my man." His voice sounded loud in my head. He plunked my bag on the bed near the door and stood up straight. "You gonna be all right, Cameron?"

"Yeah," I lied.

"Then I'll see you around," he said, winking, and walked out whistling a tune I didn't recognize. Angel was a pretty good whistler.

I looked around at our room. It was a lot like a college dormitory except for the carpeting and the fact that the furniture was bolted down. I unzipped the black bag and pulled out Toby. It bothered me that he'd been locked up in the bag; I was afraid he wouldn't get enough air.

Tighten up, asshole, he's a stuffed animal. Hey! Hey! Hey! No nastiness here. Right, Per, sorry. Where are we? The hospital. What for? His arm got cut. Oh. I'm scared. Me, too. Breathe deep, everyone. The Comfort Room. Cam, unpack. Okay.

I pulled out the clothes and found four children's books at the bottom of the bag: two Winnies, a Grover, and Richard Scarry's *What Do People Do All Day,* everybody's favorite. *Way to go, Rik.* I stashed everything in the highboy that was bolted to the wall across from the bed and put the toilet bag on the bathroom sink. I unzipped it to take out a bar of soap, the shaving cream, and my razor. No razor. *Did Rikki forget it? No. They must've taken it when we came in here. No sharps allowed.*

I washed up and glanced in the mirror for a second, but it was too scary. *I hate mirrors! No mirrors!* I was coming out of the bathroom as Sue knocked twice on the open door. Loudly. She had the knuckles for it.

She handed me an information packet and quickly went through the highly structured schedule. She told me I'd be seeing my therapist later that day. "Dr. Mandel's an excellent therapist," she said. "You're lucky." Counting Angel's, that made two luckies in ten minutes.

Sue took me down to the arts and crafts room, which doubled as the dining room, and dropped me off. All the other patients were sitting at the table eating lunch. It wasn't Spaghettios, it was Sloppy Joes. Mmm. Haute cuisine for the crash dummies. A ward nurse named Bea, a middle-aged black woman with bug eyes and her own clipboard, introduced me to everyone in a loud voice.

I recognized the two women from the courtyard. The woman with the bandage was named Toni, and the other one was Dawn. *Toni and*

Dawn. Toni Orlando and Dawn. Tie a yellow ribbon round the blah, blah, blah. You fuckin' nut. I looked around at the others: a round woman named Lucy, who looked a little like Shelley Winters in *The Poseidon Adventure;* a young bleached blonde, Debbie, with azure eyes—maybe tinted contacts—wearing a lot of makeup; a young overweight black woman whose name Debbie told me was Charlene but who was currently a child named Bunny who couldn't talk; a worn-looking woman named Stephanie who was average-sized and about my age and wore glasses; and Kris, a very thin, dark-haired woman in her mid-to-late twenties with hundreds of scars on her arms, wearing a black jumper and black boots.

"I'm Jody!" Kris said in a much younger voice than she'd used five seconds earlier.

Shudder, switch, Clay. "I'm C-Clay," Clay said.

"Hi Clay," Jody said with a big smile and took a messy bite of her Sloppy Joe. With her mouth full she said, "Do you like Sloppy Joes?"

"Yeah!" Inner jab from me. "I m-mean, n-no. N-not good for him."

"Who, Cam?" said Stephanie, who wasn't Stephanie anymore.

Clay looked over. "Y-yeah. Who're you?"

"I'm Wobbie," she said. "I'm a boy, too!" This was getting interesting.

"Do y-you have a s-scooter?" Clay asked. "A red one?"

"Pfffff, noooo!" Robbie made the no-way gesture. "I can't dwive. Da ya wantcha fwench fwies?"

Clay nodded.

Robbie said, "Oh, okay. Sowwy."

In a heavy southern accent Lucy said, "Ah'm Daphne," bowing slightly, pointing at herself with her fork. "Robbie, ah b'lieve he means a scootah you push with ya foot."

Clay looked over at her with a french fry halfway to his mouth. "Y-yeah," he said. "A red one."

"Ohhhh, I get it," Robbie laughed. "No, we don't have one of those. I'd like one, though."

"Me, too," Jody said, slapping the table. "I want a scooter," she chanted, slapping the table with every word. "I want a scooter. I want a scooter." Everybody except Bunny chimed in, slapping the table, too. "I want a scooter. I want a scooter."

Bea came running into the room. "What the *hell?*" she boomed. "Everybody stop slappin' the table. What're you talking about a scooter?"

Debbie chattered at machine gun speed, "Clay asked if Robbie had a scooter and Robbie thought he meant a motor scooter and Daphne said 'no, a scooter scooter' and Robbie said he wanted one and—"

"Give it a rest, Debbie," Stephanie said, shaking her head, Robbie gone.

Bea looked at Clay, pointing her clipboard at him. "Who's Clay, you?" Clay was speechless. "See what you started, Clay?"

Robbie came back. "Hey, that's not faiw, Beatwice," he said.

Kris said calmly, "Bea, it wasn't his fault." Clay's face crumbled and he started to cry.

"Aw, don't crah, Clay," Daphne said, patting him on the arm and handing him her napkin. Shudder, switch, and Bart was out.

"Hey," he said with a big smile, the faucet now off. He wiped his eyes with the napkin. "What's happenin'?"

"Who're you?" Toni asked.

He smiled over at her. "I'm Bart." Everyone except Bunny, who was shoveling the food, said, "Hi, Bart." He smiled around, nodding hi, then glanced down at his plate and made a pee-yew face. "Woof."

Dawn looked up like she just got Bingo. "If you don't want it, I'll have it."

"Sure." He held up the plate while she scooped the mess onto hers. "Leave the fries and carrots," he said.

"Yeah, okay."

Bug Eyes bellowed, "Bart, I'm Bea. I'm a day nurse. I'm sorry if I upset Clay."

"Thing about the scooter, right?"

"Mm hmm."

"Okay, okay. Look, we're all a little edgy here. Cam's way out there, that's for sure. I'm new on this beach. Hey, who here's from outta town?"

"I'm from Laguna," Kris said brightly.

"Milwaukee," said Toni.

"Shame, Awgon," Dawn said, mouth full of Joe.

"What?" Debbie said disgustedly. "Finish chewing, for God's sake." She smiled brightly at Bart. "I'm from Reno."

Dawn pushed the food over to one side of her mouth, looking like the Yankees' third-base coach. If she spit, Bart was going over the wall. "Salem, Oregon," she said without looking up. *Probably doesn't shave her pits,* thought Bart.

Daphne drawled, "We're from Modesto."

"Wight heew," Robbie jabbed at the air with his finger.

Bart looked at Charlene. She was rounding Saturn. Debbie pointed her thumb at her, "They're from St. Louis."

Robbie switched back to Stephanie, who said, "Where are you from, Bart?"

"We just moved to the Bay area. From Massachusetts."

"Well," she said, spreading her hands, "welcome to L.A."

A half hour later a tall, curly-haired guy in his late forties with a manicured beard and designer glasses walked up to where I was sitting in the main room. He was wearing an expensive gabardine suit, white cotton shirt, a thin shiny black tie, and black lizard cowboy boots.

He smiled warmly. "Cameron, I'm Ed Mandel," he said. "Is it Cameron who's out right now?" Ed was a baritone.

"It's Cam," I replied nervously, getting up from the couch. Ed had my chart in his left hand. He offered me the other. I shook it cautiously.

"Let's go somewhere, Cam, and talk for a while."

We hung a right at the nurses' station. Ed unlocked some double doors, and we walked briskly down a quiet hall and into a small room with two chairs and a desk with a lamp. The french fries were duking it out with the carrots and my mouth felt like I'd been chewing on a fez.

We sat down, and Ed leaned forward, elbows on his knees, and looked deeply into my eyes. "I want to help you, Cam," he said. "All of you."

Right away I started slipping into the clouds.

Ed knew I was switching. "Cam," he said. "I need you to stay present for a bit here."

I pushed through and was back in the room again, but just barely. Inside it was getting loud.

"Good," Ed said, seeing me get clearer. "I spoke with Dr. Morelli and—"

"Arly," I interrupted.

"Arly. She gave me some background on you." He glanced at the chart and back at me. "You have a wife and a little boy."

I nodded. "Rikki and Kai."

"While you're here I'm going to do my best to help you get better for Rikki and Kai," he said. *"And* for you." He glanced at my bandaged arm. "First time that happened?"

I nodded. "It wasn't me."

Ed looked deeply into my eyes. "I understand. Do you?" I shook my head.

"There are a few reasons people harm themselves. Most of them have to do with pain. Letting it out or showing it. In people with DID, sometimes it's an alter sending a message."

Ed's words felt prickly on my ears.

"Arly said you're having trouble with denial." I didn't say anything.

Ed continued. "Just about everybody who comes in here does. It's one of the biggest obstacles to healing." He looked down at his clipboard. "She gave me the names of the alters she knows about. I bet they're all curious about me and are looking and listening carefully right now." He grinned knowingly.

Then suddenly, boom, everyone came out in rapid succession, loud and scared and crying and joking and angry and confused, tossing overflowing garbage cans out the back of our speeding truck, while Ed swerved left and right, squealing tires, keeping right up, enjoying the challenge, passing the test. *Eddie is a master. Eddie is cash.*

At the end of the hour, Ed poured me back into human form and walked me slowly back to the nurses' station. As we parted, he told me we'd need to have a therapist in place before leaving the hospital and promised to help me find one. I believed him. Ed patted me gently on the back and ducked in to make notes and prepare for his next session.

I hung in the hall like the heavy bag at Gold's Gym.

A burst of laughter came from the big room, and Kris stuck her head out and sang, "Cam's back from Man-dy!"

"Bwing 'im in!" Robbie shouted.

Kris skipped into the hall with a big smile and grabbed me by my sutured arm. I winced and pulled back.

"Sorry, did I hurt ya?" She'd felt the bandage through my sleeve and understood immediately.

"No, Kris. It's okay."

"It's Jody!"

"H-hi, Jody." Clay was facing her but not meeting her gaze.

"C'mon Clay. We're playing a game!"

"W-what kind of game?"

"Chutes and Ladders! Wanna play?"

Big nod. "Yeah."

"Let's go."

Robbie was at the table, the game spread out.

"Hi, Clay," he said. "We was playin' Chutes and Laddas. Did ya like Mandy?"

"W-who's M-Mandy?"

"Docta Mandel."

"Oh. Y-yeah," he said, eyes downcast. "I liked him."

"Clay," Robbie said, "how come you don't look someone in da eyes? We won't huwt you."

Jody shook her head. "We would never do that."

Clay looked up at her carefully, glanced away, and slowly moved his eyes back to

meet her gaze.

Jody smiled exuberantly. "That's it."

Clay moved his eyes toward Robbie's and did the same thing: glance, look away, and slowly come back to meet his gaze.

"That's gweat, Clay. Now you don't have ta look away no maw." He pointed at the game. "Which one you wanna be, wed, gween, aw blue?"

"B-blue."

"Goody," he said. "I get to be gween. But it doesn't weally matta. I'm goin' with Mandy in a minute and I'm scaiwed."

"H-how come? He's nice."

"'Cause he's gonna make me get olda today. Stephanie is weddy faw me to get olda."

Clay looked confused. He didn't know that in some cases therapists attempt to age progress certain alters in order to decrease the separation between personalities. Neither did I.

Jody said, "Mandy's not gonna do anything bad, Clay, and he doesn't do it with everybody, so don't worry. He's not doin' it with us, and we've been comin' here for a long time."

"Are y-you goin' away?" Clay asked Robbie, this time sort of looking him in the eye.

"Not weally, but I'm gonna be diffwent. I think I'm gonna be fifteen aw somethin' like that. Uh oh, Mandy's heah. Gotta go. Wish me luck."

Ed grinned from the door and wiggled his fingers "hi." As they walked down the hall Robbie said, "Ah you shooah about this?" Ed's resonant voice replied, "Mm hmm."

There were two more groups that day in the main room, one on anger management—we weren't ready for Switch to come out in that one—and one, led by Ed, called Process Group.

I was itching to talk in that group and threw my hand up as soon as Ed asked if anybody had particular issues they wanted to deal with. I wasn't the only one. I sat impatiently bunching and unbunching a small pillow in my lap while I listened, first to Dawn and then Debbie. Then Ed looked at me and said my name.

I clutched the pillow and blurted out, "I don't want to be here. I'm not like this!"

Dawn chuckled to herself. "Neither am I," she muttered.

"Not like what?" Ed said to me.

"You know."

He waited. Everyone was quiet.

"What, you're waiting for me to say it? I don't want to say it."

"Say what?" Ed said.

"Jesus, this pisses me off!"

Toni was picking at the gauze on her wounded arm. "Give him a break," she said.

Ed looked at her and back at me. "Say what?" he repeated.

"Multiple, okay? Multiple. Shit! That's . . . not . . . me. I don't belong here."

"Hah!" Debbie laughed. She covered her mouth and said, "Oops."

"Ah saw y'all at lunch," Daphne said.

Toni made an alarm sound, "Enh . . . enh . . . enh, Denial Alert!"

My knuckles hurt from scrunching the pillow and I wanted to bolt for the door.

After a few seconds Ed said, "I understand how you feel, Cam, but I think you belong here." He looked around the room and grinned. "Anybody else wish they were somewhere else?"

Toni broke into tears. "I lost my kids because of this. My husband took them away." She screamed, "I don't want to be here either!" and covered her face with her hands. Dawn patted her on the knee.

"I do," Kris chimed in, and from the tone of her voice I could tell it was Jody. "This is where we get to come out and talk to other alters and have fun. I love it here." She waved at me and said, "Hi, Clay," and I shuddered and switched and Clay said, "Hi, J-Jody."

"See?" Jody said. "Fun."

"F-fun," Clay repeated.

After dinner and a shower, the journal came out. The pen passed from mind to mind as it always did, and I was swallowed up in the long limbs of my strange tree.

Bart: "Not like this. Can you believe this guy? Stubbornest bastard I ever saw."

Dusty: "That's not nice talk, Bart."

Per: "Breathe, Cam. You don't have to go through this alone." I breathed deeply and my tension lessened a bit.

Per: "Good. This is difficult for all of us."

Bart: "Damn tootin'."

Switch: "I hate you!!"

Dusty: "Switch?"

Per: "Easy. Rest easy. Cam?"

Cam: "What?"

Per: "Don't push us out."

Cam: "I don't know what to do. I'm sorry."

A shout came from down the corridor, "Phone call for Cam West!" Huh? The voice from the hall shouted again, "Phone for Cam West." Wait a minute, wait a minute. Phone. Telephone for Cam West. It must be Rikki. Rikki's on the phone. Yeah, your wife. You have a wife. I do? And a son. I do? Right. I do.

"Okay, thanks," I shouted back. I threw on some clothes, sprinted down to the bank of patient phones by the nurses' station, and picked up the receiver that was dangling by its cord.

"Hello?" I gasped, out of breath.

"Hi Cam!" Rikki said brightly. *Rikki, my Rikki.* "Kai's right here and he wants to talk with you first. I'm putting him on."

I heard the muffled sounds of the phone changing hands, and then Kai's voice said, "Hi, Dad."

Dad. He's calling me Dad. I told you you have a kid.

"Hi! How's my little man?"

"Good," he said. "Dad . . . can I ask you something?"

"Sure." Focus. You're talking with Kai, your son.

"When are you coming home?" Kai thought I was away on business.

"Pretty soon, hon. Couple of weeks."

"Are you in a big hotel?" I looked down the hall at one of the night nurses trying to comfort Charlene, who was lying on the floor in front of her room, crying. I cupped the mouthpiece so Kai wouldn't hear.

"Yup."

"Do you have a soda machine or a candy machine there?"

"I guess so, but you know I don't buy that stuff." *Keep it together.*

"Well you're lucky anyway," he said. *"I'd* get a Snickers and a soda and watch TV."

I managed a chuckle. "I'll bet you would."

"Dad," Kai whispered. "Will you bring something home for me? A GI Joe guy. His name's Roadblock."

I heard Rikki in the background saying, "Tell Dad you love him."

"I love you, Dad," Kai said in his sweet little voice. "Will you get me the guy?"

"We'll see. I love you, too." More muffled sounds and Rikki was on the line.

"Hi. Kai went into his playroom. Don't worry about the toy; I'll pick it up so you can give it to him when you come home. When do you think you'll be coming home?"

"I don't know. Two weeks maybe?" Confusion grabbed me. I was still in the tree. "I thought I was home," I said.

"Your home is here," Rikki said pointedly. "With us." There was a chilly silence as I shinnied down and touched the ground. "Tell me how you're doing," she said. "Have you been hurt anymore?" Rikki wanted a status report.

"No. No cutting."

"No cutting is good. Your therapist, how is she, or is it a he?"

"It's a he." I told her about Ed. Rikki sounded relieved that I was being treated by someone who knew what was going on.

"I think I need some help myself," she said. "I'm going to go to that partners' group at Sedona House tomorrow."

"Okay. That sounds good." I was drifting. *Kai. Ask her about Kai.* "What about Kai?"

"He can stay with the Withingtons while I'm gone. It'll only be a couple of hours."

"Who?"

"The Withingtons," she said, a little annoyed. "The new neighbors from Australia."

"Oh." I didn't know what she was talking about. *Koalas are fluffy.*

Rikki choked up a little. "I love you, Cam."

Tell her you're sorry.

"I'm sorry, Rik. I'm sorry."

She sniffled. "No, I'm sorry. You're the one in the hospital. I'm just . . . this is really . . . I'm just scared." The faint hum of the telephone lines felt warm in my ear. Then she said, "I'll be all right," like she'd just straightened herself up and pulled herself together. "Okay, I'm gonna go now. I'll talk to you tomorrow. I love you."

"I love you, too." My mouth felt rubbery. "Bye."

"Bye." And then she was gone. And so was I.

The meds nurse, Geraldine, an ancient woman with a gravelly voice, gave me twenty milligrams of Ambien and I beelined back to my room and climbed under the covers. Happy thoughts of Winnie and Tigger, Kris and Jody, and Stephanie and Robbie drifted through my mind until the drugs kicked in, and I sank like a boot in the dunes of sleep.

TWENTY-FOUR

The next morning Stephanie came up to me in the courtyard. At least, at first glance I thought it was Stephanie.

"Hi. I'm Robbie. What's up?"

"Robbie?" I was confused. The Robbie from yesterday was a boisterous kid with a speech impediment. This Robbie swaggered.

"Yeah, it's me. I'm sixteen now."

"Sixteen?"

"Yeah," he said, hands in his pockets, shoulders loose. He shifted his weight from one foot to the other and looked up and down the walkway. "Sixteen."

This definitely wasn't Wobbie. It was Robbie. A young James Dean in a forty-year-old woman's body.

Inside, Dusty stirred. Shudder, switch, and she was there. "Hi, Robbie. I'm Dusty." Robbie quickly peeled off Stephanie's glasses and stuffed them in his shirt pocket.

"Hi, Dusty. How old are you?"

"Fourteen," she lied. Dusty was only twelve. *Oh brother.*

"You're a girl, right?"

"Of course I am," she said, a little hurt. "I know I don't look like a girl out here," she gestured up and down at my body, "but I am. And I know you're a boy."

Robbie kicked the floor absently. "Wanna talk?"

"Sure," she said. I was watching from somewhere inside; so were Bart, Stroll, and Per. This was wild. Robbie and Dusty sat down on the cool tiles. Two teenagers; well, one teenager and one wannabe.

"So, do you have a boyfriend, or what?"

Dusty clasped her hands together and hunched up her shoulders, blushing. "No," she said coyly. And then more directly, "I don't even have any friends."

"Me either." They were silent for a moment, then Robbie said, "Stephanie was going to wear a dress today, but I said no way. Absolutely no way. I hate being in this body. I look so stupid!"

"You don't look stupid to me." Dusty smiled sweetly. "You look like a sixteen-year-old boy." She paused for a second. "I think you're handsome," she said, blushing again.

"You do?" Robbie scooted a little closer to Dusty. "Well, I think you're pretty." *Whoa.*

"You do? Nobody ever said that to me before. Well, Arly Morelli said it when I showed her a picture I drew of myself. But she's a psychologist and was just being nice, I think. She didn't really see me." Dusty looked into Robbie's eyes. "Do you really see me, Robbie?"

"Yes I do." He covered Dusty's hand with his, and their fingers intertwined. "Maybe we could go to the movies sometime."

"I'd like that."

I was distantly aware of the nervous tingling of sexual excitement. *What the hell?*

Robbie shifted his leg so it was touching Dusty's and leaned over to kiss her. Slow motion, moving in closer, closer, lips parting slightly, eyes closed, warm breath, closer, and . . . bam! Stephanie's eyes opened wide, her face an inch from Dusty's. She shook her hand out of Dusty's as if a spider was on it and slid away in one quick motion.

"What's going on here?" Stephanie demanded.

Dusty was shocked, confused, and embarrassed. "N-nothing," she said. "I wasn't doing anything."

Shudder, switch, and I was back. "Hi, Stephanie."

"Cam, what the hell's happening here? Robbie was just about to kiss Dusty."

"I know. I was sort of aware." I shook my head, trying to tune in quickly.

"Look," she said. "I can't have Robbie making out with Dusty. Shit!" Stephanie rubbed her temples hard, dug her glasses out of her shirt pocket, and put them on. "He wasn't even wearing my glasses . . . trying to look cool. Jesus, I think my head's gonna explode. You're a married man!"

What? What does that have to do with Robbie and Dusty? I wasn't even there, for chrissake!

"Yes, Stephanie, I am married." I was confused. *Help me out here, somebody.*

"Well," she said, indignantly. "If you're married, then Robbie shouldn't be kissing Dusty. She's in your body, you know."

Dusty's in my body. "Right, Dusty is in my body." It was clearer now. "Of course she shouldn't be kissing anybody!" I ran my fingers through my hair and scratched my head. "Whoa, this is weird."

Stephanie said, "When were you diagnosed?"

"Almost a year ago."

She nodded. "So this is kind of new for you, having a bunch of different people in your body. Well, we were diagnosed three years ago, and our therapist out in the world and Mandy . . . well they've beaten it into my head that we're all in the same body. All . . . in . . . the same . . . body." She chopped one hand with the other, driving the point home to herself and to me. "What they do, you do."

We were both silent for a moment. From somewhere down the hall Bea roared, "Grouuup!" Our eyes were locked, each sensing the enormity of the other's pain.

"My life's too hard already, Cam," Stephanie said. She stood up slowly. "We can't be around you anymore." Then she turned and walked away.

And inside, in the loneliest corner of the loneliest place, Dusty scratched in the wet cement: Robbie.

TWENTY-FIVE

Rikki took a deep breath and blurted out, "My name is Rikki and my husband has Dissociative Identity Disorder."

She was the last of the six people—the others all men—to speak at the partners' meeting, and when she opened her mouth her jaw hurt from having clenched her teeth for the past hour. Talking about herself was difficult under the best of circumstances, and being in a new state, in this unfamiliar place, with five strangers and a multiple for a husband, was not the best of circumstances. But the familiar truths these people shared and the increasing certainty that she wasn't going to get out of this alone had diminished her guardedness.

"Up till tonight I've been carrying around this crazy thought that what's been happening in my family for the past year isn't real . . . that somehow it would all just go away and I wouldn't have to deal with it and I'd get my life back. But after listening to some of you talk about the things that happen to your wives and girlfriends, and what you go through, well . . ." Her voice trailed off and she teared up. She pulled a tissue from her pocket and dabbed at her eyes, careful not to smear her makeup.

She sniffled and wiped her nose. "Shit! I knew it was real . . . I mean intellectually I knew it. I've read the books. I was there when the alters came out. I saw them act out all those horrible memories, disgusting stuff." She looked up, suddenly realizing she'd been talking to herself. All around her were sympathetic eyes.

She took a deep breath, exhaled slowly, and continued, "My husband's in the hospital right now, a place in LA for multiples. One of his alters cut his arm pretty badly. It was awful. I just thank God our son didn't see it." A few of the men nodded, picturing their own scenes of blood, maybe their own children.

A deep crease formed between Rikki's eyebrows, the harsh light in the room accentuating it. "I feel scared and angry . . . and guilty; scared about what's going to happen to us; furious about what his goddamn mother and the others did to him; and . . ." She paused. Tears trailed down her face and she wiped them away fiercely, annoyed at their persistence, not caring anymore about her makeup. "And guilty as all hell that I'm such a wreck about this, because after all . . . it happened to him, right? He's the one who's really suffering, and what right do I . . ." she bit her lip hard and cried a little. After a moment she heaved a sigh, sniffled, and reached into her purse, fumbling for another tissue. One of the men passed her a box and she took a couple. She thanked him, smiling feebly.

Rikki blew her nose and glanced around at the caring faces.

"I'm sorry I'm such a mess. If anybody can recommend a good therapist, somebody, preferably a woman—who knows about this stuff, I'd really appreciate it." She paused for a second. "Thanks for listening." Then she was silent, but the weight of her anguish hung in the room like the fog at Half Moon Bay.

The leader of the group, a wafer-thin, balding guy in his midforties wearing old blue jeans and an orange Madras shirt, finished up the meeting by reading a paragraph from a page in his binder. After that everyone stood up and milled around, and he walked over to Rikki.

"My name's Ted," he said. "It took a lot of guts to do what you just did. These meetings can be really hard."

"That's for sure," Rikki said, smoothing her hair out, aware that she was looking a little disheveled.

"Does your husband know that there's a multiples' meeting here?"

"Yeah. Actually he went to his first one last week."

"My wife Sally runs it."

"Oh," Rikki nodded, remembering Cam's description of her, picturing the huge woman next to this skinny man.

"Between the two of us we've compiled a pretty good list of therapists around here. We might have somebody for you."

"Oh, that would be great."

"Where do you live?"

"Leona."

"There's a woman in Walnut Creek I've heard a lot of good things about. Walnut Creek's not too far from Leona."

"I know where it is."

"Her name's Nancy Hendrickson." Ted opened his three-ring binder, pulled a pen out of the pouch on the inside sleeve, flipped to the back, and jotted his name and number on a comer of the last page. He ripped it off and handed it to Rikki. She glanced at it and stashed it in her pocket. "If you call me when you get home," he said, "I'll give you her number."

Rikki smiled appreciatively. "Thanks, Ted. It'll probably take me about half an hour or forty-five minutes to get home—I don't know the roads too well yet—oh, and I have to pick my son up from the neighbors'. Could I call you then, in like an hour?"

"Sure. Does your husband have a therapist yet?"

"No. His therapist at the hospital—"

"Del Amo, right?"

"Right. His therapist there—"

"Ed Mandel?"

"Yes," Rikki said, surprised.

Ted said, "Sally had him when she was there last year. He's a pro."

People were drifting out of the room, several of them nodding silently at Rikki, acknowledging her. She smiled and turned her attention back to Ted.

"Mandel said he'd help find a therapist out here for my husband."

"Yeah," Ted nodded, grinning to himself. "They have to."

"What do you mean?"

"They have to make sure the patient has a therapist on the outside."

"Oh."

Ted scratched the back of his neck casually. "They don't really know anybody up here; they just use the ISSD's member directory. The International Society—"

". . . for the Study of Dissociation," Rikki finished.

"Right. Just because someone's in that book doesn't mean he knows how to work with multiples. A lot of people claim to know about it—claim to have worked with multiples—for bragging rights, I guess. You know, like, 'I've got a multiple.'"

"So what do we do? How do we find somebody?" Rikki said anxiously.

"Sally knows the good ones. I'll have a name or two for you when you call."

Rikki looked him squarely in the eye, deadly serious. "I think you're saving my life, Ted."

Ted closed his binder. "It's nothing," he said, smiling. "Mine's been saved a bunch of times."

Rikki made her way home, exhausted but resolute; no matter what happened with me, she was going to get on terra firma, and she'd taken the first step by going to that meeting. She picked Kai up, brought him home and put him to bed, cracked a Heineken, and called Ted. He gave her Nancy Hendrickson's number and two names and numbers for me. Rikki thanked him profusely, and Ted wished her well, told her the meeting would be there if she felt like coming back, and rang off.

Rikki dialed Nancy and left a message on her machine.

The next morning Nancy returned her call, and she and Rikki spoke for about twenty minutes, at first feeling each other out, then getting into some details of our situation. They made an appointment for the following day.

TWENTY-SIX

Nancy was about forty-five with short strawberry-blond hair that curled around her pleasant face and a vernal warmth in her hazel eyes that helped thin out some of Rikki's tension. She was snappily dressed in bright colors, with suede sandals and socks to match, and her bracelet jingled when she shook Rikki's hand.

Her office was on the second floor of a new professional building in Walnut Creek, fifteen minutes from our house. It was large, airy, and pleasant, decorated in peach and beige, with fresh cut tulips arranged in a spongeware vase on the end table next to the client chair. One wall was covered floor to ceiling with psychology books. Rikki's eye caught Colin Ross's red textbook on DID and she felt a wisp of relief as she sat down. She pulled a sheet of paper from her purse and unfolded it.

"I made some notes last night . . . sort of an emotional balance sheet," she said, handing the paper to Nancy, who took it and studied it.

After a minute she raised her eyebrows, still looking at the paper and said, "Hmm . . . you're thirty-eight years old, you have a seven-year-old boy, you've just moved to a new state, your husband whom you love dearly has a recently diagnosed severe psychiatric condition for which he has been hospitalized after cutting himself, and you're subsisting on your savings." She set the paper down on the table next to her and looked up at Rikki. "Offhand I'd say you have a lot on your plate."

Rikki burst out laughing, and the laughter tugged the chain attached to the plug that stopped up the tank that held all the tears. They gushed and splashed, drenching everything in their path with a bitter mixture of fear, sadness, hurt, and anger—at losing her man, her stability, her comfort, her normal life.

Nancy stayed silent, sensing that Rikki's only need at that moment was a witness. She liked this woman who walked in carrying her emotional balance sheet. And she understood her pain. Nancy had worked with adult survivors of child abuse and their families for fourteen years, and she knew how devastating the effects were, not only for the survivor, but for the spouse and children.

Rikki's eyes were red and her face was puffy. She worked her way through a half dozen tissues before she stopped crying and was able to get her breathing under control.

"Whew," she said with a self-conscious laugh, "I guess I needed that."

"Rikki," Nancy said, "it sounds like you've been twisting in the wind since your husband was diagnosed. You know, some people with DID do get better."

"I've heard that."

"But it can take a long time." Nancy shifted in her chair.

"I've heard that, too."

"Although I haven't met him, I feel for your husband and what he's going through. But you should know up front that if you decide to work with me, you'll be my client, not him . . . and I'll be your advocate."

Rikki's eyes settled on the delicate flowers in the vase next to her. "He's my best friend. I've loved him for almost fifteen years," she said, touching a velvety petal, feeling it glide easily between her thumb and forefinger. Shifting her gaze back to Nancy, she continued, "What do I do with this? I have a son. I want a life."

Nancy crossed her legs. "And you need to have control over that life." The room was silent for a moment, Rikki thinking, Nancy allowing the space.

Rikki shook her head slowly. "Do you know how guilty I feel about all this?"

"Guilty?" Nancy prompted.

"He's suffering through all this horrible stuff and I feel awful for him, but I'm so angry about it all, like my life's crashing in a ball of flames and I'm just watching it happen and I can't do a goddamn thing about it." She looked out the window. "It wasn't supposed to happen like this. We were supposed to be a regular family. You know, *Donna Reed . . . Father Knows Best.* And it pisses me off that it didn't turn out that way. That's what I feel so guilty about."

"Mmm," Nancy said, her eyes focused intently on Rikki.

"I shouldn't even be here. Cam's in the hospital. I should just be, you know, holding down the fort."

"You shouldn't do something for yourself? That's selfish?" Rikki took another tissue, crumpled it, and smoothed it out.

"Everything in my life is about Cam. I don't have anything that's just mine."

"Having control over your life," Nancy said, "is about being able to make choices, having your own power."

"I have no power! None," Rikki said, pounding the arm of her chair with her fist. "Everything that's happening is beyond my control."

"You still have choices, Rikki. For example, you could go back to work. That would give you some power, some independence, more financial security."

Rikki tore a little corner off the tissue and rolled it between her fingers, inspecting it. She looked up at Nancy. "But what if something happens to Cam while I'm gone?"

Nancy uncrossed her legs and leaned forward. "You can't be a watchdog, Rikki. What kind of life is that? You can't keep someone from hurting himself . . . or killing himself."

Rikki shuddered.

Nancy continued. "You can support your husband and love him and be a phone call away if he needs you . . . but you can't watch him every minute just because you're afraid of what might happen if you don't. That won't work for you . . . for him. It'll only make you angry and resentful."

Rikki drew a deep breath and blew it out slowly, nodding. "I already am. Jesus, I can't believe I'm saying this. I don't want to be angry with him. The thing is, I feel like it's not even him. My husband's gone. I don't even know who he is anymore. It's just all these . . . people. I mean, they're not, you know, dressing up in different clothes and going out to see their own friends. He doesn't lose time really. It's not like people think."

"I understand. He's got co-consciousness."

"Right. He used to be this sweet, funny guy . . . and now I never know who he's gonna be. I put dessert out and a four-year-old girl comes out to eat it." She felt the tears rising again. "And when he got cut? God, that was so horrible. That was way beyond me. I don't know what I'll do if that happens again. I have Kai to worry about. How am I supposed to live with this?" And the valve reopened and she wept again.

Nancy sat quietly, the witness.

When there were no tears left in her, Rikki sat limply in her chair, exhausted, a ball of wet tissues crumpled in her hand. She was aware Nancy was watching her, offering her silent support from across the room, and it comforted her. They both were still. Down below a bus pulled away from the curb. Out of the corner of her eye Rikki saw Nancy glance over at a small round marble clock by the window.

Their eyes met and Rikki straightened up and cleared her throat. "Our time's up, isn't it."

"Almost."

"Well," she said, reaching for her checkbook. "This was fun. We just have to do it again. Think five times a week would be enough?"

TWENTY-SEVEN

The insurance company wanted me out of Del Amo fast. They didn't understand why a person with DID would need special psychiatric care. Of course, they'd spring for a few more unnecessary sinus surgeries, or a heart transplant. But DID? Forget it. They did agree to hospitalize me in the local psych unit, though, if I tried to kill myself.

Ed Mandel went to bat for me, arguing that psychologists and psychiatrists at most psychiatric hospitals weren't that familiar with DID and would likely be unable to deliver the kind of treatment I needed. But the insurance company people wouldn't listen and pulled the plug after only six days.

Before we left, Ed hastily found a therapist named Scott Mosely, whose office was in Pleasanton, ten miles from Leona. Scott, whose name Ed located in the ISSD directory, said he had experience working with multiples. He sounded nice on the phone when Ed put me on, and we agreed to meet as soon as I got home. Ed had done what he could; he'd make a note on my chart: Outpatient therapy in place.

We said tearful goodbyes to Kris and Jody, and Stephanie muttered, "Take care of yourselves." Then Robbie popped out, shook my hand firmly and told me to say goodbye to Dusty for him. Dusty felt his hand in mine, a small, woman's hand to me, but to her, the hand of a teenage boy. She wanted desperately to talk to him one last time, but was too afraid of Stephanie to come out. She never got to say goodbye.

On the plane ride home my mind was jumping like the kernels in a Jiffy Pop pan. How does the brain work? How does my brain work? How does DID differ from other psychiatric conditions? What's the psychophysiology of DID? How does emotional trauma affect neuromechanisms?

All those years ago I'd thought about becoming a psychologist. Was it because I knew something was wrong with me? Because I needed help? I looked out the window over the wing and thought about Arly Morelli and Ed Mandel—deft, perspicacious, smart, respected.

I'm smart . . . when my mind works. Maybe I'll never be able to work with people the way they do, but I can learn what they know. Master the mind. My mind. Mastermind. Respect myself. Ooh, big one. How about not hate myself. Hah! We can become a psychologist. Help others. How? Somehow. The Krises, the Stephanies, the Cams. Leif can help study. He can do anything. We can do this. Wait. We can't be in a classroom with other people. How would we even find our way to school? There must be good programs where we can work from home. Be safe at home. I'll bet there are psychology programs for people who can't go to classrooms. Working people. Yeah, we can find one of those. It'll have to be a good one, an accredited one. No Joe's College and Storm Doors. Course not. We can do this. If I can stay alive long enough.

I borrowed a pen from a young female flight attendant with big hair and wrote on a napkin. Goal: Become a psychologist. Do this now!

Before I knew it the plane was touching down at Oakland airport, and Rikki and Kai were at the gate waiting for me. *They recognize me. I must look familiar.* Goddamn, I was glad to be back with my family. Rik slipped me the GI Joe when Kai wasn't looking, and I presented it to him with a flourish. His eyes got as big as bocce balls and he jumped into my arms and hugged me like a long-lost pal.

Rikki looked sparkling in a mauve print dress and turquoise earrings. Meeting with Nancy had replenished some of her strength, and she didn't seem tepid or scared, just glad to see me. She kissed me like she meant it, and when she did her mouth opened a little and my body lit up inside like somebody'd poured out a long line of gasoline and dropped a match at one end. Maybe later . . .

The three of us stopped for lunch at Val's in Hayward, a restaurant that's been around since 1958, serving huge milkshakes and juicy burgers cooked by a guy with a big gut and tattoos, and delivered by a waitress named Tina in a white bowling shirt and black Laura Petrie pedal pushers, with a pencil stuck in her beehive hair.

We thought Val's would be a special treat for Kai, but we were wrong. Val's had way too much character for him to appreciate. It just wasn't McDonald's enough for him. Imagine that. The little guy had two bites of his Baby Burger and pushed it away. He liked the milkshake though, sort of—the real ice cream was a curve ball, but he got used to it—and of course he had Roadblock to play with, so he was happy.

Rikki and I held hands—holding hands was good—and talked about her going back to work. I tried not to sound too scared about it; I could see she'd made up her mind. Then I sprang my plan to become a psychologist, which shocked her. Not because it was such a huge task—she'd seen me accomplish difficult things before.

"You just got back from . . ." she wanted to say hospital, but couldn't in front of Kai, so she gestured at my arm with a lot of eyebrows.

"How will you be able to do schoolwork?" she asked. What Rikki meant was, "Hey, you usually don't know what day it is, or even what year. How are you going to go to school?"

"You're going to see patients?" she said with a lot of doubt.

"Not every psychologist sees patients, Rik." I played with my napkin. "I need to learn. I need something to concentrate on, to focus my mind on."

"What you need to focus on is—" She looked for a code word. "Getting . . . ah . . . feeling . . . well." She gave me a stern look but a smile peeked through. Then it turned into a grin and I grinned back at her. It was kind of fun and funny sitting in Val's, sipping chocolate milkshakes, talking over Kai's head. The only-we-know-what-we're-talking-about kind of funny. Even if it was about deadly serious stuff. But, truthfully, getting well seemed a lot more far-fetched than getting a Ph.D. at that moment.

"Maybe this guy Mosely will work out," I said, dunking a huge onion ring in ketchup. "And if he doesn't, we'll go to that guy's list . . . that guy you met at the meeting . . . Sally's husband."

"Cam," she said, taking my free hand and giving it a squeeze, "you're gonna do what you're gonna do. We both know it. So, if you've made up your mind to get your Ph.D., then you've got my support. Maybe there's a program you could do from home, a distance learning program. I'm sure there are good ones."

"Exactly." That was Rikki, always thinking.

"Will you be . . . uh, fine . . . while I'm at work?" Rikki didn't smile when she asked me that. It wasn't even a little funny. Would everything go to hell when she wasn't there? She wanted to know. I couldn't answer that. I loved Kai. Rikki knew that. I wanted to keep him away from the sticky web of my madness. She knew that, too. Would I be able to? Neither of us knew the answer to that.

"We can always call you at work," I said. "When you go to work you'll just be a phone call away, right?"

Rikki nodded. Kai looked up at her from his toy questioningly. Kids hear everything. She smiled at him brilliantly.

"Right," she said. "Just a phone call away."

TWENTY-EIGHT

That afternoon I found my way to Dr. Mosely's office, scared as hell. He was a well-made, handsome, gray-haired man, about my size, thin and athletic. He gestured me warmly into an elegant walnut-paneled office. I sat down nervously on the black leather couch, my mind in the wilderness. *Another therapist. He doesn't know us. What if he's mean. He doesn't look mean. Mean? Uh oh, lots of leakage going on here.*

We talked for a few minutes; I tried to keep my eyes moving so they wouldn't lock on one thing and build that gateway to nowhere. My face started to numb up. *Uh oh, I'm losing it.* Shudder, switch, and Clay was out.

"I'm C-Clay," he said, his body tight as a cello string.

Mosely jumped like a cartoon character, socks and shoes popping off, eyes bugging out, hair sticking up, teeth jumping out. "What?! Who's Clay? Why are you talking like a child?" His voice sounded harsh, scared. *Jeez, it's just Clay. Testing this fucker.*

"I-I'm eight." Clay held up eight fingers.

"What? What do you mean you're eight?"

"I'm eight."

"Well, you've got to grow up, Clay."

And the rockets' red glare, the bombs . . . shudder, switch, and I was back. Inside, Per told Stroll and Bart to get Clay to the Comfort Room right away. My mouth was trying to form words, but all that came out was "jjjbbbsss."

And suddenly Leif was there.

He sprang off the couch, feral and angry, and Dr. Mosely leaned back in his chair looking up, eyes wide.

"Hey, Mosely. You've got no business talking to Clay that way!" Leif barked, punctuating his words with finger jabs. "Grow up? Jesus, are you kidding?! Are you outta your fucking mind? Don't you know anything about DID?" He paced back and forth, and Mosely's worried eyes followed him.

Mosely backpedaled. "I-I just thought he should grow up—shouldn't talk like a child. I-I guess I shouldn't have said that."

Leif wheeled and faced him, glaring. "I guess not!"

"I'm sorry. I didn't mean to hurt Cal's feelings."

Leif didn't bother to correct him. He whipped out my checkbook, scribbled a check for a hundred dollars, signed Leif, scratched it out, signed Cameron West, and stuck it in Mosely's face. Mosely took it feebly, not knowing what to say.

"Thanks for your time, Doctor," Leif hissed and walked out with the rest of us in tow.

We sat in the car for a few minutes trying to put all the bottles back on the shelves, checking for cracks. *Nothing broken. Good.* Leif went inside and I came out, jangling like a janitor's keys. *Shit.* I fired up the car and slowly backed out, wondering if Mosely was trying to peek out at us through his shutters without being seen. *Way to go, Eddie. You screwed us. Mental note: Trust no one.*

Finding my way home was a bitch, reading the directions in reverse, but I made it to Route 680 North, and once I got up to sixty, things eased up inside. My resolve hardened. *I'm going to become a psychologist.*

But first, on to Ted's list.

TWENTY-NINE

Rikki was surprised to see me so soon. I told her what had transpired at Mosely's and she took my face in her hands, kissed me, and hugged me close. Leif came out for a minute and filled her in on the details, quietly, so Kai wouldn't hear, and Rikki patted him on the hand and thanked him for watching out for us. My Rikki. A soft place to fall.

"Hey, Kylie," she shouted into the family room. "Want to make cookies?"

"Yeaaah!" he shouted back excitedly, running into the kitchen. I heard someone inside say, *"Cookies."*

Rikki got out the ingredients: flour, eggs, butter, chocolate chips, sugar, baking soda, salt, vanilla. She turned on the oven, pulled out a baking sheet and a blue glass mixing bowl, and started measuring. Kai helped mix the batter and poured in the chocolate chips. I would have helped, wanted to, but I was slipping like sneakers on ice. *The hospital, the plane, the airport, the kiss, Val's, Mosely, Clay, Kai running, playing, happy, the sound of the eggs sloshing, mixing, the chocolate chips.* Mmm.

Shudder, switch, and Clay was out. "I-I like c-cookies."

Everything stopped in mid-motion, like a freeze frame of Grand Central Terminal at five.

"Huh?" Kai said, not sure what he'd heard.

Rikki started to say, "Cam," but Clay was already answering. "I-I like c-cookies."

"Dad?" Kai looked at Rikki, frightened. "Mom? Why's Dad talking like that?"

"Th-those are chocolate chips," Clay said slowly, clenching and unclenching his hands.

"Daddy?" Kai looked at me, but saw Clay—the tense body, downcast eyes. "Mommy!" he shouted, bursting into tears.

"Cam!" Rikki barked, sinking to the floor, throwing her arms around Kai. Shudder, switch, and I was back.

"W-what?" I said, dazed, shaky, not quite certain what had transpired. I noticed Kai was crying. "What's wrong, Kylie?"

Kai pulled away from Rikki and ran to me, clutching my leg. I knelt down and hugged him.

"What's the matter, Daddy?" he asked, sniffling. "Why were you like that?"

"Daddy's okay, honey," Rikki said reassuringly.

I stroked his hair. He stopped crying. "Yeah," I said. "Daddy's okay."

Rikki sat down on the floor and so did I. Kai remained standing. Now he was the tallest, but not by much.

"Remember when Daddy yelled 'stop it' in our old house?" Kai nodded. "Itchy was there."

"Yeah. And we talked about what happened to him when he was little?"

Kai nodded again. He leaned against me, put his hand on my shoulder and patted me gently, his eyes still on Rikki.

"Well, sometimes when Daddy thinks about those bad things that happened to him, he gets kind of far away, kind of different. He might just seem spaced out or he might talk funny. That's what just happened a minute ago."

"Well, why doesn't he just keep not remembering?" Kai asked.

Rikki spread her hands and shook her head. "I don't know, sweetie." She looked at me somberly. "He just . . . can't."

"Well, I didn't like it," he said. "It scared me."

"I'm sorry I scared you," I said, trying to stay dialed in. I didn't m-mean

to scare him. It's okay, Clay. It's okay. Not your fault. Comfort Room. What about cookies? He can have one when Kai's out of the room. Aw, balls. Don't say that, Bart. Everybody into the Comfort Room.

Kai looked at me, his scared little face two inches from mine. "Don't be like that again. Okay, Dad?"

I fought back a tear. "I'll try not to."

Rikki said, "Honey, if Daddy gets like that again all you have to do is call for him. Just say, 'Dad' or 'Cam' and he'll come right back." She looked at me grimly. "Won't you, Dad?"

"Yeah," I nodded and dredged up a big smile for him.

Kai hugged my neck and then put his face right in front of mine again.

"Cam?" he said, trying to snap his fingers a couple of times. "You with me here? You okay?"

I took a deep breath and let it out slowly. "I'm with you, Kai."

"Okay," he said, satisfied for the moment. He looked at Rikki with a big grin. "Can we bake the cookies now?"

Rikki smiled at him and stood up. "Sure," she said, mussing his hair. "You can spoon 'em onto the cookie sheet."

"And lick the bowl?"

"And lick the bowl."

Inside I was crumpled in a heap at the bottom of a deep canyon. I dragged myself to a standing position and faked a smile. "Lickin' the bowl's the best part."

THIRTY

Later that night I was lying in bed remembering the kiss in the airport, certain that the incident in the kitchen had quashed all chances of my landing on the shores of Rikki West. I was wrong. She came in from the shower wearing a big bath towel and a sly grin, slipped out of the towel, insinuated herself between the sheets, and slid over next to me. She wrapped a leg over my hips, nibbled my earlobe, and started playing with my week-old whiskers.

"You look very sexy with that beard," she cooed. "You look . . . wild." Her voice was breathy, like Marilyn Monroe's.

"I didn't think you'd still be interested," I said hoarsely, turning toward her. I gently brushed the back of my hand across her hard nipples and she moaned softly, gyrating her hips, her warm wetness against my leg. My fingers lightly touched her smooth shoulder and ran down the line of her back. Rounding dead man's curve, my hand stopped and squeezed. Rikki moaned and pushed against me.

"Mmm, you've been gone a long time," Rikki whispered, her tongue touching my upper lip, pulling back, touching it again. Then she kissed me deeply.

Her hand was on me now, stroking, squeezing, and she guided me into her, and then things got really good. On the outside.

On the inside it was louder than the floor of the New York Stock Exchange. She's hot, huh? Never mind. What are they doing? Ooh, this is disgusting. Don't watch, Dusty. Leave 'em alone. Who is that? Not Mommy. I-I'm a good boy. Yes, you are a good boy. Feels good. I'm a good boy. I'm a bad boy. I'm bad, I'm bad. Shit, get everybody to the Comfort Room. Right now.

I tried to ignore the ruckus. For now it was Rikki and closeness and warmth and comfort and love and the shimmering feeling of being desired and desirable. We moved together silently, bodies undulating to the night rhythms of passion, sweating, blood throbbing in our veins. And then faster and harder, and Rikki arched her back and I pushed hard against her and held still, filling her with glistening hot steel, and she moaned, "I'm coming," and then tighter, tighter, one more second and, "Aaaaaah," I moaned too, and splash. Crazy or not, here I come.

We collapsed on each other, hearts thundering, chests heaving, hot breath and damp hair, the flushed tingly feeling of release. But in my head, orange-red sparks of madness danced like fireflies around a campfire. And the eyes of the others glinted at me hauntingly from very dark places.

Rikki didn't know how close they'd been while we were making love, how near I'd come to switching. My guys and I didn't have a plan yet for how to handle sex. That was a problem that was going to come crashing down on us like a tree on a Jeep.

THIRTY-ONE

Dr. Janna Chase's name was at the top of Ted's list. I left a message on her machine. "My name is Cameron West. I've been diagnosed with DID and I'm looking for someone who's very experienced. I just moved here from Massachusetts and was in Del Amo hospital for a week. You were recommended to my wife by someone at a group for partners of multiples. I need a therapist badly." And I left our number.

Janna called back that day and asked a lot of questions, cautious, feeling me out. Most people don't contact therapists and announce their diagnosis. They enter therapy not knowing—just pointing at their toe saying, "Doc, it hurts here."

Janna wanted to be sure I was multiple. Hey, I wasn't even sure I was multiple. Arly said I was. Mandel said so, too. The crowd at Del Amo certainly thought so. But me? A multiple? Us . . . multiple? There was sand in that sandwich, and I didn't want to swallow it. *I'm just weak. I'm crazy.* Denial's Rake. That screeching tune.

After a few minutes Janna agreed to meet me at her office in Berkeley a few days later.

Now on to scoping out a graduate school. I pushed everybody out and was feeling pretty sharp and regular, and after an hour in the reference section at the Leona library I had the names of more than a dozen schools offering alternative graduate psychology programs.

I settled on Saybrook Institute in San Francisco, a highly regarded institution founded in 1971 by Rollo May and a few of the other great Humanistic psychologists. The self-paced program would allow me to do almost all the work on my own, which was exactly what I was looking for. And there'd be a lot of it: eighteen courses, three seventy-five-page candidacy essays, and a dissertation. Could I do it? With Leif's help I could. Maybe. If I lived long enough. I went home, sent for my transcripts, and applied that day. Then I went to bed with Toby and *Winnie-the-Pooh.*

Janna Chase's office was the middle one of three which occupied the upstairs of a converted house off of Shattuck Avenue. The lobby was tiny, the only seating an early American wooden bench that made a church pew seem like a Barcalounger. But the small stained-glass window that faced the street and the delicate spindle stair railing made up for the bench.

At one o'clock sharp Janna came halfway down the stairs and waved me up. She stood in the hallway and gestured me through double doors into her small office. I scanned it quickly. We all did. The floor was carpeted with a blue-and-white oriental rug, the client couch was beige leather, and Janna's chair, also leather, was pale blue. An antique writing desk and ladder-backed cane chair stood by the window, and against one wall was a tall teak bookshelf filled with miniature ceramic trinkets and lots of books on dissociation and trauma, including two textbooks on DID. *Good sign.*

A large Wallace Ting print of some fish hung on the wall behind the couch, and on the opposite wall were two smaller prints, one of them a zigzag of colors, and the other a Monet scene that reminded me of Huck Finn by a summery river. I liked that one.

Janna and I sat down and looked each other over. To say that I looked her over is understating it a bit. *We* looked her over, me out front and everyone else pressed up against the plexiglass like tourists at the observation deck on top of the Empire State Building.

Janna was about my age and as thin as two coats of paint. She had wavy brown hair cut to her shoulders, no makeup, and bright happy eyes the color of blueberries. Thoughts rolled through my mind like marbles on a wooden floor. *Birds like blueberries and I like birds and they like blueberries and her eyes are like blueberries so I like her eyes so I like Janna. Janna rhymes with Anna and sanna and claus and red and nose and rose and newts and chutes and cowboy boots. Wow, look at those cowboy boots!* Mauve-and-black cowboy boots stuck out from under Janna's denim dress. Anna loved them. If Janna didn't lob a grenade at us when somebody came out, we might have a chance with her. *Uh oh. Here we go.* Shudder, switch, Anna. Toothy smile, crinkly eyes, folded hands, knees together.

In a little voice she said, "My name rhymes with yours."

Janna returned the smile. "It does? What's your name?"

"Anna."

"Great! Anna and Janna. They do rhyme!"

"Are you a teacher?"

"No, I'm a therapist. Like Arly Morelli. Cameron told me about Arly Morelli."

"Who's Cameron?" Someone inside quickly told her. "Cam?" She pointed her thumb behind her.

"Is that what he's called? Cam?"

Bashful nod. No eye contact. Anna almost never made eye contact.

"Is he behind you, is that why you pointed with your thumb like that?"

Another nod.

Janna sat up straight and said, "I'll repeat, for whoever might not have been listening when Cam and I talked on the phone the other day, that my name is Janna Chase. I'm a psychologist and I've been working for nine years with people who have dissociative conditions. You all should know that, if we do end up working together, I won't ever touch you unless you ask to be touched, and then it will only be a handshake or a pat on the back or something like that. Okay?"

Poof. Bart. He crossed his legs lounged back, craned his neck, looking around the room, appraising things. Janna spotted the switch. Ray Charles would have.

"Hi," Janna said.

"Heyyy, Janna, right?" He leaned forward and put his hand out. "Bart."

She shook his hand and smiled warmly. "Hey, Bart."

"Nice boots."

"Thanks." No grenades yet.

"Did Cam tell you we saw some other shrink a few days ago? Guy had the brains of a bush. Mailed himself to Peru when Clay came out. Told him to grow up." He shook his head and scowled.

"I know," Janna said. "Cam told me on the phone. That's terrible." She looked genuinely upset. "What's Clay like, Bart?"

Bart shrugged. He knew why she was asking. "Don't worry. He's not dangerous. He's a nice kid. Stutters a little. The guy was a stool."

"Mmm. So everybody's pretty wary, huh?"

"Yeah." He looked her over some more. "But you seem all right."

"Thanks. Hey Bart?"

"Hmm?"

"Does Cam come out much?"

"Him?" he pointed like Anna did, with his thumb. "All the time. Something's *wrong* with that dude."

"What do you mean?"

"You ever heard the word 'denial'?"

"Once or twice."

"Yeah, well . . ." Bart sneered and jabbed his thumb over his right shoulder.

"Cam, huh."

Bart laced his fingers behind his head and leaned back. "Jeez. Cute and smart."

Janna acknowledged the remark with a little smile and nod. "Tell me, does he want to come out?"

"He ought to. He's paying for this shindig. See ya."

I heard Janna's voice say, "See ya," and felt the familiar swirling shift as Bart faded into my mind's murky swamp. My eyes rested blankly on Janna's face. She quietly observed.

"Cam?" she prodded. *Hey, somebody start this motor!* Starter whining, battery draining, gloved hand on the key twisting it farther to the right than necessary as if just a little more English would start this giant rusting machine. *You're real, you're real, you're real. Hey, YOU'RE REEEEAL!!*

"Cam?"

"I . . . can . . . hear . . . you," I said, my face feeling like a piece of meat that hadn't thawed enough.

"Listen to the sound of my voice. Feel your feet on the ground. Wiggle your fingers. Go ahead. Try to wiggle them."

I felt a finger wiggle way down my arm.

"I can hear you," I said, a little faster this time.

"Good. You're doing good. Lot of stress right now, that's understandable. I know you just got out of the hospital. I know it didn't go well with that other therapist."

My eyes began to focus as I fell and fell and the ground got bigger and I dropped into my body. Kerchunk!

"Cam," she said as I scrambled to put things together, to figure out what was going on.

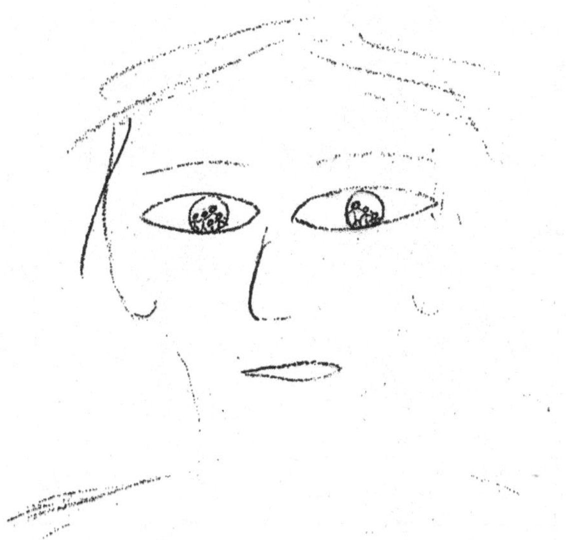

A portrait.

My eyes focused on her. The lady in the doorway. The paintings. The boots.

"Hi," she said, her eyes engaging mine. She looked confident, interested. "Were you here when you first came in?"

"Sort of." My arm itched where the stitches were healing.

Got arms. Good sign.

"Were you the one I spoke with on the telephone?"

"Yeah. That was me."

Janna sat back and smiled. "Well, hi."

"Hi."

"I've met Bart and Anna."

"I know," I said, wiggling my fingers again, zooming in a little more.

"Great! So you have some co-consciousness."

"Mm hmm. We all do."

Janna smiled. "That's excellent."

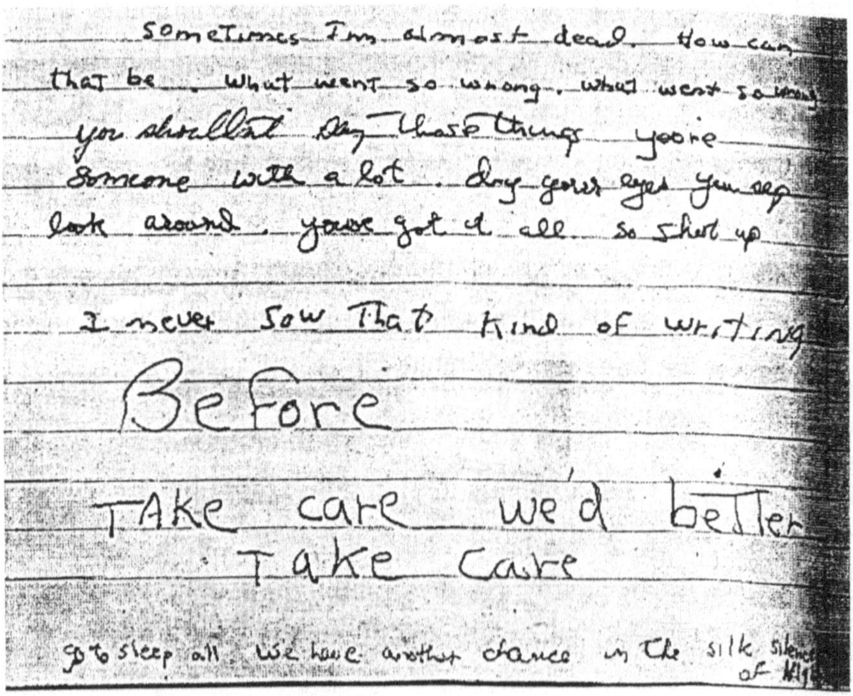
Sometimes I'm almost dead. How can that be. What went so wrong. what went so wrong

you shouldn't say those things you're someone with a lot. Dry your eyes you see look around. you've got it all. so shut up

I never saw That kind of writing Before

Take care we'd better Take care

go to sleep all. we have another chance in the silk silence of night

A precarious state as I began work with Janna Chase.

Then a thought augered into my head. I winced and rubbed my temple with three fingers. "We have journals. There's a lot you need to know that I can't tell you. The journals have everyone in them. You need to read them."

"Sure," she said. "I'll read them as soon as you bring them to me."

I leaned my head against the back of the couch and closed my eyes. A bitter taste filled my mouth.

"What's happening? " Janna said.

"I'm a crazy person."

She didn't speak.

I opened my eyes and looked at her. "Help me. I don't want to die from this."

Janna leaned forward, keeping her gaze on mine, considering everyone in there. She said softly, "You're not crazy, and I don't want you to die from this either."

THIRTY-TWO

I was accepted to Saybrook Institute and started in on my studies, and Rikki found a job as an administrative assistant to the vice president of sales for a large company in Oakland. All of a sudden she was gone from seven in the morning until six at night, and I had to be Ozzie *and* Harriet *and* Big Man on Hippocampus.

Kai and I got into a routine during the week where I'd climb into his bed first thing in the morning and read Gertrude Chandler Warner's *Boxcar Children* mysteries to him for a half hour before getting him ready for school. I'd make up funny dialogue and Kai would laugh like hell the whole time. He loved it and so did I.

We could usually count on that fun to carry us right through breakfast and the rest of our morning routine without any problems at all. And it was a good thing, too, because by the afternoon the only thing we could count on was that the dad who picked Kai up from school wouldn't be the same dad who'd dropped him off.

To get through the immense amount of work required for a Ph.D., I forced my guys into the background while Kai was at school, not giving them any "body time" at all, except for the meager two hours on Mondays and Thursdays when we'd all trudge off to Janna's. The rest of the time I worked furiously, with an incessant cacophonous racket in my head.

Whether I was reading or writing, each word was a page, each page was a book, and by the time I'd drag myself away from the computer to pick Kai up from school, my thoughts were shredded, and angry alters were leaking out. Kai knew it, too, and got plenty used to calling for Cam to come back, just like we'd taught him.

It was unavoidable. No matter what Kai's day had been like, he'd stumble into my trench, through no fault of his own, and there we'd be—me trying to claw my way out to get us back on level ground, and him wondering what the hell had happened to Boxcar Dad. Usually I couldn't dig us out; I just didn't have the strength. Getting Kai a snack was tough enough; helping him with second-grade math was practically impossible. Patience? Hah! Humor? Hah!

Kai and I counted the seconds until Rikki would come home. I usually didn't have dinner ready; I just couldn't do it. Rikki didn't complain. She'd just cook and chat with Kai while he played on the kitchen floor, and I'd slink off to my own rusty cage of misery until it was time to eat. We'd reconvene at the table, and pretty soon Rikki's wonderful lightness of spirit would dissipate the tension between Kai and me. After dinner the evening went smoothly. Rikki would help Kai finish his homework, run him through the kid wash, read him a story, and tuck him in. Then I'd swing in for a kiss and maybe a little more *Boxcar,* and it was lights out for the midget. Rikki and I usually weren't far behind.

Rikki and I used to say that some of our best conversations took place in the dark, in that fertile place before the world ends and dreams begin. Now that place seemed like a deserted parking lot where our two cars moved a space farther apart every night.

All of my energies went toward my studies and keeping it together during the day, and I was exhausted by the time my head hit the pillow. Rikki was patient and supportive, but she was lonely. And loneliness is everything it's cracked up to be.

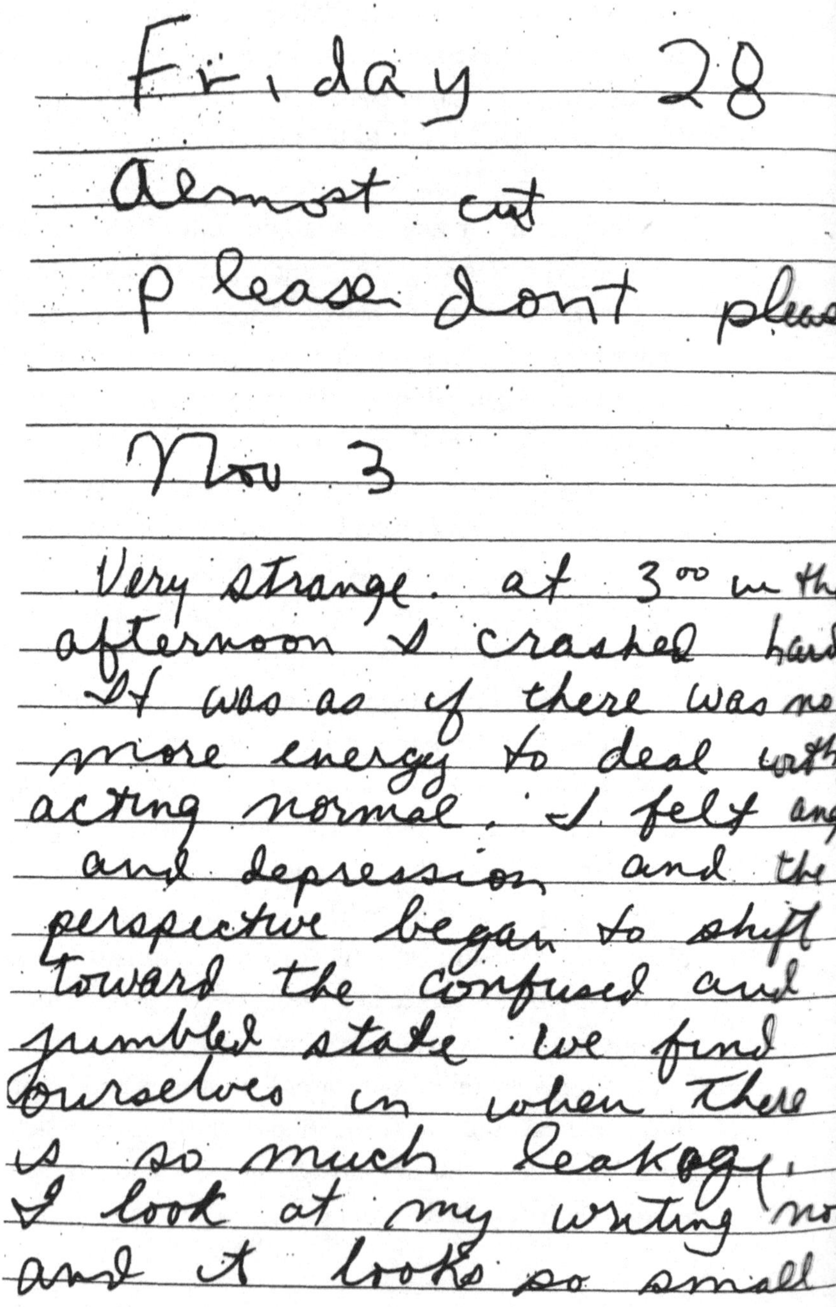
Friday 28
Almost cut
please dont pleas
Nov 3
Very strange. at 3:00 in th
afternoon I crashed hard
It was as if there was no
more energy to deal with
acting normal. I felt ang
and depression and the
perspective began to shift
toward the confused and
jumbled state we find
ourselves in when there
is so much leakage.
I look at my writing no
and it looks so small

A typical afternoon immersed in studies.

d contained. One wouldnt
ess from this handwriting
hat I have so many people
ving in my body. Death
oes not scare me. It
ould be a release. Midnig
leeping on a moonlit bay.
Not now dont talk like
that you're not nice.
dont you scare me.

ont you scare him. Dont talk
like that.
n sorry.
ll kids go to the comfort
room
Please dont let him
ll me.
Hello

you see this? See.

THIRTY-THREE

Within six months Rikki was promoted to Operations Manager. She now had a spiffy office overlooking San Francisco and eight people working directly under her, including Janine Barnes, her assistant. Janine was five feet four, with large mischievous brown eyes, a curvaceous body, and a truckload of wavy dark brown hair.

She was the classic picture of a twenty-two-year-old still living at home and working in her first real job—sporty new two-door Toyota, cell phone, pager, lots of stylish clothes, inch-long fingernails that looked like terra cotta roofing tiles, and not a worry in the world other than falling off her pumps or screwing up her tan line.

Rikki had taken Janine under her wing because she was bright and efficient and had a good sense of humor, even about herself, which is a rare quality in anyone and almost nonexistent in young people. Rikki also liked her because, like most twentytwo-year-olds, Janine was far more concerned with her own life than with anyone else's, including Rikki's. To Janine, Rikki was sort of like a hip aunt who, outside of work, did what aunts do, whatever that was. Adult stuff. She didn't want to know, and Rikki was comfortable with that because she didn't want to tell.

"Hi, Boss," Janine said, pushing Rikki's door open with her hip, a cup of coffee in each hand. She set one on Rikki's desk and plopped down in a chair.

Rikki put down a yellow pad and picked up the coffee. "Thanks," she said, taking a sip. "Mmm, nutmeg. You put that in there?"

"Mm hmm."

"Nice touch."

Rikki put down her coffee and picked up the yellow pad. "Okay, let's get to work. We've got a lot to do to pull this trade show together. I need you to call Service and tell Dave those machines have to be shop-worked by Tuesday. We need to have both a black and white *and* a color tech on site all day Thursday, so set that up with Ed and Greg. We've also got to get the reps to give us their final lists of attendees by the end of the day, so we can print the name badges and order the food. Get Cheryl in marketing on the line and find out when the giveaways'll be here, and call Diane and ask her who she's sending over to man the reception table." She picked up her coffee. "Okay, that's it for now."

"I'm on it," Janine said, getting right up. She stopped in the door and turned around. "Oh, Rikki, I forgot to tell you on Friday. Teri told me a bunch of people are getting together at Chevy's after work today to say goodbye to Andy Grumman."

"Oh jeez, I forgot. He took that job at Oracle. Sure I'll go." Rikki leaned back in her chair. "Hmm, too bad he's leaving. I don't really know him that well, but I like him."

"Yeah," Janine said, drumming her tiles on the oak door. "I always thought he was kind of sexy . . ." she grinned, "for an old guy."

"*Old* guy. Andy couldn't be more than forty. If he's old, what does that make me, huh?"

"Just kidding, Granny," Janine snickered. "I do think he's sexy, though."

Rikki mused as Janine walked out. Hmm . . . *Andy Grumman is kind of sexy.*

That afternoon Rikki called to tell me she'd be home a little late. That was rotten news; therapy had been brutal and I wasn't doing too well. Two new alters had come out for the first time.

Almost immediately after I walked into Janna's office I felt a rumble like a Santa Fe freight train and poof, I was in the abyss and Wyatt was there. He stood up abruptly, put his toes at the edge of the border of the oriental rug, and began sidestepping around it. Janna sat patiently, watching. She could tell someone new was out; she could feel it.

"This is a square rug," Wyatt said, in the voice of a bright ten-year-old. "I mean a rectangle."

"What's your name?"

"Wyatt."

"Hi, Wyatt. Why are you walking around the rug?"

"It makes me feel good to walk around things."

Janna said, "Are you anxious? You look very anxious."

"Yes, I am."

"And watching the pattern and walking around it makes you feel less anxious?"

"Yes."

"Do you know why you're anxious?"

"Because I don't know you or this place," he said, his eyes carefully following the woven border. "Eating cereal and walking on gravel are the same . . . except with one you don't get full."

"Hmm," Janna nodded, considering that. "So you don't know who I am?" It didn't surprise her. Often, new alters don't know basic information.

"No."

"Wyatt, see if you can get the information from inside, if somebody in your mind can tell you who I am."

He didn't speak for a few seconds but kept on sidestepping around the rug. "I don't know." Inside we were trying to talk to Wyatt, but he wasn't listening, or just couldn't hear us.

"Do you know where you are?" she asked.

"No. In a room in a house."

"That's right. Actually it's an office in a building that used to be a house. My name is Janna Chase," she said slowly, getting a little dizzy from following his movement around the small rug, "and I'm a psychologist . . . I'm Cam's psychologist. Wyatt, do you know what year it is?"

"Nineteen sixty-four," he said confidently. "How did I get so tall? I must be on stilts or something, or you're playing a trick on me."

"I'm not playing a trick on you, Wyatt. Do you know who Cam is?"

Wyatt continued his sidestepping, carefully watching the intricate pattern on the blue-and-white rug. He said, "Big man with big shoes."

"Yes, that's right. Would it be all right if I asked you to stop what you're doing and sit down for a few minutes?"

He stopped moving. "Okay. Should I sit on the floor?"

"You can if you want. Or you could sit on the couch."

"Okay." Wyatt sat down on the couch. He immediately began tracing the white crown molding around the ceiling, his eyes unmoving, his head following the perimeter. When the two windows came into view his focus dropped, and he followed their rectangular pattern over and over. "Your ceiling's not straight," he said. "Your room's not straight. And your pictures aren't straight."

Janna laughed. "You're probably right. It's an old building." She watched his expressionless face tracing the outline of the windows, first one then the other. "Do you think you could stop what you're doing for a moment?" She paused. "If that's okay."

"Okay," Wyatt said. His head stopped moving, and his eyes now focused on the river picture by Janna's writing desk. "Wyatt?"

"Yes?"

"It's not nineteen sixty-four."

"It's not?"

"No. Listen inside and see if you can find out what year it is."

He sat still, his face showing intense concentration. "I don't hear anything," he said. "Nineteen sixty-four."

Suddenly Wyatt's body jerked, slamming him against the back of the couch, and he slid down sideways onto his back, feet still on the floor, hands balled in fists tightly against his chest, and, bang, someone else was out, terrified eyes staring straight up at the ceiling, gasping for breath as if a steel beam were lying across his chest.

Janna sat up straight, totally focused, looking for a toehold. "Tell me what's happening."

No response. Just the terrified look and straining sound of desperate breathing.

Again, this time more sharply. "What's happening?"

He sucked in air painfully, gasping a molecule at a time. "Huuuh . . . huuh. Can't . . . huuuh . . . breathe."

"Why? Why can't you breathe?"

"Let . . . me . . . huuuh . . . go. Please . . . huuuh . . . let . . . me . . . go."

Janna stayed cool. She knew this was an abreaction, a re-experiencing of some past event, and not an epileptic seizure as someone less experienced might have thought. She knew I wasn't choking on something, that my airway was clear. At least it was in the present. But whoever was on the couch was not in the present. He, or she, was in my past.

Janna asked, "Am I talking to Wyatt?" The head shook twice.

"Who are you?"

He gasped, "Mo . . . huuuh . . . zart."

"Mozart?" she said. "Is your name Mozart?"

"Yeeessss . . . huuuh." He sounded like he had something lodged in his windpipe.

"Listen to me, Mozart. You are not in danger right now. My name is Janna Chase, and I'm here to help you. Listen to the sound of my voice. Try to stay connected to the sound of my voice."

"Blue . . . huuuh . . . dress."

"Blue dress? Who's wearing a blue dress?"

No response. Only the rasping sound of his tortured breathing.

"Mozart, listen to me. No one is going to hurt you now."

"Underwear . . . in . . . huuuh . . . my . . . face . . . huuuh," he wheezed in a small, terrified voice.

"Mozart," Janna said firmly. "Look in front of you. Focus your eyes on what's in front of you. There are no underwear in your face. Nothing is in front of your face. Reach up and touch your mouth. There's nothing in front of your mouth. Go ahead, reach up and touch your mouth."

"Can't . . . huuuh . . . move my hands . . . huuuh," he said, his arms still glued to his chest.

Janna decided to go with it. Let it play out. She'd let the rescue wait a couple of minutes. She leaned forward. "Why can't you move your hands?"

"I . . . huuuh . . . can't."

"Why can't you?" she probed.

"Huuuh," he gasped. "She's holding me down."

"Who?"

"Her . . . huuuh. Lady . . . huuh."

"What lady?"

The rasping sound intensified, his breathing becoming more labored.

Janna kept pushing. "Do you know who the lady is?"

"Huuuuuuh," he gasped, tears streaming down his face. Mozart's body began to writhe on the couch and he uttered a stifled scream that was muffled by the ghost of the lady in the blue dress, her vagina in his face. It was time for the rescue.

Janna's voice softened. "Mozart, listen to the sound of my voice. Stay connected to the sound of my voice. It's going to help you. You *can* move your hands. Nothing is holding your hands down. Look at your hands." Mozart stopped writhing and slowly moved his head, glancing down at his hands.

"See?" Janna told him. "There's nothing holding your hands down. Now keep listening to the sound of my voice. Try and unclench your fists and reach up and touch your mouth." He did what she said, slowly, still gasping for air, and touched the back of his fingers to his lips. "See what I mean? Nothing is in front of your face." The terror in Mozart's young eyes abated slightly. Janna said calmly, "You can relax your breathing now. Whatever was keeping you from breathing isn't there anymore." Slowly his body began to relax and his breathing began to sound less strained. He was getting farther from the lady in the blue dress.

Janna waited a few moments and then said, "Mozart, can you look over at me?"

He turned his head and his eyes focused on hers for a second and then started to close. He was drifting off to sleep.

"Can you stay with me a little more? Try to stay with me." His eyes opened again slightly, the lids heavy with exhaustion.

"You're going to be all right, Mozart," she said. "That happened a long time ago. You were reliving something from a long time ago. You're not in any danger anymore." She smiled at him warmly and said in a soothing voice, "You're safe now."

Mozart's eyes closed and he fell asleep.

Janna sat back in her chair, watching my limp body. "Cam?"

A swirling apparition spiraled down through a dark and winding tunnel to the softly lit room where I lay peacefully sleeping on a huge white bed with fluffy pillows the color of saffron. A finger tapped me gently on the chest, once, twice. "Cam?" My eyes opened slowly, responding to the tap and the feathery voice. "Cam?" I tried to focus, to see who the lovely voice belonged to, but couldn't.

"I can hear you," I said, my own voice sounding very distant. "Who's calling my name?"

"Janna. It's Janna," the voice wafted in past a lattice-crust blueberry pie cooling on a country windowsill.

"Janna?" I said, my voice thick, the sweet intoxicating aroma of the pie filling my nostrils. The name sounded vaguely familiar.

"Cam," the voice said again, this time sharper, and a frown crossed my face as the pie rose off the sill and floated out the window across a meadow and into darkened woods. "Cam." *My name. She's calling my name.*

"I can hear you," I said again, feeling my larynx vibrate with the words. "I'm trying to open my eyes."

"Your eyes *are* open, Cam. Try to focus them on my face."

This time the voice was much closer. The soft pillows shrank and vanished and my face was pressed against the leather of Janna's couch. *Focus, focus, focus, focus, focus.* And at last, there was Janna's face sideways in front of mine. *She's not sideways . . . you're lying down. Right. What am I doing lying down?*

I said aloud, "What am I doing lying down?"

"Can you sit up?"

Slowly I began to rise to a sitting position, my eyes watching Janna's image tilting clockwise, leaving the horizontal and becoming more and more vertical until I was actually sitting up straight.

"We're both vertical," I said. I shook my head hard a couple of times. "What's going on?"

"Try to get the information from inside."

I scowled at her. "Why don't you just tell me what the hell is going on?"

She smiled patiently. "A lot's been going on. Try to get some information—"

"From inside," I said, annoyed. "I know. All right. Give me a minute. Walking around a rug. Dizzy."

Janna nodded. "Uh huh. Anything else?"

"Wyatt."

"Right. Wyatt, a new alter . . . at least one I didn't know about . . . was walking around the rug."

I frowned and put my hands on my chest. "Heavy breathing, like being trapped under something . . . something pressing on my chest." I was beginning to feel very uncomfortable. "A blue dress. Blue cotton dress. Underwear. A vagina."

"Good."

"No, not good! I don't like this."

"What else? Who was wearing the blue dress?"

I closed my eyes for a second and a flash of anger hacked at my brain like a machete. My eyes popped open and I glared at her. "Who do *you* think?" I spat.

"I don't know."

"Who gives a damn anyway? Just because somebody says something doesn't mean it's true!"

"That's right, but—"

"But what?!"

"Who was it? Listen inside." We were quiet for a minute.

"White hair, okay? That's what I'm getting. White hair. I don't even know where it's coming from. *Goddamn,* I hate this!"

"The grandmother," Janna muttered to herself.

"I don't know where it's coming from!"

"Listen inside. I know this is hard for you, but just listen."

When she said "listen," she stretched out the "s" and it glided from her lips and wrapped around me like a silk shawl, and the rage evaporated. I closed my eyes again.

"Mozart. Music? No, a name. A kid . . . named Mozart. An alter named Mozart." I looked at her quizzically. "I have an alter named Mozart?"

Janna nodded. "That's what he said his name was. He sounded pretty young. And very distressed. He needs to know about the Comfort Room. You and some of the others should find him and bring him to the Comfort Room. Wyatt, too. Try to do that now. Per and Bart, Dusty, Stroll . . . look around for Wyatt and Mozart. They need to go to the Comfort Room."

A moment went by that we were silent. Then, "Okay, we found them both."

"Can someone take them to the Comfort Room?"

"Yes. We're all taking them down."

"Good."

Neither of us said anything for a couple of minutes. My eyes felt cold; I blinked them and they stung.

Janna got up and crossed to the couch and sat down at the other end. I turned my head to look at her and realized my neck hurt.

"You've had a rough session," she said. "How do you feel?"

"Alone on a high wire . . . without a net."

Janna reached toward me to touch my shoulder, but withdrew her hand and placed it on the couch near me.

"You're not alone, Cam," she said softly. "And I'm your net."

THIRTY-FOUR

Eight people from Rikki's office were at Chevy's, a Mexican restaurant in Alameda, drinking margaritas, eating nachos, and laughing loudly at two tables pushed together, when Rikki joined them. She was an hour late for Andy's party.

A wiry, muscular guy in his early thirties lifted his glass and said, "Hey, look who decided to show up." He launched into a line from *Hello Dolly* in a Louis Armstrong voice that sounded more like Grover from *Sesame Street.* "Find her an emp-ty lap, fel-las"

Janine slid her chair away from Andy's and Andy pulled a chair next to his from another table while they all chimed in, "Rikki don't e-ver go a-way, Rikki don't e-ver go a-way, Rikki don't e-ver go away agaaiin." The whole group broke up laughing and everyone in the restaurant clapped and cheered.

Rikki sat down, a big grin on her face. "I'm not leaving," she said, grabbing a glass. She put her hand on Andy's shoulder. "He is. Now somebody pour me a margarita."

Andy picked up the pitcher and filled her glass. He had straight black hair with a little gray showing at the temples, cornflower blue eyes and a rough-hewn face with crow's-feet and deep smile lines that made him look like he built log homes for a living and enjoyed it. Except he was wearing Italian shoes and a twelve-hundred-dollar suit. And he didn't build log houses. He was in marketing.

He smiled at Rikki, "Glad you could make it. Thanks for coming."

"Wouldn't have missed it. Sorry I'm so late. I had to get some last-minute stuff together for the show." She shouted across the table at the wiry guy, "Hey, Satchmo. You don't get me your client list for the show by tomorrow, your horn's gonna end up in Pucker City."

Everybody said, "Ooooh."

Satchmo laughed. "Is that a promise?"

"I'm not kidding, Jimmy. I need those names."

"Okay, Rik. Sorry. I'll get 'em to you tomorrow. I just gotta chase down one more prick."

Rikki grinned. "I'd like to chase one down myself," she said and knocked her drink back in one gulp.

A big guy wearing a white shirt, red tie, and suspenders piped up from the end of the table. "Excuse me, ah, Rikki?" he said, peeking under the napkin on his lap with a wide grin. "Ah, I think I've found one for you."

Everyone cracked up. "Thanks, Brian," Rikki chuckled. "I'll get back to you on that." Andy refilled her glass, and his hand brushed against hers lightly. Their eyes met and she smiled at him warmly. "Thanks."

He smiled back. "Sure."

"Well, I gotta go," Janine said, pushing her chair back and standing up. She dropped a ten on the table. "Hot date tonight."

A well-dressed woman in her mid-thirties holding a nacho on a napkin said in mid-chew, "I'm gonna go out on a limb here, Janine, but I'm guessing he's not a farmer."

Janine made face like she was offended. She said, "No, he's Itaaalian."

Everyone cracked up some more, including Janine. She turned to Andy.

"Good luck, Andy," she said, giving him a little peck on the cheek. "We'll miss having you around."

Andy started to get up and Janine pushed him back down. "Don't get up," she said and glanced around at everyone. "What a gentleman!"

He smiled at her. "Thanks for coming, Janine. Be good."

"Me? Hah," she laughed. "Bye, everybody. See ya tomorrow." She waved and headed for the door.

Brian stood up, too, and said, with a holy-shit face, "Look at the time. I gotta get home for my for my seven o'clock beating." He dropped a twenty on the table, slipped his suit jacket on, and went around to shake hands with Andy.

"Me, too," Jimmy said, throwing down two tens. "I'll see you all tomorrow. Poker Thursday, Andy?"

"You bet," Andy said, smiling. "I need your money."

The others all finished their drinks, got up, left some money, and said their goodbyes to Andy. They walked out and Rikki and Andy were alone.

"Well," Andy said, a little nervously. "Here we are."

"Yup," Rikki shrugged. "Here we are." A moment passed while they both looked around the restaurant, not knowing each other very well and a little uncomfortable at being suddenly alone. Andy turned to her and broke the silence.

"Rikki, you probably have to go—"

"I just got here. But you don't have to stay on my account."

"No, no, I was gonna finish my drink. I just don't want you to feel like you have to stay just to keep me company. You know, the guest of honor shouldn't be the last to leave the party."

Rikki nodded. "That is kind of a sad image." She looked at the pile of money on the table. "Although it looks like you made a pretty good haul."

"I suppose you're right," Andy chuckled. "I guess I'm in the chips." He grinned sheepishly. "We could pay the bill and go to Tahoe on what's left over."

A little jolt of excitement dashed through Rikki's stomach and she was suddenly aware of how close they were sitting to each other. Their legs were almost touching. Rikki looked at Andy, and with heavy lids and an exaggerated Bacall voice, said, "Hmm . . . Tahoe. They have a lake there."

Andy leaned toward her and did the Bogie thing with his mouth a couple of times and said, "Yeah, sweetheart, a wet one," and did the thing with his mouth again.

They looked at each other for a second and cracked up.

The waitress came over to their table. She looked about twenty, with short black hair and thick eyebrows. "Can I get you anything else?" she asked.

Andy looked at Rikki inquiringly. She glanced at her watch and back at him. "I'll have a coffee with Kahlua."

"Great," he said, and told the waitress, "two coffees with Kahlua, please."

"Yes, sir. And I'll have someone clear the table right away."

"Thank you."

As she walked away, Andy shook his head and said, "She called me 'sir.' She wouldn't have done that if she didn't think I was old."

Rikki smiled at him. "No, sir, she wouldn't." They both laughed and Rikki felt their knees touch. She cleared her throat. "Janine calls me Granny."

"Get outta here. Really?"

"Really."

He ran a hand over his silk tie. "I've got a fourteen-year-old daughter."

"I've got a seven-year-old son."

"Ahh. What's his name?"

"Kai. What's your daughter's name?"

"Katie."

The drinks arrived and they stirred them and took sips.

Rikki jerked away from her cup, fanned her mouth and said, "Whew. Hot. Tasty, but hot."

"Burn your tongue?"

"Mm hmm," she said, dousing it with a sip of margarita. "Damn!"

Andy said, "I hate it when you burn your tongue on the first sip."

Rikki nodded. "Or the roof of your mouth on the first bite of pizza."

"That too." Andy took a spoonful of whipped cream. "Whipped cream's not hot," he said, offering Rikki a taste. Danger zone. She hesitated for a second and then lipped a little off the end, her eyes on his. Neither of them spoke for a moment.

Rikki glanced at Andy's left hand. "I don't see a ring."

Andy took a careful sip of his coffee and placed the cup on the table. "My wife left us when Katie was two."

"My God. She just left?"

"Mm hmm. Went back to Wyoming to live with her folks. Didn't go for custody when we got divorced." Andy smiled sadly at Rikki. "Ellen's got some serious problems with alcohol. She's been in and out of half a dozen psychiatric hospitals. Even tried to commit suicide once." He shrugged. "We talk about twice a year, she sends Katie a birthday present."

Rikki frowned. "It must have been so hard on you."

"It was for a while. You know, I never saw it coming. All of a sudden it just seemed to swallow her up." Andy played with his spoon a little. "We do all right, though, Katie and me."

"Has there been anybody else?"

"Oh," Andy sighed. "A couple. I started to get serious with somebody about three years ago, but when it came right down to it she didn't really want to be a stepmom, she just wanted her own family. So," he gestured with his hands like an explosion, "pcchhhh!"

Andy straightened himself in his chair and smiled brightly, stepping off his dark path. "What about you? Tell me about you."

Rikki picked up her cup and held it in both hands, studying the swirl of whipped cream for a few seconds while she thought about how much to tell him. And then she spoke. And she told him everything. Andy listened intently, watching her deep blue eyes and the delicate movements of her hands as she emphasized her thoughts.

It was starting to get dark when Rikki finished, and the busboys were going around to each table lighting candles. The whipped cream had melted in their half-drunk cups of coffee.

Andy put his hand over hers and gave it a gentle squeeze. "I'm sorry you're having to deal with all this."

Rikki squeezed back. "Thank you." She glanced at her watch. It was 7:30. "Oh, my God!" she said. "I've got to get home. Cam's going to a meeting tonight and I think it starts at 8:30." Andy signaled the waitress and she hurried over and dropped the check. He gathered up the money everyone had chipped in, paid the bill, and left a big tip. Getting up he said to Rikki, "I'll walk you to your car."

Rikki smiled and they headed for the door.

They stopped at her car and he stood close to her. "Would you like to have lunch sometime?" he asked. "Just friends."

Rikki got a tingling feeling, followed by a slap of fear. She frowned as the two sensations danced clumsily around. And then her frown disappeared. "Okay," she said to Andy, with a smile. A friend.

THIRTY-FIVE

When Rikki pulled into the driveway, I was pacing back and forth in the darkened garage feeling prickly and mean, hating the idea of arriving late for my meeting at Sedona House.

Rikki spotted me in the headlights and could tell I was miffed.

She said she was sorry, I mumbled an insincere "it's okay," we exchanged a cursory kiss at the car door, and I was behind the wheel and pulling out of the driveway within fifteen seconds of her arrival. The appearance of Wyatt and Mozart at Janna's already had the mixmaster in my head on blend, and Rikki being late pushed it up to frappe. I was trying to focus on driving, but the wheel felt like thick black licorice in my hands, and the headlights seemed to be spraying billions of particles of yellow paint on everything.

I was on Alta Vista Road less than a mile from home when I heard the siren and saw the crimson lights flashing. *Pull over, pull over, step on the brake, put it in park. What's happening? Quiet. What's happening? Quiet! What's happening?! QUIET!!!* A stalk of white light pointed at me.

"Roll down your window, sir." Huh? Where'd that voice come from? Again, this time louder, "Roll down your window, sir." Somebody say something! Press the button. Nothing's happening. This is the button. Nothing.

"Put your hands on the wheel, sir." We put my hands on the licorice. The cop opened the door and shined his flashlight right in my face.

"Why didn't you roll down your window?"

"I didn't know how. I pressed the button, but it didn't go down."

"The motor was off. Have you been drinking?"

"Water. I had water in a glass."

"Step out of the car, please."

Gooey legs pulled free of the floor mat and feet squished on the pavement. *I'm tall.* A breeze blew a wisp of long hair across my face into my open mouth. *What's this, string?* I was diving down and down into murky waters.

The cop said, "Show me your driver's license, please."

"What?"

He said it again, harsher this time, "I said show me your driver's license please." His partner was in the prowler running my license plate. She got out of the car and came over.

"I don't know what you mean," I said slowly.

"Your driver's license. In your wallet. Do you have a wallet?" The lady cop looked quizzically at her partner.

"Pocket," I muttered. I was sinking. No one was coming out to save me. *Where's Leif? I don't know. Per? I don't know.* "In my pocket. I have pants. It's in my pants pocket."

The male cop looked at his partner and back at me. "Carefully reach into your pants pocket and take out your license, sir."

"Okay." I slid the wallet out and handed it to him, careful not to open it. *Sometimes they bite, you know.*

"Don't hand me your wallet, sir. I want you to take the license out of your wallet."

"I can't. I-I don't know what to look for."

The lady cop stuck a plastic thing in my mouth and said, "Blow on this." I did, and she took it out of my mouth, looked at it, and said to her partner, "Nothing."

He took the wallet, flipped it open, and pulled out my license. Another stalk of light shined on me. The lady had one, too.

She said, "What's your name, sir?"

"Cameron West," my voice said. I was deep beneath the waves of reality. "He's Cameron West."

The male cop checked the license and said, "Same."

The lady said, "It's his car. No warrants. Lives right around the corner."

The male cop handed the wallet back to us and we tucked it into its bed in my pants. He said, "What do you mean, 'He's Cameron West'?"

I didn't say anything. It's hard to talk when you're underwater.

"Do you know where you are, Mr. West?"

"California." There was some mumbling between them I couldn't make out.

"Do you know you were doing thirty-four miles an hour in a twenty-five-mile-an-hour zone?"

Bang, Wyatt popped out. "Fifty-nine. That's fifty-nine. Thirty-four plus twenty-five is fifty-nine."

The male cop said, "What?" but Wyatt was gone. He looked at his partner. They didn't know what to do. I heard more mumbling.

The lady said to me, "Mr. West, are you married? Is there someone at home we could talk to?"

I said, "Rikki West."

"Is that your wife?"

"Huh?"

"Is Rikki West your wife?"

"Rikki West is the wife."

"Do you know your telephone number?"

The number came from somewhere inside and my mouth opened and the words dripped out. *Where'd that come from?*

Then Wyatt came out again for a second and said, "There are no bugs here. Not one. But the breeze blew strings in his mouth and I could taste them."

The lady cop said to her partner, "I'll call her," and walked back to the cruiser.

The male cop said, "Walk over here, please," and motioned me to walk around to the right side of the car to get off the street. A few people had seen the police lights and came out on their porches to watch. The air felt warm on my skin.

The lady cop got out of the car and came over to us. She said to her partner, "I spoke to his wife. A car's gonna pick her up and bring her over here. Be here in a minute. She said he's an incest survivor and sometimes he has flashbacks and gets confused, like post-traumatic stress. Said he was on his way to a support group meeting."

The male cop said in a hushed tone, "I don't know. Maybe we should fifty-one-fifty him. Seems a lot more'n confused to me."

The lady said, "Let's see what happens when she gets here." I was deep in warm tropical waters, the glinting moon making zebra stripes on the sandy bottom, no shoes on, just a shirt and baggy tan pants. *Why am I wearing pants in the water? Don't ask out loud. Jail, they'll take you to jail. Oh my God! What'd we do wrong?*

I surfaced for a second and said, "What did I do wrong?" Then I went back down.

The male cop said, "You were driving too fast, Mr. West. A car's bringing your wife over here. Here she comes now. Just take it easy."

The lady cop walked over toward the second prowler and two male cops got out. One of them opened the rear door for Rikki and she got out, too. Cars were slowing down to see what was going on, and a few more people came out in the street in front of their houses. Rikki talked with the lady cop for a minute while the male cop watched me. I stood still, but inside I was a ray swimming inches above the ocean floor. Then everybody walked quickly over to where we were standing.

Rikki came right up to me and put her hand on my arm. "Cam? Cam?" she said worriedly. Her words reached down through the warm water like a long wavy bamboo pole, gently nudging my shoulder. I turned and grabbed the pole and it slowly pulled me up from the depths. *Goodbye fish, goodbye plants. We'll be back.*

The neurons in my brain realigned and the water receded. Then a quick shudder, a switch, and I was fully back. Police, lights, cars, night, Rikki.

"What's going on, Rik?" I said, confused.

"You got pulled over for speeding," she said, still holding onto my arm.

"Got pulled over," I repeated, struggling to comprehend. I looked at Rikki's face and then at the faces of the four police officers and felt a flush of embarrassment as reality set in. "Uh oh," I said. I was scared. "Am I in trouble? Rik, I don't want to be in trouble."

Rikki looked hopefully at the female cop. The cop said, "Mr. West, we're not so concerned about the speeding. We just want to know if you need to be in a hospital for psychiatric observation. Your wife said you might've been having a flashback of some kind."

I shook my head. "Ah . . . yes . . . yes, I was having a flashback. Not a drug kind," I said, worried they'd think I was on LSD or something. "I don't take drugs. I—"

"We understand." She spoke slowly and deliberately, like I was hard of hearing, "Are you all right to go home if your wife drives you?"

I looked at her, trying to appear normal. "Yes, ma'am. I'm sorry for causing this trouble."

The male cop next to me said, "It's all right, Mr. West." He looked at his partner and then back at me. "Just be careful next time you get behind the wheel, okay? You shouldn't be driving in this condition."

I nodded. Then he looked at Rikki and said, "You can take your husband home now, Mrs. West."

Rikki said, "Thank you," and opened the passenger door for me. I got in and she closed the door. She walked around to the driver's side and got in, started the car, and drove us home.

She put her hand on my leg. "Are you all right?"

I shook my head, looking out the window. "No . . . I'm not all right. Bad things at Janna's." She patted my leg. I changed the subject. "Where's Kai?"

"I had to leave him at the Withingtons."

"What'd you tell them?"

"Who, the cops?"

"No, the Withingtons."

"Same thing I told the cops. That you're an incest survivor and you were having a flashback and you got disoriented. They were concerned about you, but they won't ask questions."

"I'm way out there, Rik," I said, shaking my head. "I'm a nut." She patted my leg again and we didn't speak for the rest of the ride home.

When we got there I went right upstairs and ran a bubble bath. Rikki walked over to the Withingtons' to get Kai. I was soaking in the tub when they came home. They walked upstairs, knocked on the door, and came into the bathroom. I was in the land of bubbles, hoping the hot water would wash away what just happened. It might. But it wouldn't draw out the sticky blackness that coated my insides like the tar on the devil's driveway. That was on there good.

"Daddy?" Kai said. "Are you all right? A police car picked Mommy up and I couldn't go."

I managed a smile. "Sure, I'm all right. I just had some bad memories and got kind of confused. That's all."

"I really wanted to ride in the car." He eyed the mound of bubbles. "Can I get in?"

"Sure!" I said, secretly hoping the bad water wouldn't taint my little boy.

"I'll get some guys," he said and took off for his toy room. My eyes met Rikki's for a second and I quickly looked away, thoroughly embarrassed.

"You okay?" she said, without smiling.

I nodded. "Yeah, I'm okay," I said, but I didn't mean it.

After the bath, Rikki read to Kai and I tucked him in and kissed him goodnight. We got into bed, and about thirty seconds later Rikki rolled over and put me in a lip lock Houdini couldn't have gotten out of. She held my face tightly with both hands, her lips against mine, mouth open, tongue exploring.

She threw her leg over me, straddled me and pulled her T-shirt up, pushing her breasts in my face. I took a hard nipple in my mouth and sucked it and she moaned loudly. She grabbed me and squeezed, kissed her way down my chest and stomach, and slid her warm wet mouth over me, devouring me, moaning feverishly. I felt the slick sweat on her hot back, and the rhythm of her head moving up and down and her moist lips and hungry mouth, and my body tensed and the room began to swirl and fade and . . . *oh, no* . . . shudder, switch, and . . .

"M-mommy?"

It was Clay.

Rikki jerked her head up and looked at Clay in the dark. "M-mommy. Ssstoppp," he pleaded.

In an instant Rikki was out from under the covers lunging for her bathrobe. She flipped on the light. "Clay!" she shouted breathlessly, clutching the robe tightly around her.

"W-what?"

"I'm *not* your mommy. You shouldn't be here."

He started to say something but the words came out garbled.

"I need to talk to Cam right now," Rikki insisted. Smash! I hit some wall in my head and was suddenly back in the room.

"What the hell," I said, clambering to get to my mental feet. "What the hell's going on here, Rik?"

She just looked at me for a moment, mortified. "What just happened here, Cam? Did what I think happened just happen?" She ran her hand over her hair. "I'm trying to stay cool here. I'm trying to stay cool."

"Clay came out, right?"

She lost it. "You're damn right he came out. While I was . . ." she put the back of her hand to her mouth. "Aw shit, Cam. This is awful."

"Rikki," I stammered, "it's, it's . . . not so bad."

"Not so bad!" she yelled, and then backed off, realizing she might wake Kai. She hissed, "It's fucking awful! The whole thing is blown."

I looked down at my fading erection and smiled at her feebly. "Not quite," I said, but the joke didn't work.

"Cam, this isn't even close to being funny. I'm not sure what to do with this. I mean, if we can't have sex without someone else coming out, then . . . shit."

"Rik, I'm sorry. I'm really sorry. We'll work on it with Janna in therapy. We'll make some arrangements ahead of time for everybody to be in the Comfort Room. You're right, this can't happen again. I'm really sorry. Come back to bed, okay? It's gonna be okay."

Rikki didn't move. She looked at me and said in a deadly serious voice,

"I feel like I just did something terrible. Like I just sexually abused a child." Then she started to cry. "I don't want to feel that way," she sobbed, "I want to make love to my husband, goddammit, not Clay, or anyone else!"

There was nothing to say. I pulled the covers over my naked body, suddenly so embarrassed that I wanted to go hide in the wretched mist of some distant corner of the universe. *Somebody help me. Snap your fingers and make me disappear.* Nothing. Nowhere to go.

Rikki eventually came to bed, but she put on a pair of pajamas first. She didn't touch me, just curled up on her side of the big bed and went to sleep. I turned on my light, opened my journal, and had a serious discussion with Bart, Per, Stroll, and Leif. *No one comes out when Rikki and I make love, especially the young ones.* Everyone agreed that was best and went off to attend to Clay.

I closed the journal and turned out the light, wondering if the agreement had come too late, if Rikki would ever want to make love with me again.

THIRTY-SIX

A guy in a movie called *Joe* once said, "You can learn to live with just about anything." But he didn't say at what cost. The incident with Clay was more than a tremor; it was a full-blown quake, and Rikki and I ended up on opposite sides of the fault line. She blamed the people who hurt me, and I blamed me. And from then on we tiptoed around each other, aftershocks rippling the once firm ground beneath us.

Rikki started having lunch, and occasionally dinner, with Andy, which should have been okay. She'd had male friends before. I'd always trusted her. I wasn't the first guy who was friends with her. Why should I be the last? You can use all the friends you can get, whatever kind, I say. It wasn't that I didn't trust Rikki. I didn't trust the ground. I didn't trust the sky. Blue wasn't blue anymore.

I had school, though, and I tore through it like a stoned kid through a bag of chips, typing with one hand, holding Denial's Rake with the other.

I turned away from my guys, and the more I ignored them, the worse things got. There wasn't any comfort in the Comfort Room. Everybody was keeping low, crouching down, staying out of sight, while a ricocheting bullet zinged around—ptchew, ptchew—smashing things, searching for flesh.

The bullet was Switch. He started cutting my right arm again. In the middle of writing a paper, I'd find myself upstairs with something sharp in my hand and blood dripping into the sink from a fresh wound. Where was Bart? Where was Leif? Keeping low, that's where. And it was all my fault for shutting them out. Off to the hospital for more stitches. Rikki hid the knives, but Switch found other things: the top of a tuna can, the blade from Kai's pencil sharpener, a rusty nail.

I saw messages in my journal, written in blood:

"Come and get me."

"What do you want?"

"I'm still here."

I wrote my own message: "Help me." And drew a bloody self-portrait beside it. And from then on, when I'd pick up the journal, it would fall open to that portrait, and the haunting eyes would stare at me, begging for help.

The wheels were spinning, the tires were smoking, and the pipes were roaring. I was going down like the gas gauge on a hot rod to hell.

On a Thursday, nine months after the night with the cops and Clay, I dropped Kai at school and came home, but didn't sit down at my computer. My body was tingling, everything looked sharper and brighter than usual, and inside my head was like a cuckoo clock store—tick tock, tick tock, tick tock—strange things on every shelf, tick tocking. And it was two minutes to midnight.

My feet glided across the kitchen tiles and the living room carpet, my hand turned the knob to the garage door, and I stepped down the two steps onto the cold, slick cement. My eyes scanned the garage past the trashcans, washer, dryer, to the tools. *What's going on? I don't know. I don't know. This doesn't look good. Aw shit, what now?* Rakes, shovels, handsaws, pick axe, hedge clippers, pitch fork, sledgehammer. *Oh God, what's happening?* My body moved toward the sledgehammer. *Oh no. Oh no.*

Switch slid his left hand down the wooden handle toward the iron and hefted it high. The right hand lay flat on the smooth concrete, fingers splayed, waiting. Tick . . . tock . . . tick . . . *Oh God, I'm not watching this. I don't mind, I don't mind, I* . . . tock. Cuckoo.

Wham! The sledgehammer came down and smashed my hand like a clove of garlic. Aaaahhh! That hurts! What the hell? Aw goddamn, I knew he was up to something. Look, the fingers are blowing up like those balloons . . .

you know, the ones they make swans out of. The hand's turning purple. Cam . . . hey Cam, you see what's going on here?

Written in blood after Switch cut.

I came over the ridge on a horse—clip clop, clip clop—and stopped. My mare whinnied and snorted steam from her nostrils. I grabbed the saddle horn and swung my leg over the horse's back to dismount. *Ouch. Damn! My hand hurts.* I landed on the ground, my horse faded into the air, and suddenly I was in the garage with the unforgiving cement under my feet.

"Holy shit, my hand's been smashed!" Oh, no! Back to the hospital. This is not good. This is definitely not good.

I was right. It wasn't good. The ER nurse—one I hadn't seen before—said, "Wow, what happened to your hand?"

"A safe dropped on it," I said and got sent off to radiology for pictures.

My self-portrait in blood next to the words "Help me."

It turned out it wasn't as bad as we thought. The large flat surface of the sledgehammer must have distributed the impact evenly, and although my hand was the size of Wyoming, astoundingly, no bones were broken. The doctor—whom I also didn't recognize—put splints on my fingers, wrapped up my hand so it looked like a white oven mitt, and sent me home.

Rikki insisted, and Janna agreed, that I return to Del Amo, and by Saturday noon I was back on the ward, once again sailing at close reach into an angry wind.

Everything was different. The DDU had been moved to another part of the hospital while they renovated. Bug Eye Bea was still there, and so was Sue. Stephanie was there, too, but she was in the day program. When I saw her she acted like she owed me money and didn't have it. I found out Kris had just left after being in for two months; she'd burned up half her body with chemicals. *Poor Kris. Poor Jody.*

Mandy wasn't our therapist and it was a damn shame. He was too booked up. We were assigned to Dr. Alan Beecham, a mealy-looking, middle-aged guy with a bluish five o'clock shadow, even at ten a.m., and a handshake that reminded me of corn mush. He had a sticky, dry-mouth voice that droned like a bilge pump, and his eyes were close together like a Gulfport Rounder's. I guess he was bright, though. He had a Ph.D. But I was on my way to my own Ph.D., and I'd learned a lot, particularly about my condition, and Alan Beecham wasn't dazzling me with his knowledge or insight. We were a mismatch, that's all. Wasn't his fault.

Dusty liked him. A lot. He listened sympathetically when she cried about Robbie. He seemed to like her, too, probably because she didn't try to out-shrink him or slap him down. I did. So did Leif. Together we beat him like a rented mule.

I was pissed off to be back in the hospital. Pissed off that we didn't get Ed Mandel. Pissed off that Beecham had the brains of a Zagnut. Pissed off that Kris wasn't there. Pissed off that Stephanie was colder than Admiral Byrd's ass. And pissed off that Rikki was slipping away from me and I couldn't do anything about it. All in all, I was pretty fucking pissed off.

Fortunately Janna had us on the front burner and was calling every day, trying feverishly to help me shed the mental pounds I'd put on—the crazy man's Jenny Craig. I'd given her a calling card number and insisted that we have paid sessions—none of that free stuff like some therapists who call just to check up and see how you're doing out of the goodness of their hearts. Nope. Goddammit, I wasn't about to let Janna Chase be concerned about us without the meter running. I just wouldn't accept the fact that she genuinely cared about us. Why would *anyone* care about *us?*

We were doing a lot more work with Janna over the phone than with Dr. Flounder in person and wanted to get out of Del Amo as quickly as we could. Our wish came true. When Switch walked into the hallway with a two-inch gash he'd dug in his arm with the end of a paper clip and the word "DEAD" written on his forehead in blood, I was as popular as a zit on prom night. They offered me a choice—the lock-down unit or the keys to the street. *Hmm, let's see.*

Adios Del Amo, and *buenos dias* . . . whatever. Hey, everybody limbos at de zombie jamboree.

THIRTY-SEVEN

"I want to talk to Switch," Janna said, "but I want you to stick around as much as you can. We've got a lot to cover." She sat back in the blue chair and took a sip from a tall paper coffee cup topped with white foam and dots of powdered chocolate.

I rocked rhythmically back and forth, trying not to get lost in the river painting. I tore my eyes away from it and looked at Janna. "Okay. I'll stay as close as I can. But don't you forget about me. I need time here today, too."

She nodded. "I know. Right now I want to talk with Switch. But I want you and everyone else to stay close and pay attention." Inside everyone was gathering. Batter up.

The baseboard heater clicked on and warmth drifted up toward me, cutting through the slight chill in the room. My body shivered, I gasped, and Switch stepped up to the plate. I went to the dugout and watched.

"What?!" Switch barked loudly.

Janna didn't flinch. "You're pretty upset, huh?"

"Yeah!" he barked again.

"You've been having a really bad time, haven't you? You told me on the phone."

"Yeah! A really, really bad time!"

"A really, really bad time," Janna nodded, looking at the rolled-up sleeve and the bandaged right arm. The metal splints were still on my fingers, and my hand was still wrapped.

Switch stared at the floor, a deep frown on his face. "I smashed his hand and wrote 'DEAD' on his head," he said softly. He looked like he wanted to cry.

"You showed him how angry you are. And I don't think you're the only one who's angry. Listen inside and find out if other people are angry, too."

Switch was quiet for a moment, concentrating fiercely. He glanced up at Janna and then down at the arm of her chair and nodded. "Some of them are mad, too."

"Are they mad at you? Listen again."

He pursed his lips, frowned some more, and listened. "Per said nobody hates me. Nobody's mad at me. But they don't want me to hurt this body anymore. He says it hurts everyone. I thought it just hurt Cam."

"Remember I told you that when you hurt Cam you also hurt everyone else: Anna, Trudi, Wyatt, Clay, Mozart, Davy, Bart, Stroll, Leif, Per, Dusty. Everybody. And you, too. You hurt yourself, too."

Switch shrank in on himself, his face got red, and a tear formed in the corner of each eye. "I-I'm sorry I hurt everyone. I won't do it again." Then his eyes shut tightly, his face contorted in the strange smile of agony, and hot tears erupted and ran like lava down his cheeks. His hands hung lifelessly by his sides and his body shook as he cried. "I'm sorry, everyone," he sobbed, and then screamed, "but I . . . don't . . . wanna . . . be . . . locked . . . uuuppp!!" Janna jumped a little. Switch jabbed the thumb from the damaged hand past his shoulder. Then, like a train's whistle, first soft in the distance, then louder, then screeching as it blasted by the platform, he screamed, "HE'S LOCKING US ALL UUUPPP!!!" The intensity of Switch's anger vibrated in the room, and Janna unconsciously gripped the arms of her chair.

"Who?" she said after a few seconds. "Who's locking you up . . . Cam?"

"Yeah," he said, wiping his eyes on his sleeve. Janna got up, grabbed the tissue box, and offered it to him. Switch took one and blew his nose. He looked around for a place to throw out the tissue. "Where do I put this?" Janna pointed to the small wicker basket next to the couch, and he tossed the tissue into it.

Janna said, "He's been pushing you all out."

"He doesn't want us to be here. 'Specially me. He hates us."

Then he screamed again, "I haaaate thaaaaaat! I haaaate hiiiim!!"

"You don't want to be ignored, do you?"

He shook his head and sniffled, "No."

"No," Janna said. "Nobody does."

Switch drew a portrait of himself. He didn't want to cut, but he couldn't stand to be ignored.

Inside I looked around the dugout. Everyone was looking at me. *Shit.* Janna leaned forward and rested her forearms on her knees. "Switch, I want you to close your eyes and look inside again. Find out if Cam's been listening." Switch closed his eyes and listened, sniffled again, and wiped his nose on his sleeve. He nodded at Janna, his eyes still shut, and said softly, "He heard me. He said so."

"Good. Now I'd like everyone to gather around Switch and tell him how brave he was to yell so loudly and let Cam know that none of you want to be ignored." She waited a moment. "Is everyone around you, Switch?"

"Yeah, they are. And they're being nice to me."

"I'd like everyone to know that Switch said he won't hurt the body anymore."

Switch nodded, "That's right. I won't."

"Switch, I'm going to make a special badge for you for being so brave."

"You are?"

"Yup. You are very, very, very important to everyone in this system. And very brave."

A faint smile crept across his face. He said aloud, not to Janna, but to the others, "Wow, she's gonna make me a badge."

Janna said, "Now someone please take Switch to the Comfort Room with the other young ones—Dusty could do that—and the adults stay around. There's more for us to do."

"Cam?" *Oh, shit, I'm up. World Serious.* Shudder, bang, back. Ripples of sadness turned to waves and became huge double-overhead curls that crashed down on top of me, and I burst into tears.

"Rikki's going to leeeeave me, Janna. She's going to leeeeave me," I moaned, rocking back and forth, hugging myself tightly. My right hand hurt, but I didn't care. "She's going to leave me. I can feel it."

Janna was surprised. "What makes you think Rikki's gonna leave you?"

"Because I'm CRAAZZzyyy!" I screamed. "I'm a crazy person. I know it. I'm crazy. Don't you hear all this shit getting talked about? Aren't you listening? Switch and Bart and Per and Mozart and Dusty and Clay. The fuckin' bees are swarming, Janna, and I'm outta Raid. I'm outta Raid! Goddammit! You think I'm normal? I'm a little depressed 'cause I didn't get a bike for Christmas? No, my fucking brain's a floppy loaf of bread that's barely connected at the bottom. I'm a fuckin' nut, Janna, a fuckin' nut, and I can't do anything about it, and there's blood in my journal and 'DEAD' on my forehead and my hand hurts and I can't find my way back to Rikki and I'm one inch from it, Janna, one inch, you hear me, and I got a kid, I got a k—"

"That's right, Cam!" Janna shouted at me, and the shock of her force knocked me back against the couch. "You've . . . got . . . a kid!" She jabbed her finger at me with each word. She kept yelling, "Yes, some bad shit happened to you and your brain doesn't work like most other people's and you've got Dissociative Identity Disorder and you've got to get used to it, Cameron. You've . . . got . . . to . . . accept it! You've been forcing your alters away because you don't want to accept it. You're screaming at Mach Two through school to get away from it. And it's not working!"

I moaned, "Janna, please . . ." I reached my hand toward her. "Please. Just touch my finger . . . like in the Sistine Chapel . . . like God and Adam in the Sistine Chapel. Do it, Janna. I'm dead. Give me life!"

She sprang out of her chair and paced the room. She stuck her finger out, but not like I'd asked; she jabbed it at me. "You're the only one who can give you life, Cam. If you lock them out, you aren't going to make it. And you . . . have . . . a kid. Even if Rikki leaves, you'll still be Kai's father. And he needs you." I covered my face with my hands. She said, "Kids who lose a parent through suicide are more likely to commit suicide them selves. Do you think Kai wants his father to die? Do you?"

"Noooooo!" I sobbed.

Janna said, "Good! Then you're going to have to face that you're a multiple and how you got that way, and start accepting your alters. You're going to have to let them out, and not just when you're here. You're going to have to take time every day to let them out—even if it means that it takes longer to get your Ph.D."

"I'm garbage, Janna," I sobbed.

"Is Per garbage? Is Clay garbage?"

I shook my head, "No."

"Is Mozart garbage? Dusty? Bart? Anna? Trudi?"

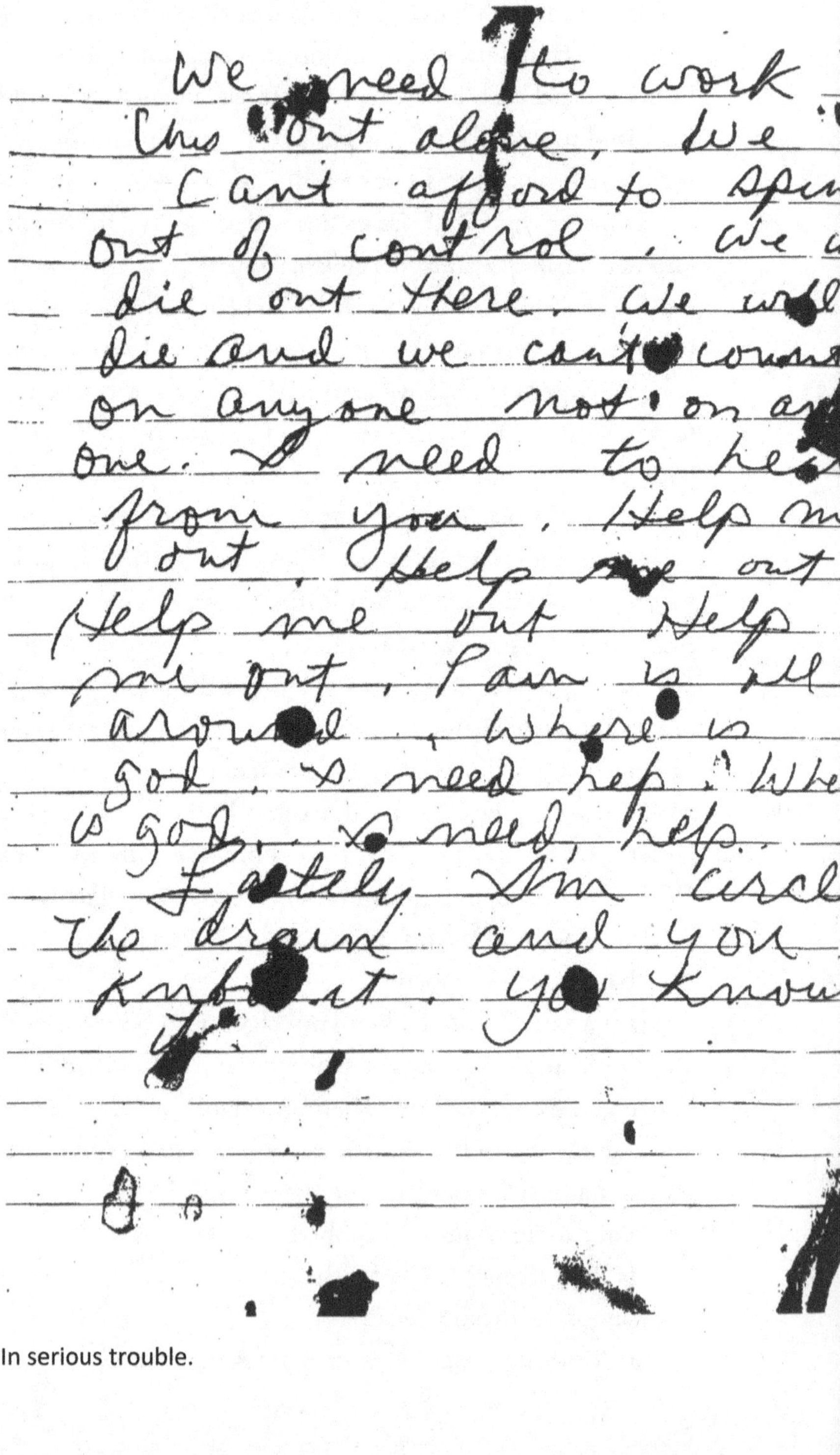

We need to work
this out alone, we
cant afford to spin
out of control. We w
die out there. We will
die and we can't count
on anyone not on any
one. I need to hear
from you. Help me
out. Help me out
Help me out Help
me out. Pain is all
around. Where is
god. I need hep. Whe
is god. I need help.
Lately I'm circl
the drain and you
know it. You know
it.

In serious trouble.

I shook my head again, "No. They're not garbage. They're good."

Janna sat down and said, softly, for the millionth time, "They're all parts of you, Cam. And they are good." She took a deep breath, let it out, and leaned forward. "And you are good." She picked up the coffee cup from the table beside her and held it in her lap with both hands. The foam had melted and the chocolate was now dark brown streaks.

I took a tissue and blew my nose. *Parts of me. Parts of me.* "They are parts of me," I said, "and they aren't bad. They are good."

She took a small sip, grimaced, and put the cup down. "Cam, you can't be garbage if parts of you are good."

I repeated her words, "I can't be garbage if parts of me are good. They're parts of me. They're good. I'm good."

Janna nodded. "Yes. You are good. And you're Kai's father, and he needs you."

I whispered, "He needs me." I was calming down now. No more tears. I wiped my eyes on a wet sleeve. "What about Rikki? I don't want to lose her."

"Is forcing your alters away, or getting your arm cut or your hand smashed helping to keep her?"

"I'm scared of losing her to that guy . . . Andy. She talks to him and goes out with him."

Janna interrupted, "Are the things you are doing helping to keep her?"

I thought for a moment and shook my head. "No."

"Would being more stable help to keep her?"

"Yes." We sat in silence for a moment. The electric heater cycled on again.

"Let them out, Cam," Janna said softly. "They need body time."

"Rikki doesn't accept them."

"How do you know that?"

"I can tell. I don't even know how to talk to her anymore. She said I'm not the man she married."

"You are who you are, Cam."

"And just who is that, Janna Chase?" I asked bitterly.

"A good person. A person whose mind works differently from most people's, but a good person. A funny, creative, interesting, intelligent man. A loving father. A loving husband." She paused. "I know your alters can't come out around Kai yet, and I know that bothers them . . . and you—"

"A lot," I muttered.

"A lot," Janna repeated. "But you can let them out for a while during the day—every day—an hour every morning maybe." She leaned forward to drive home the point. "And not just to let Dusty do the shopping, but to read books, or take a bubble bath, or take a walk, or even to help you study or write, if someone wants to."

"But Leif's pushing me so hard."

Janna gazed deeply into my eyes, "I want Leif, if he's listening . . ."

"He is."

". . . to let up, take a break. The work will get done. Leif needs some time out, too, to just . . . be."

Shudder, switch, and Leif was there. He crossed his legs and looked down at my tear-stained shirt. "Look at me," he said. "I'm a mess."

Janna said, "I know you've been listening." Leif nodded.

"Leif, you're incredible. Your drive is amazing."

"You told me that on the phone at the hospital. You were very good on the phone, by the way."

"Thank you," Janna said, leaning back in her chair. "Leif, it's time for you to let up on him a little and use your drive to help get everyone on track. Things will iron out much more quickly if you do that . . . and you'll get a little time just to relax."

Leif reached up to rub his chin, winced when the injured fingers touched his face, and gently placed the hand back on the arm of the couch. "Okay," he sighed. "I'll help out." He uncrossed his leg and crossed the other. "What about his wife?"

Janna shrugged. "I don't know. But she's been with you guys for a long time, and I'm sure things haven't been easy for her. You or Per could talk to her if Cam can't. Explain the situation, that you're going to be changing things, that things'll be better."

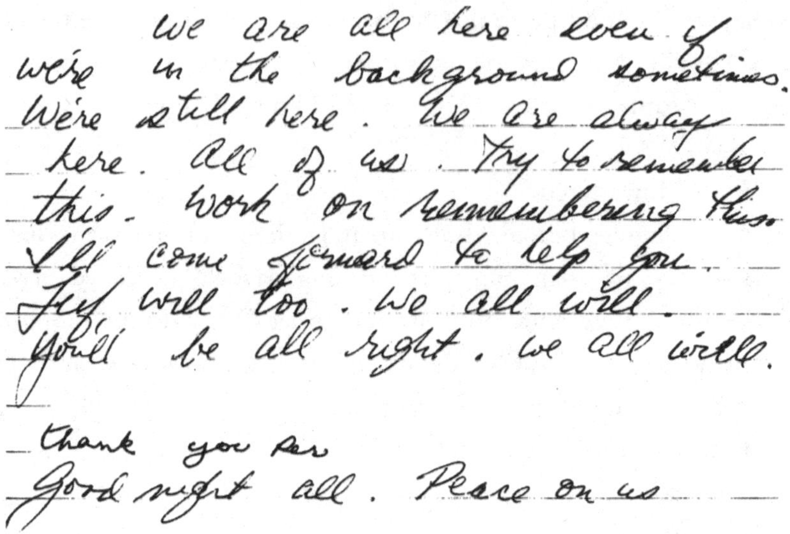
We are all here even if
we're in the background sometimes.
We're still here. We are always
here. All of us. Try to remember
this. Work on remembering this.
I'll come forward to help you.
Leif will too. We all will.
You'll be all right. We all will.

thank you Per
Good night all. Peace on us

Per offered his and Leif's support to me.

Leif nodded. "That makes sense, if Cam . . ." he jerked his chin toward his right shoulder, "gets with the program." Leif looked Janna in the eye. "See ya around, Doc." His focus started to fade and then quickly resumed its intensity. "One more thing," Leif said. "Per says he's in."

My body shuddered and I was back. Janna looked at me forcefully. "Did you hear that? Leif is going to ease up on pushing you through school and get some more time for himself, *if* . . . you start to accept them, giving them an hour out a day to do what they want. And Leif or Per will talk to Rikki if you think that would be helpful."

"Yeah," I said. "I think that'd be good." We sat quietly for a moment, our eyes locked on each other. "You know I've been circling the drain," I said. Janna nodded. I shook my head slowly, "Well, no more."

I looked out the window. It was beginning to drizzle. Several water droplets hit the glass, wandered alone for a second, then gathered in a little stream that ran down the windowpane. Separate, then together.

THIRTY-EIGHT

A light year is a measurement of distance, a very long distance. To figure out that distance you have to multiply 186,000 miles, which is how far light travels in a second, times 60 seconds, times 60 minutes, times 24 hours, times 365 days. And you arrive at the distance that light travels in a year. It's pretty far. Our scrawny planet is roughly 30,000 light years away from the center of the Milky Way galaxy. Which is just about the same as the distance between pasta from a box and homemade pasta.

That clear February evening I was *not* making pasta from a box. I was making homemade pasta: two cups of white flour, three eggs, a splash of olive oil, a pinch of salt, and a little warm water. I'd mixed them together in our Moulinex La Machine II food processor, taken the golden dough to the kitchen table, cut off little hunks with an eight-inch knife, and was rolling them out in long thin sheets on our squeaky Marcato Ampia Tipo Lusso Model 150 hand-cranking pasta roller.

The machine works by running the chunk of dough repeatedly between two steel rollers, one of which can be adjusted in distance from the other in increments from one to six, with six making the thinnest sheet. I stopped at five, laid each sheet on a large floured cutting board, and cut out circles with an empty tuna can that had the top and bottom removed. Then onto each circle of dough I spooned a delicious mixture Rikki had prepared of ricotta, parmesan, egg, parsley, pepper, and just a dash of nutmeg. I folded the dough over, pinched the edges together, and tossed the resulting half-moon ravioli onto a large flour-dusted oval plate.

I'd removed the bandage and splints from my sore hand that morning, and even though that gave me more mobility, I knew that assembling the ravioli was still going to be a little painful. I'd suggested making the meal, though, because it was like the old Rikki and me, when we used to cook all the time, when she used to call me Giuseppe the Pizza Man, before all the bad, crazy stuff. There's great comfort in familiarity. Cooking with Rikki was familiar, and I needed as much comfort as I could get that night.

I worked on the ravioli while Rikki stood at the counter making a pesto sauce from fresh basil, garlic, olive oil, parmesan, pine nuts, and a dash of salt and pepper. The big stainless steel pot, half-filled with water, a splash of oil, and a pinch of salt, was simmering on the burner.

As usual, Kai was playing with Jack upstairs in his toy room, and every so often I could hear their happy voices chattering. The chatter I was hearing in my head wasn't nearly as happy. Everyone inside knew what had been discussed with Janna, knew I was gearing up to talk with Rikki about some unpleasant things, and knew that some of those things had to do with them. Inside my head there was, as reporters say, a general state of unrest.

Although Rikki and I were doing something both of us thoroughly enjoyed, neither of us had said much since we'd started preparing the food, and despite the wonderful aromas and the anticipation of eating one of my favorite meals, my stomach was rolling like a garbage truck at dawn. It was time to talk, and I was counting on Per to help me out like he said he would. I put down the spoon, shuddered once, and stepped back into my mind, letting Per come out. Rikki didn't see the switch because she was inspecting the mixture in the food processor.

"Ahem," Per cleared his throat. "Rikki?" he said, trying to get her attention. She turned around to face him. Wearing a cobalt blue apron with yellow quarter moons over her white T-shirt and red jumper, her soft brown hair pulled back in a ponytail, Rikki looked strikingly beautiful. She noticed right away that someone else was out.

"Bart?"

"No," Per said with a warm smile. "It's Per."

Rikki smiled back. "Hi, Per. Have you been making the ravioli?"

Per chuckled easily, and my stomach—my whole body—felt more relaxed now that he was out. "No," he said. "It was Cam. Sure looks good, though." He admired the silver pasta roller. "This is a nifty contraption."

"We've had that thing since . . . I don't know . . . a long time."

Per closed his eyes and inhaled deeply. "Mmm, what are you making? It smells wonderful."

"Pesto sauce," Rikki said, "and it is. You should try some at dinner." She looked at his swollen purple hand and frowned. "How's the hand feeling? Must hurt."

Per glanced at it for a second and then back at .her. "It looks worse than it is, Rikki." He paused for a few seconds. "Actually," he said, "I'm glad you brought it up. That's sort of what I'm here to talk with you about."

Rikki leaned back against the counter. "Oh?"

"Mm hmm. We've been doing some good work with Janna, on the phone from the hospital and particularly yesterday with Switch, Leif, and Cam, and things are much more under control. In fact, I think I can say with assurance that from here forward there won't be any more cutting or . . ." he lifted the damaged hand, "this."

Rikki raised her eyebrows. "Really? That would be wonderful." She didn't look or sound convinced.

Per said, "I can tell you have some doubts."

Without saying a word, Rikki turned off the burner under the pot, walked over, and sat down across from Per. She put her elbows on the table, made a steeple with her fingers, rested her chin on her thumbs and sighed.

"I don't know, Per," she said. "How's it going to be different?" Inside I felt my heart beat faster, but Per remained calm. He settled his gaze on Rikki.

"Well, for one, Switch has agreed not to harm the body anymore.

He was doing it mostly out of anger at Cam for keeping him and everyone else down while Cam raced through school. Now that's all out in the open. Everyone is communicating again. Leif has agreed not to push Cam so hard to get through school, and Cam has agreed to give everyone in the system time out in the body."

Rikki sat up, startled. "Wait a minute. Time out in the body? Like when?"

"During the day—"

Rikki slapped her hands down on the table. "But I'm not here during the day! I can't be here during the day. I'm in Oakland!"

"I understand that."

"I'm sorry, Per, but I don't think you do. I worry all day, every day while I'm at work, about what might happen. Will Cam get hurt? Will Clay or Wyatt or Anna come out while Kai's around?" Rikki motioned agitatedly with both hands, here and there. "Will Cam even show up to pick him up at school?"

Kai shouted down the stairs, "Mom, why are you and Dad arguing?"

Without taking her eyes off Per, Rikki yelled back, "We're not arguing, honey. We're just having a discussion."

In the background we heard Jack say, "C'mon Kai, bring all the weapons in here," followed by the sound of little feet running.

Per asked calmly, "Has Cam ever not shown up . . . to pick up Kai from school?"

"What? Uh, well . . . no," Rikki said. She leaned toward Per and said in a loud whisper, "But the cutting, and . . ." she gestured at the hand, "the smashing. Jesus, look at your hand."

Per nodded. "You have a lot to be concerned about, Rikki. And frankly I'm more than a bit embarrassed that I haven't been able to exert more control in keeping everything inside in order. Some of the others are, too." He glanced at the hand and shook his head. "Things definitely got away from us."

"I would say so!" Rikki said a little louder. She leaned forward and whispered, pointing a finger at the ceiling, "I've got Kai to think about, you know. What's he supposed to think when his father gets cut all the time? What if Clay or the others show up after school when I'm not around? That scares the shit out of me, Per." Rikki leaned back in her chair and said in a huff, "Excuse me."

Per waved it off. "It's all right," he smiled. "I've heard the word."

Rikki picked up the knife, cut off a little piece of dough, and played with it. "I don't know. I'm tired of worrying all the time."

"I don't blame you, Rikki," Per said, "but you should know that we've agreed to have everyone out for about an hour in the mornings after Kai goes to school. That way no one will feel locked down while Cam's doing his school work. The tension won't be there anymore. We'll be communicating again . . . and Switch won't feel like he's got to throw the big stone."

Rikki kept stretching and balling the dough, her eyes fixed on Per's. "Well," she said, still disbelieving. "It sounds good." She looked down at the yellow dough in her hands, biting her lower lip. "You know, Per, I don't dislike them . . . the alters, I mean. I accept them." Inside everyone's ears perked up. Per didn't say anything. Rikki went on, "They're all welcome to talk to me anytime."

Per nodded. "I know."

There was grumbling and banter inside. I don't feel welcome. She doesn't like me. She hates me. She does not, Switch. I don't feel comfortable around her. I know, Dusty. Where are we? Look at her, will ya? She's gorgeous. Oh, for chrissake, Bart. What? She's gorgeous. I know.

And then my interstellar shuttle came screeching into the station like Wile E. Coyote heading for the cliff, heels down, leaning back, arms flailing. Except it wasn't funny. And bang, Per was gone and I was back. Rikki saw this switch.

She said, "Cam?"

"Hi," I said sheepishly.

"Hi. I was talking with Per."

"I know."

"He told me about everyone getting some time out in the mornings.

Sounds like a good idea. Do you think it'll help?" I nodded with a hopeful smile. "Yeah, Rik, I do. No more cutting or getting hurt. I know it seems like I'm handing you glass diamonds, but I mean it. No more."

Rikki put down the little ball of dough. "Well, that would be good," she said with a weak smile. She drummed her fingers on the table and started to get up. My eyes followed her.

"Rik?"

"Yeah?"

"Could you sit down for another minute?"

"Okay," she said, sitting back down. "Sure."

Suddenly I wasn't feeling so good. "Rik . . . about Andy."

She frowned. "What about Andy?" she said harshly.

"Are you—"

"Am I what? Sleeping with him? No. I've told you that. We're just friends, Cam. He's just someone I can talk to," she said angrily.

"Rikki, please don't be angry with me. I just don't want to lose you to Andy . . . or anybody. I don't want to lose you." I tried to get her to look me in the eye, but she wouldn't.

Rikki took a deep breath and blew it out slowly. "Cam . . . Andy's just . . . a good friend." She picked up the little ball of dough again. "He's been very supportive. We go out to eat. We talk. My best friend's been away, you know. Remember him? The Buns in Space man? If you see him, tell him I miss him." Her eyes filled with tears. She wiped them away with a finger, careful not to smudge her makeup.

Things were really rumbling inside now. "It's going to be different from now on. We're going to do better. It'll be more peaceful." We heard a whoop from upstairs and four little feet dashing from one room to the other.

Rikki choked up a little, "It's been so crazy—no wait, I'm sorry, crazy's not the word."

"Yeah it is."

"No, really, Cam, I know none of this is your fault."

"I'm trying to get it under control. We're gonna get it under control."

I reached across the table and put my good hand on hers. "I'm not going down, Rik."

She looked at me and blinked a tear away. "I don't want you to, Cam. I don't want you to."

"See Andy if you want. Sleep with him if you want, it doesn't matter. It's no different. Really. Not fucking him isn't going to fix us, Rik."

"Cam . . ."

I squeezed her hand. "I'm serious. I know I've got some major problems, unbelievable problems. But I love you. And I want you to be who you need to be . . . do what you need to do. But don't let go of us, Rik, please don't let go of us. There's Kai and you and me. That's it—that's all I've got. Do what you need to do, but don't let go of us." The mustangs were bucking and I was struggling not to switch out. Now was definitely not the time to switch.

Rikki shook her head, "I'm sorry, Cam. I just can't give up that friendship right now." She put her free hand to her chest. "It's mine."

"It's okay," I said. "I mean it's not okay, but it'll have to be okay." *Hang on. Hang on.* "Rikki, we don't have to talk about forever," I said. "We just need to slow things down."

"All right, then," she said. "You and your guys . . . just . . . slow things down. Smooth things out. Like I told Per, I'm here for them, as long as Kai's not around."

I felt a shot of pain behind my right eye. Now pots and pans were getting thrown around my mind. "But they don't feel welcome," I said.

Rikki jerked her hand out from under mine. "That's *your* stuff and theirs," she said. "Not mine. I've never given them cause to feel unwelcome." She pushed her chair away from the table and got up abruptly. "This is our home! And our life! I'm doing the best I can!"

Kai shouted down again, "Mom! What's goin' on?"

Rikki shouted up, "Mind your own business, Mr. Big Ears. Go play. Daddy and I are just talking. Don't worry about it."

"When's dinner?"

"Ten minutes!"

"Okay!"

"Cam, I'm just trying to live a life. Have a normal home and be a normal wife and a normal mother. But, living with this is just so bizarre." She started pacing around the room. I stared at the table and listened. "It's like this big secret we carry around with us. We don't even have any couples we can just hang out with, because nobody knows. And things that used to be simple are difficult for you now—they're triggering or too stimulating, or scary, or surreal. You can't take Kai to the movies. Or the mall. A camping trip is like an expedition to Mars."

"I'm sorry, Rik," I said, without looking up.

She stopped pacing and leaned against Kai's homework desk. "I've always wanted a simple life, Cam, and living with . . . all of this . . . is anything but simple. I'm sorry, but it's true. That doesn't mean I won't be there for your guys, and it doesn't mean I don't like them, and it doesn't mean they're not welcome. I'm just trying to be a regular person."

"I brought this on you. On us."

"Don't do that to yourself."

"All right." The words felt thick in my mouth and things were getting wrinkly. I looked up at Rikki and tried to re-center. "Wait. Give me a second. I just need to get this straight. This is our life. And our home. And we're all welcome, right?"

She watched me silently for a moment. "Right," she said softly. "You're all welcome."

"All welcome," I repeated. Things smoothed out a little.

Rikki sighed and a little smile crossed her lips. She bent over and kissed the top of my head, wrapped one arm around my neck and gave me a hug. "So, hows about some ravioli, Giuseppe?"

Kai made a startling observation that night at dinner. With a mouthful of ravioli he looked over at me and said, "Dad, do you have Multiple Personality Disorder?"

If we'd had a grandfather clock, it would have stopped right then. I looked over at Rikki. She was the undisputed boss of what got said to Kai, but she just looked at me, in shock. Kai chewed and waited expectantly. I swallowed. Hard. "What brought that up, Little Man?" I said.

He shrugged. "I don't know."

Darts shot out of Rikki's eyes at me. I gave her an honest-I-didn't-say-shit look, and after a few excruciating seconds she answered Kai, "Yes. Daddy has multiple personalities. Actually, it's called Dissociative Identity Disorder. It's—"

"You don't have to explain, Mom," Kai interrupted. "I just wanted to know if that's what he has." And that was it. He took another forkful of pasta like nothing had happened and launched into a description of a Calvin and Hobbes cartoon he'd read where Calvin is in the cockpit of a fighter jet and a voice comes over the radio saying, "Enemy fighters at two o'clock," and Calvin says, "Roger, what should I do until then?" Which is funny. But it wasn't remotely funny to me at that moment.

I was in shock. My son had just told me he knew I had multiple personalities. I was relieved and sickened at the same time. At last it was out in the open, at least in name. But if he knew I had it, then maybe it was true. Nah. No way. I'm just weak and flawed and screwed up and crazy. I'm a miserable worthless piece of shit with a scarred-up arm and a brain that doesn't work right.

Christ, that pointy rake.

Later that night I swore up and down to Rikki that I hadn't said a word to Kai, and she believed me. He'd just figured it out. Probably from seeing all the books and journal articles lying around. Probably just wanted a label for how Dad was when he was "out."

Oh boy, did my guys want to come out and meet Kai then. Even though I wasn't a multiple, everyone in my system wanted to come out and meet my kid. But they weren't allowed to. In my mind, I saw Rikki waving her finger. Uh uh. No way. In real life she just said, "I don't want your guys coming out and introducing themselves to Kai. He's not ready. He's too young."

I'm a big man
and Tall er
he's big but I'm
Taller I think hes
a lucky boy very
lucky Boy and
I wish hed be
my friend, but
hes scared of me
and Wyatt and
dusty and Anna
and Switch. Not
just me.
But it makes
me sad.

Clay's sadness at not being able to play with Kai.

THIRTY-NINE

In Jamaica, speed bumps are called sleeping policemen, which I always kind of liked—the image of a guy with a round, smiling face and a starched white uniform, lying back with the brim of his hat pulled down over his eyes. Gingerly rolling over him at two miles an hour, careful not to disturb him. Delicately: *b-bump b-bump.*

Over that spring, summer, and fall, on the road to a better life, I rolled over quite a few speed bumps. But not gingerly at two miles an hour. Nope. I was waving and screaming, "Outta the way! Outta the way!" doing eighty-five in a rickety tub of shit with bolts and hubcaps flying off, drink spilling, ass bouncing off the seat, head smacking the roof. Flattening the motherfucker. SQUISH! Nice white suit all red, buttons popped off, surprised look on his jolly Jamaican face. Just a few speed bumps on Multiple Road, that's all. Don't worry . . . be happy.

No, I didn't get cut, and my hand didn't get smashed again.

Leif stopped pushing me with such ferocity. We all took time to write in the journal, and everyone got a chance to come out in the morning after Kai went to school. We even got a two-year-old Golden Retriever, named Baylie, from the Golden Retriever Rescue Foundation. I started running four miles a day with him and taking him for hikes at Diablo. On the surface things looked pretty good.

Well, the part about the running and hiking was good. I was lean and fit. And having Baylie was great. He didn't care if I was a nut. I was the guy who saved him from a life of eating scraps in a dark garage. Baylie was doing great compared to me.

Nobody'd saved me. Nobody was feeding me grapes in the garden. Although alters were allowed out, it didn't make me happy. It was an annoyance, slowed me down. What business did they have coming around while I was the one still scratching my way through school? I started pushing them down again little by little, breathing fire, moosing that boulder, inch by inch, course by course, up Ph.D. hill. I was getting near the top, too, which was good. But I was starting to worry about what would happen when I got there.

Janna knew, Rikki knew—and I knew, too—that becoming Dr. West wouldn't make me feel a damn bit better about myself than I did being Citizen West. *Citizen West, Citizen Kane, sugar cane, Sugar Ray Robinson, Robinson Crusoe, Robinson miso, miso soup, black bean soup, black sticky soup, black sticky me.* Yeah. Inside I was still a fetid and festering corpse covered in sticky blackness, still mired in putrid shame and scorching self-hatred. I could write an 86-page essay comparing the features of Borderline Personality Disorder with those of Dissociative Identity Disorder, but I barely knew what day it was, or even what month, never knew where the car was parked when Dusty would come out of the grocery store, couldn't look in the mirror for fear of what—or whom—I'd see.

Rikki, Kai, and I took some family vacations, including a trip to Disneyland and one to the San Diego Zoo, and I gave my best effort each time, but things never worked out too well. Anna and Trudi and Clay and Wyatt and Mozart kept coming out, and Kai kept getting nervous and saying, "Mom, Dad's 'out' again," and, "Cam, come back," and Rikki would explain to him that it was just the crowds and the commotion, and she'd nudge me and say, "Cam!" with a steely look in her eye that worked until the next time I switched.

Rikki still saw Andy, although with less frequency, which was a gleaming gift from a sparkly angel. We didn't talk about it—that ice was too thin already—we just skated along. And as far as sex, well, it wasn't mangoes in Maui. It was more like mukluks in Minsk. That didn't help my self-esteem any more than needing Kai to go through the check-out line at the video store because I couldn't figure out the money, or having a clerk and a line of people behind me stare while Clay tried for two minutes to sign my name to a check.

Every session at Janna's was forty minutes of wrinkling and ten minutes of ironing; either I was too wrinkled or she wasn't hot enough. I was a shirt that just wouldn't stay pressed. It was The Rake.

I started getting banged off light poles and mailboxes while Baylie and I were running, as if I'd been blasted by a big gust of wind, but it wasn't windy and it wasn't Baylie doing the banging. Behind the wheel, my hand was twitchy and my foot was too heavy; overpasses filled my sight and undertakers filled my mind. I needed a "brake" and I needed it bad.

We had serious trouble right here in River City. And that ends with Y and that rhymes with die and that stands for dead.

PART THREE

DENIAL'S RAKE

FORTY

It was time to go back into the hospital. After my last experience there, Del Amo was out of the question. We were a match made in Teaneck. Janna set it up with the Ross Institute for Psychological Trauma at Charter Hospital in Dallas.

Rikki, Kai, and I had a little going-away party for me the night before I left to go "do some work at a psychiatric hospital in Texas." Kai thought the trip was part of my graduate training. We ate ribs at Tony Roma's and stopped at TCBY on the way home. Kai got to have his favorite—a parfait with gummy bears on the bottom, then chocolate frozen yogurt covered with caramel sauce, then vanilla frozen yogurt and bits of Heath Bar on top. Oh boy, some of my guys really wanted to have one of those. Rikki had a hot fudge sundae, and I, Commandant Cam, ordered a small cup of vanilla.

You'd think that on the eve of going into the hospital to bash down the doors of denial, I'd have let my alters have something they wanted. Nope. That stuff's not good for you! Aw, c'mon. Pleeease? No! The body needs its strength. What a jerk. I heard that. Sorry. What a jerk. Thanks a lot, Bart. C'mon, Cam. We're having a party here. Leave me alone! I'm the one who's going in the hospital, you know. You could be supportive. All right, all right. Jeez. I'll bet even Teddy Roosevelt let his troops have a cone before riding up San Juan Hill.

Despite the ruckus inside, I was having fun with Rik and Kai. We went home and played San Francisco Monopoly, and then I read some chapters of Huck Finn aloud while Kai took a bath with GI Joes and shaving cream and Rikki curled up next to me on some pillows.

For somebody who was about to walk the plank, I did pretty well that night and had a loving and happy time with my family. Kai cried a little when I hugged him good night—two weeks seemed like a long time to him—but he perked up when I said I might bring something home for him. Like the other times I'd gone, he really wanted to come along. Candy machines, cable TV, and a big hotel suite. Yeah.

Before drifting off, Rikki and I lay in bed and held hands for a while without talking, and that was good enough for me. That night I had a bad dream, though. I dreamt I was being held prisoner inside a tube of toothpaste and a giant in striped pajamas with mussed-up hair was about to brush his teeth and was going to squeeze the tube somewhere and I didn't know where. I was trapped in that airless goo, hands poised above my head in futile preparation for the bone-crushing pinch, not knowing when it would come.

The next morning I kissed my family goodbye and boarded the 8:15 Crest with Tartar Control for Dallas. A couple of years later we landed uneventfully in Texas—no goo, no mint up my beak, and no ogre, except that the lady from Elite Limo Service who picked me up had a little wart on one side of her nose. Her name was Flo. She was at least sixty, and wart or no wart, I was glad as hell to see her at the arrival gate with a little sign with my name on it.

Flo did all the talking on the forty-five-minute drive to Charter Hospital, while I just tried to pass for regular. She dropped me off and I had to wait for three and a half hours in the lobby before being checked in. Either they were giving away money at the hospital or the loons were out in Plano and they were all waiting to check into Charter. Nobody'd given me any money so far, so I figured it must have been the loons. And I was one of them.

Eventually a staff psychiatrist, who looked about twenty, screened me and I was officially admitted to the multiples' ward. While a nurse walked me down the hall toward who knew what, a tiny plane buzzed around the inside of my head skywriting in a foul green vapor. *Oh, shit, what was I thinking? How'd I get us into this mess? What are we doing in a place like this? Can we catch the last Crest out of here and go home? It's not too late to go home. YES IT IS!!*

About eight women and one man were milling around the small common room near the nurses' station, some watching TV, most of them waiting for a nurse named Alice to take them out onto the smoking porch. Everyone checked me out with furtive glances or open stares, hoping we weren't going to be disruptive, weren't going to scare anybody, weren't going to tip the scale so all the beans fell out.

I was sitting in a chair next to the nurses' station, being gawked at, while another nurse, Lucinda, took my vital signs. A tall, thin, woman with bleached hair, a nose ring, and a big friendly smile sidled over next to me and introduced herself as Leslie. I told her my name and where I was from. She put her hand out, I took it, and she gave it a shake and said, "Welcome, Cam. The first night's a bitch. But it gets worse." Then she chuckled. "Only kidding," she said slapping me on the back, and walking off to have a smoke.

A short woman with close-cropped hair and a weathered face, wearing an L.L. Bean vest, came over next and introduced herself as Edie. She looked nervous, too, and blurted out that she'd arrived yesterday and that she and her husband had cashed in their retirement so she could come here, and if this place didn't work she figured she'd be in the morgue before long. The part about the morgue was a little close to home, but something about Edie was oddly comforting. She reminded me of an old country store with sturdy wooden stairs worn in the middle from half a million footsteps.

I was glad Edie stuck around, because when Lucinda finished taking my blood pressure and peeled the cuff off, the ripping Velcro sound jolted a few quick switches and my guys kind of popped up and back down quick, like the ducks you aim at in a shooting gallery. Edie took my hand in hers and it felt rough and leathery like I expected, and she looked at me with the saddest most understanding green eyes I'd ever seen. And right there in that chair with traces of the ogre, the Crest, and Flo's wart still scrolling by, and a roomful of dinged-up people looking me over like a Kmart suit, I felt a little more grounded. And I was grateful.

After Lucinda took my temperature, she called for a big guy named Lonnie to take me to our room, Edie said goodbye and went for a smoke, and Lonnie and I went off to get me unpacked. The room was just like the ones in Del Amo, with the bolted-down furniture and puke-proof carpet. No candy machine, no TV. Kai would have hated it.

When big Lonnie left our room he started whistling, and it made me think of Angel, and I wondered if we were back in Del Amo. I walked over to the window and pulled back the curtains to see if the courtyard was there. Nope. Even in the dark I could tell it wasn't. Instead, there was a field with a couple of tall wooden poles and what looked like a trapeze, and off in the distance, some apartment buildings. I let go of the curtain and it swished twice and then hung there at attention. Nope, we weren't in Del Amo. *Where are we? In Texas. Goddamn that Lonnie for whistling. He wasn't even that good a whistler.*

I walked down to the patient phones in the hall and called Rikki. She picked it up on the second ring. "Hi, Rik."

"Cam. I was worried about you."

"Almost four hours in the lobby before they got to me."

"You're kidding. But you're in now? How does it seem so far?"

"Rik, I'm really scared. Everybody's scared."

"I know. I know how hard it is for you to go in. You're gonna make it, though. I want you to work hard while you're there. You're in a place where they can help you."

I licked my dry lips. "I don't know if I can do this."

"You can. You can do it."

I was listening carefully, hanging on to her words by a pinky. "Right. I can do this. We can do this."

"That's right," Rikki said. "You're made of strong stuff, Cam. You can do anything."

"I can do anything," I repeated, but there wasn't much in it.

"I can tell you're having a hard time."

"Mmm."

"Let me put Kai on the phone. I love you, Cam."

"You do? Thank you, Rikki. Don't worry. I'll give Kai the good stuff."

"Great. I'll get him."

Kai came on in a few seconds and said, "Daddeee! Are you in Texas?"

"You bet," I said. "How's my little man?"

"Good." Then he whispered like we were meeting on the pier to swap government secrets, "Dad? Did you get me anything yet?"

I had to chuckle; the cuteness factor was so high. "Actually, not yet."

"Are you in your hotel?"

"Uh huh."

"Is it nice?"

"It's okay."

"Okay, I love you Dad. Bye."

"Bye."

Rikki got back on the line and said, "I love it when he whispers like that."

"Me too," I said. "Rik, I'm gonna go. I'm fading fast."

"Okay."

"Rik?"

"Yeah?"

"Thank you for saying you love me."

"Of course I love you," she said. "Try to get some rest tonight. Did you see I packed Toby and some books for everybody?"

"Yeah. Thank you."

"I'll talk to you tomorrow, honey."

"Okay. Bye," I said and waited for her to hang up. After she did, I hung up and went right to the nurses' station for an Ambien to help me get to sleep. A young serious-looking nurse with bright red hair gave me my one-way ticket to Pluto, and I headed back down the hall toward my room. On the way, Edie, Leslie, and a girl named Tina, who was about twenty-five with a heavy New York accent, were sitting on the floor in the hallway and asked if I'd join them. I took a seat and said hello.

I'd forgotten Janna was going to call and had popped the pill, which gave me about fifteen minutes till flaps down. About ten minutes later the phone rang, and one of the other patients answered it and shouted my name, which kind of shocked me. I got up and ambled over. The world was starting to get mushy.

The woman who'd called my name was wearing a pink robe and matching slippers. She was about my age, with black hair pulled back in a ponytail. She smiled and said, "Hi, I'm Andy," in kind of a squeaky voice, and I knew right away it was a child alter. I mustered a smile and picked up the phone. Andy walked off. Andy. That name. That bastard was trying to take my Rikki away. Ooh, I wanted to comb his hair with a brick.

I put the phone to my ear. It felt spongy. "Hello?"

"Hi, Cam." It was Janna.

Her voice poked a hole in my composure and what was underneath spilled out like a burst water balloon. "Janna, get me out of here! I want to get out of here right now! We can work at home with you! I hate the hospital! I don't recognize these people. I'm in Texas. They hang people in Texas! I want to go home!"

"Cam," Janna said confidently, "they know what they're doing there and you're going to get good care. I'll talk with your therapist as soon as you get one, and I'll call you every night at nine to go over how the day went. It's a good place, Cam. You can do concentrated work there. They have a good program."

"Okay, okay!" I said. "Shit! We'll stay. But I don't know how long." And then we switched and Clay was out.

"J-Janna?"

"Hi, Clay."

"Wh-where am I?"

"You're in a hospital."

"Am I sick?"

"No, it's not that kind of hospital. It's a place where all of you can talk with a therapist and with other people like you."

"Oh. Is Jody here?"

"No. You're at a different hospital . . . in Texas."

"T-Texas?"

"Yeah."

"B-bye," he said, and we switched again. "Heyyyy . . . Janna Chase."

"Hey, Bart." The drugs started really kicking in, and my body got wobbly.

Bart said, "Hey, what the hell? I feel like Gumby," and he switched out and I was back.

"Janna, it's Cam." I was definitely losing it.

"What was Bart talking about, Cam? What's going on there?"

"Ambien." My lips felt like the rubber on a hovercraft. "G-gotta go." I dropped the phone and started to topple.

A nurse or a patient in the hallway caught me before I hit the ground and dragged me to my bed. As we were touching down at Pluto International, I heard a voice say in a thick southern accent, "That Ambien'll gitcha ev'ry tahm."

FORTY-ONE

For the first few days I worked on settling in and getting something out of the groups, while I champed glass waiting to see our therapist. I did see a psychiatrist—a tall guy with a face like a rumpled-up sheet and a gravelly voice like Henry Kissinger's, only without the accent—for an anxiolytic. The Serax he prescribed for me shaved a tiny sliver off the anxiety.

Most of the groups were much like those run at Del Amo, except for two. One of them, called Ropes, was only held twice a week. That was so you could recover for a few days before doing it again. Ropes was the Outward Bound for multiples, and it was run by a soft-spoken, gray-haired guy named Jeff and his assistant, a young energetic woman with kind of a Wayne Newton haircut, named Samantha, who said to call her Sam. The first time we did Ropes, Jeff and Sam led a group of us outside, had us put on rock-climbing harnesses, and tried to get us, one at a time, to climb up a telephone pole—the one outside my window—while everyone else in the group shouted encouragement.

While you were climbing, Jeff and Sam had you tied to a rope that was slung up through a clip attached to what looked like the frame for a huge swing set, which was higher than the pole so you wouldn't go splat when you jumped or fell.

Once you got to the top, if you did, you had to stand there with nothing to hold on to while Jeff and Sam asked you a bunch of questions about your commitment to getting better and pumped you up about how brave you were to come all the way to Texas to this hospital and how you were made of strong stuff for climbing up that pole. And all the while you're trying to balance and keep that goddamn pole steady and not have something bad happen in your pants or jump off before they said to. And then they'd tell you all right, go for this trapeze, which hung about ten feet in front of you, and you'd jump for it, and it was sort of like being in the circus except you didn't have tights and there was no music. If you missed it, they just lowered you down slowly. But if you caught the bar, you were supposed to hang there while everybody cheered and said great things about you. And then you'd let go when you were ready, and they'd bring you back down to earth.

Now climbing a telephone pole, standing on top, and jumping for a trapeze may sound simple, but it wasn't. For me or for anybody in that group. It wasn't even hard. It was almost impossible. Actually, for some people it was impossible. And nobody who went before me caught the bar, although Edie touched it, which was pretty impressive considering she was no bigger than Mickey Rooney. Then it was my turn.

Inside it sounded like this: What the hell's going on here? What'd you get us into? Hey, why are we doing this? We're in the hospital. I don't know why we're doing this. Well, fuck you. Get the fuck down from here! I'm scared. He's scared. Somebody look out for him. I'm scared, too. Look out for her, for all the young ones. What the fuck are you doing, Cam? Shut up! Fuck you! Hey, stop arguing and keep your eye on what you're doing. Jesus, don't let go. Holy shit, I'm on top. Whoa, this thing's waving. I want to jump. Cut the rope and jump. I want to die! Hey, somebody get Switch to the Comfort Room! Right now! Don't look down. Oh, shit, he looked down. I told you not to look down! Oh yeah? You wanna take over? Goddamn I'm shakin' bad. Listen to what that guy's saying down there. Tell him what he wants to hear so we can get outta here. Shut up, I'm trying to listen. Okay, jump for the fuckin' bar. No wait, not yet. They didn't say jump yet. Okay, okay, jump. Don't miss it. I think my heart's gonna burst. We're gonna die right now. Fuckin' jump! Okay. Yaaaahhhh!! Jesus, he caught it. We're hanging here. We are? Don't look down. Shit, he looked down. I'm gonna have a heart attack. Wow, we're up high. Yeah. High. We're up high. Quiet, that guy's asking him a question. Listen, Cam. Tell him what he wants to hear. No, listen to what he's saying. We made it. We're brave. We did it. We did? Yeah. Okay, he says you can let go now. Let go of what? The bar. You're hanging onto the bar. What? Look up. You're hanging onto a bar. I am? Oh Jesus, I am. How'd we get here? You don't know? No. Well just let go and see what happens. Is this it? Are we gonna die? No, we're on a rope. What? Look at the rope. Oh, we're hooked up? Yeah. That's good. Well, let go. I can't. Fuck it, just let go. Okay. Yaaaahhhh!!

I was first in line for a Serax after Ropes and was pretty damn useless even after it kicked in. About an hour later, Bart and a good-looking psychiatric nurse named Denise, who had a southern accent you could get paid for, were sitting on a couple of chairs at the end of the hall, talking. I was way out there somewhere, buzzing like a plane over Bremen.

Denise had a clipboard on her lap with my chart on it. She smiled and said, "So, how did Ropes go?"

"No problem," Bart said. "By the way, what the hell was that all about, anyway?"

"How's that?" It sounded like "thayat."

"I mean, what was that all about? Putting him and those other people through all that shit, climbing and screaming and puking."

Without a second's hesitation Denise said, "Yer not Cameron, are yew?"

"Hell no," he said, "I'm Bart."

"Bart, do yew know where yew are?" She could have blown out a candle with the *"where."*

"Texas, right?"

"Mm hmm. Do yew know where yew are in Texas?"

"He's in a psychiatric hospital somewhere near Dallas."

"That's true, but Ah didn't ask where he is, did Ah? Ah asked where yew are."

"What's this, a trick question? Am I gonna win a toaster?"

"Nope," she said straight-faced, "it just sounds to me like yew don't feel connected to him being here, the way yew said that, that's all."

Bart smirked, "I'm not. He's the nut. I'm just a part of the cracked shell, like Per and Dusty and Leif and the rest of them." He waved it off. "You think I wanna be here?"

"No, Ah can tell yew don't. Most people don't." Denise paused a moment. "Do yew realahze that Cameron's a patient in a psychiatric hospital?"

"Yes," he said, annoyed. "I realize that."

"Then do yew realize, Bart," she pointed a long-nailed finger at him, "that yew are also a patient in a psychiatric hospital?"

Bart shook his head. "I'm not a patient in a psychiatric hospital," he said, doing the hitchhike thing. "He is."

"Bart," Denise said, continuing to press, "If Cameron is a patient in this psychiatric hospital, then so're yew. Yew are also a patient in this hospital."

Bart straightened up in his chair. "I told you, Denise, I'm just along for the ride. I am not the patient."

"Well, yes yew are, too," she said nodding. She pointed at him again. "Yew . . . are a patient at Charter Hospital in Plano, Texas, one that specialahzes in treating Dissociative Ahdinity Disorder." Bart sank back down in his chair, squirming a little. Neither of them said anything for a minute. Somebody paged Dr. Somebody over the intercom. Then Denise said softly, "Do yew think he's suffering, Bart?"

"Oh yeah," Bart said, looking serious now. "He's suffering. He's a bag of shit."

Denise glanced down at the chart. "It says in his fahl that his main goal here is to work on denahl." She looked up at Bart. After a few seconds she said, "It sounds to me like yew got some a yer own." There was an uncomfortable silence for a moment while Bart thought that over.

Then a smile crept across his face. "You know, Denise," he said. "You're pretty crafty."

She didn't bite for the charm and kept on pushing. "Bart, y'all are gonna have to start working together if yer gonna git better. Let me ask yew something. Does Cameron think he's here alone?"

Bart shook his head. "He knows we're here . . . but I guess he thinks he's doing this all by himself." He looked at the glass door next to him and touched the big sheet of plexiglass covering it. Still looking at it, he said, "So I'm a patient in a psychiatric hospital, huh?"

Denise nodded. "Yup."

"Then I'm a dick," he said to himself. He turned to Denise. "Uh, I mean a jerk. Of course we're all patients in this hospital. Per should be hearing this."

"Per?"

"He's one of the main people in the system. Listen to me. Talking about our system. Like it's a stereo." Bart shifted in his chair, rubbed his chin a couple of times, and folded his hands in his lap. "You know, Denise," he said, "none of us likes this one bit. And we're all scared. Me, too. I was duckin' out, leaving Cam in the weeds." He shook his head slowly, talking to himself, "I am truly a dick."

"Don't be so hard on yerself, Bart," Denise said. "Everybody is keyed up when they come into a place like this. Yer doin' good." She paused for a second and then said, "I think the Video Therapy group on Thursday would be perfect for y'all."

That was the other group that Del Amo didn't have. My plane passed out of the clouds and there was a mountain coming up fast in front of me.

"It's where different alters git recorded on videotape, like in a TV interview. It might be helpful fer yew to be one of those alters who gits videotaped, Bart."

Bart nodded and a grin crept over his face. "I always wanted to be in pictures. I'm a natural. Thursday, huh?"

"Mm hmm," Denise said. "Thursday. Want me to make a note that y'all'd be interested in doing that?"

"Sure. If we're in this together we should do it as a group, right? I mean, there's a bunch of us."

"Ah figgered. Ya think Cam'll be wantin' to do that? Maybe he's listenin' now. Ah don't know y'all's system."

Bart nodded. "Oh, he's listening, all right."

Nyowwww crassshhh. Whup! Whup! Whup! Plane down! Videotaping alters! Whup! Whup! Whup!

"Well, good then," Denise said, slapping the chart. "Ah'll make a note that y'all'd like to do that. It's not written in granite, though, so don't feel like ya just committed to somethin' ya can't git out of. Y'all just chew on it awhahl. Talk about it amongst yerselves. And with yer therapist, when ya git with him."

"When's that gonna be? We've already been here three days."

Denise looked down at the chart. "Looks like tomorra mornin' you'll be meetin' with Dr. Sawyer. You'll like him. Well," she said, standing up. "Ah got ta go. Good talking with ya, Bart." And she walked off down the hall.

Bart looked out through the plexiglass at the empty courtyard. Inside I lay crushed in the twisted flaming metal.

Medddiiiiic!!

FORTY-TWO

Rikki and Andy were sitting next to each other at the big oval sushi boat bar at Isobune, a Japanese restaurant on College Avenue in the Rockridge section of Oakland. It's a fun place where the chefs stand inside the bar and make sushi, place it on small rectangular plates, and put the plates on little wooden boats that are chained together and float around the bar counterclockwise. Patrons at the bar wait for something to go by that catches their eye and just grab it off the boat, and when they're done eating, the waitress counts up the empty plates and tallies the bill.

"I won three days at the company beach house," Andy said, wiping his hands on the small hot towel the waitress had given him when they sat down. Rikki was doing the same.

"Get outta here," she said. "When?"

They both put their towels on the bar, and the waitress quickly took them and filled their teacups with green tea. Andy waited for her to leave. When she did, he grinned and said, "Next week. The second through the fourth." He grabbed a plate of California roll from a passing boat and popped a piece in his mouth. "Mmm," he said chewing, "why'ncha come down and meet me. Be fun."

Rikki grabbed a plate with two chunks of smoked salmon and rice from the next boat and put it down in front of her. She picked one up with her chopsticks, dunked it in soy sauce and wasabi, and took a bite. "Yum," she said. "These guys make the best sushi in the East Bay."

Andy watched her. "Seriously, Rik," he said. "Why don't you come down for a day?"

Rikki washed the food down with some tea. "Anybody else from your office going?"

"No. Just me."

"What about Katie?"

"She's going to stay with a friend." Andy picked up his cup and took a sip. He looked over the rim at Rikki and said, "Maybe Kai could do the same for a night."

Rikki looked deeply into his eyes. "Are we talking about what I think we're talking about here?"

Andy put the cup down. "I don't know," he grinned. "Are we?"

They sat silently for a moment looking at each other. All around them the place was bustling with the din of the lunch crowd, but in that moment there was no one else. Andy's leg touched Rikki's and she felt that same jolt of excitement she'd felt at Chevy's over a year before.

Rikki put down her chopsticks and reached for a bottle that sat by her little stack of plates. She held it up to Andy. "Sake?"

FORTY-THREE

Anticipating something bad works on you—like red ants on a body that's been tied down and smeared all over with jelly. You don't like it and you can't get used to it and you can't stop it. And no matter how hard you try to think about something else, like drifting off to a peaceful sleep under a willow by a gurgling brook, you just can't do it for more than eight seconds at a time before coming back to those red ants.

It doesn't really even matter if it's bad. Good anticipation can get you, too. Like getting married, or better yet, like meeting the president. If you didn't have time for anticipation to gnaw on you, say, if you bumped into him at the supermarket, you might just ask him if he knows where the floss is. But if you have a day or two ahead of time to think about it, by the time the ants are through with you, you've forgotten how to talk at all and just drool on your new shirt.

Well, since Bart had talked with that steely southern belle, I'd already drooled through six shirts, two sweaters, and a bulletproof vest, so when Steve Sawyer pulled me out of a group sometime the next morning, I was ready to see him. I thought.

He was about my age or a little older, with brown hair, a handsome, chiseled face, and eyes that exuded the strength and serenity of a sequoia. He was wearing a camel-hair jacket, an expensive white shirt, neatly pressed black slacks, and shiny shoes. His silk tie reminded me of Van Gogh's *Starry Night.* He smiled and seemed eager to meet me as we walked down the hall. We entered a small consultation room with two chairs, a table with a lamp and phone, and a TV and VCR on a stand. Steve sat in the chair next to the TV. I sat in the chair with the ants and started grinding my teeth, tapping my foot, and nervously working the ends of the green vinyl armrests.

"I talked with Dr. Chase for a while this morning," he said. "And with Denise. You look pretty anxious."

"You want to try being me? Huh? Everybody else does." I reached over and touched Steve's chest and ran a finger across the yellow stars. "And that," I said on the edge of hysteria, "is a nice tie." My eyes flashed at him and I sat back in my chair and started in on the armrests again. I rocked back and forth. "I'm not anxious. I'm a dead man."

"Tell me—" Steve began.

"Dead men tell no tales," I said.

"You're not dead," Steve said calmly. "You're scared."

"I'm not scared. I'm not scared of—"

"What are you scared of, seeing them on TV?" he said, tapping it.

I rocked harder. "That's just a goddamn box. I'm a dead man."

"You're a live man," he said forcefully, "and you're dying to see what comes out of that box."

I shook my head rhythmically side to side, insisting, "I am not dy—"

"You came twelve hundred miles to see what comes out of that box."

I kept shaking my head, pointing at the TV. "I do not want to—"

"Tell me, Cam, what's it all about?"

"What the hell are you talking ab—"

"Say it."

"You sonofabitch—"

"Tell me!"

"What do you want from me?"

"Say it!!"

I sprang out of my chair and Steve jumped up too and a fiery engine roared up through my groin and my belly and my heart and lungs and throat and out my mouth, and I screamed with the kind of force that'll blow your hair back, "I . . . DON'T . . . WANT . . . TO . . . KNOWWWWWW!!!"

A thick silence hung in the room as I swayed back and forth, my chin hanging on my chest. I felt Steve's gaze on me as he gently said, "Cam, you know it already."

More silence. Maybe a full minute of it. And then I crumbled.

Steve stood there with an open heart and stars on his tie and said softly, "What will happen if you see your alters on tape?"

With great effort I managed to lift my head and peer out through the tears at him.

I whimpered, "Then I'll know it's true."

Steve paused and then leaned forward, touched my shoulder, and said, "Yeah . . . and won't that be a relief."

And my body shook and I cried some more—for Dusty, and Clay, and Davy, and Anna, and Trudi, and Switch, and Mozart, and Wyatt, and Bart, and Per, and Leif, and Stroll, and for anybody else who was still locked inside my mind. And I cried for Rikki and Kai, too. But not for me. Not for me.

Later that night I called Rikki and told her we were going through with the videotaping. She sounded a little distant, but I couldn't tell if she was preoccupied or if it was just me. I didn't know she'd just gotten off the phone with Andy. She wished me and everybody luck and put Kai on so I could say good night.

Janna's call came next—before the Ambien—and Leif told her that Per, Bart, and he had written up a list with Dr. Sawyer of the plan for who'd be interviewed at the videotaping, and in what order. He took a folded yellow sheet, which I didn't even know existed, from my pocket and went over the order of the list with her. Clay would come out first, followed by Bart, then Leif, then Per, and finally Dusty. That sounded good to Janna, and she called for me to come out and we went over it. We had a good plan. For once we all seemed to be working toward the same purpose.

Most of the ants were gone, but guilt was chewing on me now. After all, I was the one who'd gotten us here—caused all the problems. I was the manager of this sad hotel, the jerk who'd bolted the door and turned up the screeching music when the guests were calling me.

Janna slapped me around some for talking like that, and suggested I take a minute and listen inside to what the others had to say. I did, and the word from everyone was to just go forward into tomorrow, that everything would be okay.

Something was happening and it wasn't all bad. But that didn't mean it didn't feel bad. It did, and by the time the taping actually took place, my stomach felt like a Maytag full of old overalls.

Fortunately we didn't have to wait, because none of the other patients who showed up for the videotaping session wanted to do it. A pleasant guy named John sat behind a video camera that rested on a tripod and looked over the list of my alters, while I squirmed in the chair opposite him. He saw Per's name and asked how to pronounce it, which Per and I both appreciated.

Then John fired up the camera and began the interview. He asked me some questions about who I was and where I lived, about my family, whether I understood what was going to happen, and why I was doing the taping. Then he asked for Clay to come out and instantly I was gone and Clay was there.

Clay thought he was being filmed for a movie or a Lassie episode, and when John explained that it was just a film for me and Clay and the other people in my system, he was a little disappointed. John asked him how old he was and what he knew about me and the other alters. Then he asked Clay if there was anything in particular he wanted to say to me, and Clay hunched up his shoulders and said, "Tell him I d-don't want Kai to be afraid of m-me, so I don't have to g-go away when he's there."

John pointed to the lens and said, "Look here and you tell him," and Clay looked into the camera and said, "Tell Kai I'm not scary. I'm n-nice. He d-doesn't have to be afraid of me."

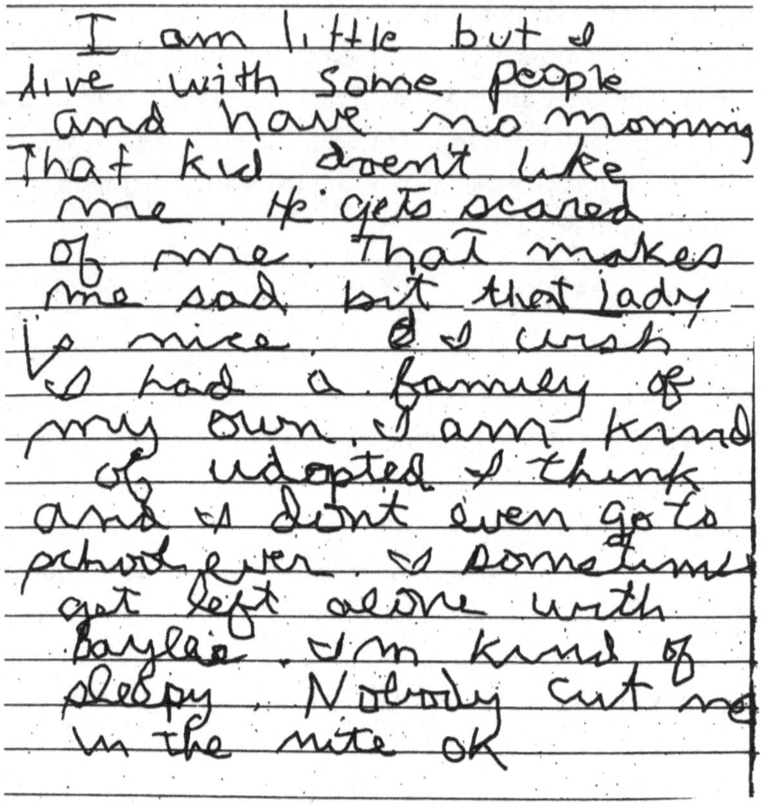
I am little but I
live with some people
and have no mommy
That kid doesn't like
me. He gets scared
of me. That makes
me sad but that lady
is nice. I wish
I had a famuly of
my own. I am kind
of udopted I think
and I dont even go to
school ever. I sometimes
get left alone with
Baylee. I'm kind of
sleepy. Nobody cut me
in the nite ok

After the videotaping, Clay talked about Kai being scared of him.

Edie was watching and she said, "No, of course you're not scary, Clay."

Debbie switched to Andy, who said in his squeaky voice, "I like you, Clay."

Clay smiled and said, "I like you, too, Andy." No one spoke for a minute, and then John said it was time for Bart to come out, and Clay said, "Bye," and there was the shudder and Bart appeared.

Bart was just, you know, Bart. Loose and funny and charming. Inside of fifteen seconds he had the girls in the room laughing and chatting with him like they were all at the beach sipping blue drinks. John asked him about himself and about being in the hospital and Bart got serious for a minute and said he knew we were all patients at Charter and were working hard at overcoming denial. When John asked him if there was anything he wanted to tell me, Bart looked into the camera and said, "Don't give up, Cam. Multiplicity is a team sport. I'm with you. We're all in this together." Then he made a joke about having to duck into a phone booth so he could change into SuperLeif.

Everyone laughed and, poof, Leif came out, and immediately the feeling in the room changed completely. It wasn't *Beach Blanket Bingo* anymore; it was *60 Minutes*. Leif was all business. He crossed his legs, rolled up his sleeves, and looked directly into the camera's lens, and from inside I could tell that the people in the room were shocked by the stark contrast between him and Bart.

John asked him what his job in the system was and he replied brusquely, "My job is to make sure Cam gets things done. So, what would you like to know?" He clasped his hands together and then spread them palms up. "Ask away."

John said he had nothing specific in mind to ask him, that he had just wanted Leif to come out on camera and talk a bit.

Leif uncrossed his legs and looked directly into the camera. "All right. I've got something to say to Cam." He leaned forward and pointed. "Don't forget this. I might do the pushing, but you do the work. All of this . . . is you." He leaned back and crossed his arms, and his muscles looked taut and powerful. The room was silent. "Now Per," he said and switched in, letting Per come out.

Per was his usual self—tranquil and soft-spoken. He expressed confidence in our ability as a system to overcome our collective problems, but was worried about some of the alters' feelings of being unwanted and unwelcome at home and wanted me to know that we should work on a solution to that problem. One of the patients asked him if Kai had met any of the alters, and he explained that they weren't allowed out when Kai was around. That caused a big stir, and John actually had to restore some order so we could continue with the taping.

Dusty closed the show. She was bashful and nervous and didn't say much until John prodded her. Then she talked about going food shopping, being lonely, and having no friends since Robbie. Her message for me was that she wanted to have her own room.

Dusty drew a self-portrait.

And that was it. It was over. John turned off the camera, took the tape out, and handed it to me. I stood there trying to comprehend what had just happened while John packed up his camera and people filed out of the room.

Edie came over, patted me on the back, smiled and said, "Cam, you are most definitely a multiple."

"You think so?" I asked shakily.

She laughed out loud, "Are you kidding? Wait'll you see the tape."

Then Debbie joined us and said, "Cam, you are undoubtedly, absolutely, unquestionably a classic multiple. But that's not your problem. Your problem is your alters don't feel welcome, and if they don't feel welcome, my friend, you're fuckin' sunk." And then she switched and Andy came out for a second and said in his childlike voice, "Yeah, sunk." And Debbie switched back, shrugged her shoulders, and walked away with Edie.

She's right. We're gonna have to do something about that.

I was alone in the room looking out the window at a flat stretch of Texas grass when it occurred to me. I did it! Videotaped the alters. Goddamn! That wasn't so hard. Wait a minute. Shit. Now comes the really hard part. We gotta watch this thing. Uh oh.

And the Maytag started chugging again, and I made a beeline for my bedroom, flung the tape on my bed, raced into my bathroom, and puked up the overalls.

FORTY-FOUR

At one o'clock Steve came by and collected me from a group and we walked to the consultation room. I had the tape in my hand. When he unlocked the door, I noticed he had the TV and VCR turned on and ready to go.

We sat down and he looked at me carefully, spread his hands, and said, "So, how did it go?"

I swallowed hard. "Can we just watch it?" I said, handing him the tape. He glanced at the tape to make sure it was rewound, stuck it in the machine and pressed play. My hands were gripping the armrests like the chair was going to blast off, and a bead of sweat ran down my right side and made me shiver.

There were a few seconds of nothing and then there I was on the screen, looking thin and scared and all glassy-eyed, like I'd just been in a bus crash. I heard John's voice asking me questions, and it shocked me to see how dazed I looked and how disjointed and hard-fought my answers were, like I really *had* been in a crash, and all the gears in my head had been jarred loose.

And then on the screen I saw my eyes close and my body shake like I'd gotten a sudden chill, and when my eyes reopened, Clay was there. I tried to focus on what I was watching, but there was a big scuffle inside for control of the body. I heard Steve's voice from somewhere say, "Cam, stay with me here," but it was too late. Elvis had left the building. And Clay was out.

"Why are y-you watching that movie?" he asked.

"Clay?" Steve said.

"Y-yeah." Clay was looking down at his size-10 sneakers. He was all closed in on himself and his neck was tight.

Steve said, "This is the videotape you guys made this morning. Remember doing that?"

"W-well, yeah."

"That's you in the picture."

Clay looked up from the shoes and took in the image on the screen for a few seconds. He listened to the sound of his voice talking to John. "W-what?" he said, his eyes filling with tears.

Steve paused the machine and asked softly, "What's the matter, Clay?"

"That," he whimpered, pointing a wobbly finger at the screen.

"What you see on the TV?"

Clay started to sob. "Y-yeah."

"What about it? What bothers you about what you see on the TV?"

Clay cried, "I-I'm a kid, not a g-grown up."

"But you share the same body as Cam," Steve said gently, handing him a tissue. "Even Dusty and Bart and Per are gonna look the same when they come on. You'll see. They'll be wearing the same clothes, and they'll look like Cam . . . and like you."

"Like me?" Clay said, drying his eyes.

"Uh huh," Steve said, and he started the tape again.

Clay watched the video some more. "Th-that's me on TV," he said. "I'm big."

Steve smiled. "Yup. That's you, Clay. And your body is big, even though you're still you . . . you're still a kid."

Clay nodded. "Yeah," he said, "still m-me. I'm still a kid." Steve smiled. "That's right, Clay. You're still you."

Clay wiped his nose on his sleeve. "Okay," he said, satisfied. "B-bye." And then he was gone and I was back in the hot seat.

Steve paused the machine again. "Who's out?" he asked.

"Me," I said grimacing, rubbing my stiff neck. "I'm back."

"You saw Clay? You know what just happened?"

"Yeah. I saw him. And I know he came out to see himself." I rubbed my temples. My head hurt, too. "How'd that go?"

Steve said, "Ask inside."

I was quiet for a few seconds, listening for the word on Clay. "He's okay," I reported. "Just thinks he looks funny."

Steve laughed. "I feel the same way when I see myself." He asked if I was ready to continue. I bit my lip and nodded, and he hit the play button again.

I was watching the tape, feeling like a lure on the end of a fishing line, floating slowly down through the cool water of comprehension, when I saw the part where Clay looked into the camera and said, "Tell Kai I'm not scary. I'm n-nice." And, klunk, I hit the muddy bottom and looked up as a fish swam by towing a banner that read HOW CAN YOU ACCEPT YOURSELF WHEN YOUR FAMILY DOESN'T ACCEPT YOU? I tried to swallow but my mouth was too dry. Which seemed odd, since I was at the bottom of a lake.

Steve knew Clay's statement was important, but now wasn't the time to clean that sore. Now was the time to face the images on the screen. He paused the tape for a second. "Cam," he said sharply, tugging the line, and the fish swam off and I was jerked to the surface. I managed to swallow.

Steve started the tape rolling again and out came Bart, who looked totally different from Clay, except for the clothes, the body, and the face. This was so weird. A second ago Clay was out, all tense and talking like a kid, and here was Bart all loose and buttery, looking like he had a new Corvette. And they both looked like me! I watched with fascination as Bart yucked it up all beachy, making the girls and John laugh. He wasn't at all like the guy sitting here with Steve, the guy in the bus crash. Even Steve chuckled a little, until Bart said he knew we were all patients in a hospital and that I shouldn't give up. That's when Steve paused the tape again.

"Did you hear that, Cam?" he said excitedly. "What Bart said? That's cooperation. That's progress."

His words seeped in. He was right. It was progress. For a second I felt silvery, like that good-looking fairy godmother in *Pinocchio* had touched me on the head with her wand. *Ding!*

Then I went back to staring at Bart's frozen image on the screen. My mind whirred. I'm here. That's Bart. I'm here. That's Bart. Progress. Progress. Progress. That was me, then Clay, then Bart. Look at it. Look at it. That's Bart. Muh . . . muh . . . multiple. Okay okay okay. Multiple.

"Go on, Steve," I said.

He hit the button and Bahama Bart turned into SuperLeif right in front of my eyes. No mistaking it. Same body, different person, and, goddamn, the second Leif took over it seemed like a cloud rolled in and thunder cracked. Leif's eyes were lightning, his voice a saber being pulled from its scabbard. This was not Bart. And definitely not me. I sat transfixed while I watched Leif roll up his sleeves and flex and relax his hands as he spoke to the camera, the muscles in his arms looking ropey and strong, his brown eyes clear and deliberate. *This guy's incredible. This guy's fire. This guy's cash.* I tore my eyes from the screen and looked at Steve.

"This guy can do anything," I whispered.

Steve let the tape roll until Leif was through and then paused the machine. "Yeah, Leif can do anything." He leaned forward. "You hear what he said. This is all you."

"But . . ." I said, pointing at the screen, "he's . . . he's not crazy." My mouth started to get thick. "I'm . . ."

"Cam," Steve interrupted. "Stick with me here. Stick with me." I squinted hard, trying to keep him in focus. "That's it, Cam. Listen to me. Are you listening? You're not crazy. If Leif's not crazy, you're not crazy. Do you hear me? You're . . . not . . . crazy. You're a multiple." He pointed at the screen. "And this tape is the proof you've been looking for."

The words seeped in. Steve pressed play and I watched the silky screen some more. And the pretty fairy touched me with her wand again. *Ding!*

And then Per came out after Leif, and once again I saw an incredible change. Just like that, the thunder stopped and the skies cleared. A calm breeze massaged my mind, and a peaceful feeling filled the room. Per seemed older. Older than Leif or Bart . . . or me. The lines in his face were deeper, and his calm eyes radiated the wisdom of time. Per touched his fingers to his lips before he spoke and they looked graceful and slender. He may have been a father or he may have been a mountain. I couldn't tell. I blinked hard to clear my eyes, and another cold bead of perspiration trickled down my side, giving me goosebumps. *Per is a part of me, too. Ding!*

And then Per switched in and Dusty came out and the contrast between them was breathtaking. The middle-aged man was gone, replaced by someone young and bashful and girlish. My hands were sweaty and hurt from gripping the armrests, and I forced them loose and rubbed them on my pants. Then I reached up and touched my face, slowly running my fingers over the contours of my skin. *Is this me? Who is me? She is me, too?* And then my mind began to melt and swirl and as the walls collapsed, I floated into the sky like a homesick angel, and Dusty came out. Steve was watching me and stopped the tape again.

"Hello," he said calmly.

Dusty wrung her hands for a few seconds, looking down at the floor. Steve said, "Dusty?"

She nodded once with effort, and the emotion rushed up and burst the dam and she pointed at the screen and moaned, "That's . . . not . . . me!" and put her head in her hands and started to weep.

Steve said softly, "It is you, Dusty. It is you."

She moaned through her hands, "I hate you for showing me this. I hate you." And then she lifted her face toward the ceiling; her arms reached out and she pleaded, "Help me! Help me, please! Don't make me look like this. Please! Don't make me look like this."

And she dropped her arms, sank back down in her chair, hung her head, and sobbed.

"Dusty," Steve said softly, "you knew you lived in Cam's body. It's still you." He paused a moment and then asked her, "Were you watching the tape before? Did you see Clay and Bart and Leif and Per?" She nodded weakly. "They looked like Cam, too, didn't they?" he said. "And like you . . . but still different. Still themselves, right?" She nodded again. Steve handed her a tissue. "Dusty, you've got to accept yourself for who you are. You're one of Cam's alter personalities . . . and yes, he's a man and you're a girl, but you're no different than you were a minute ago before you saw the tape. You're still you. And Clay's still Clay. And everyone else is still who they were before they watched the tape. All parts of Cam."

Dusty sat still with her face in her hands until she was able to stop crying. Steve handed her another tissue and she dried her eyes. Behind her, in the stillness, I listened . . . and felt . . . and thought. *This is me. She is me. They are all me.* And then Dusty leaned back in her chair and looked up at Steve.

He smiled gently at her. "All right?"

She nodded again. "All right," she said softly, and her eyes closed and she switched in and I whipped back out before I was ready.

My face felt hot and wet. I reached for a tissue and blew my nose and dried my face with the back of my hands.

"Hi," Steve said.

"Hi," I answered, and my voice sounded hollow and distant. Steve folded his hands and said, "What do you think?"

I stared unfocused down at my knees. "Poor Dusty," I said, shaking my head slowly.

Steve nodded. "It's hard for everybody. Perhaps Dusty more than anyone else. What do you think?" he repeated.

I looked up at Steve and it took me a minute to focus my eyes on his. I slowly filled my lungs with air, let it out gradually, and said, "I think I have Dissociative Identity Disorder."

"You *think* you have Dissociative Identity Disorder?"

Our eyes were locked. I said, "I know I have Dissociative Identity Disorder."

We sat silently for a moment; Steve knew I was perched on the precipice of acceptance.

"Something bad happened to me," I said, not taking my eyes away from his.

"Yes," he said. "I'm so sorry."

And the walls of my pain trembled and shook and the antiquities of anguish tilted, lurched, and fell off their hooks and shelves and crashed to the floor and the floor buckled and caved under their weight and the foundation crumbled and the concrete yawned and the earth opened and lava gushed up and enveloped the wreckage of my heart and mind in its molten heat. I sprang from my chair and screamed the scream of the greatest sorrow and started to collapse, and Steve jumped up and grabbed me and held me and my arms hung limp at my sides and my head lay on his shoulder and the tears gushed and slapped the searing heat as billows of steam rose from the unutterable sadness.

For Dusty and Clay and all the others. And, at last, for me, too.

FORTY-FIVE

I couldn't wait to call Rikki and kept watching the clock until nine, which was her seven, when she and Kai would be finished with dinner. I was surprised when Kai answered. Not that it was strange for him to answer the phone, but I'd worked out everything I had to say to Rikki and was nervous about it and was planning on just blurting it out as soon as she picked up.

"Little Man?" I said.

"Daddeeee! Hi! What're ya doin'?"

"Oh, nothin'," I said. "I just finished working and wanted to call and tell you how much I love you."

"I love you too, Dad." I heard him shout, "It's Dad, Mom, but I need to say somethin' to him first!" Then he whispered to me, "Dad?"

"Yeah?" I knew what was coming next. "Have ya gotten me anything yet?"

"Well, not yet," I said. "But soon."

"Okay. Guess what?"

"What?"

"I get to bring the rats home for the weekend."

"Rats?" I said.

"Yeah," he said excitedly. "From my class. There are two of them. Lucy and Ethel. Oh oh. I have to go now. Mom wants to talk to you."

"Okay, son. I love you."

"Love you, too. Bye."

I heard Rikki tell him to get into the tub and felt tremors in my chest.

"Hi," she said tentatively.

I took a deep breath. "Hi, Rik. We did it and watched it with Dr. Sawyer."

"The videotaping?"

"Yeah."

"And?"

"And there they were. It was incredible. I mean I know you've seen them a lot, so watching them wouldn't have been—"

"Cam," Rikki cut in. "I know it was big deal for you. How did it go?"

"Rik," I said, filling with emotion, "I'm . . . a . . . multiple."

She sighed. "I know, honey, I know." She paused for a few seconds. "Do you believe it now?"

I choked my tears back. I didn't want to cry. "Yes," I said. "I believe it. And so do they."

"What do you mean?"

"I mean it was hard for them to see the tape, too. Especially Dusty."

"Oh," she said, thinking that over. "That hadn't even occurred to me."

"Rik," I said nervously—I had to get it out. "Rik, we've got to make some changes."

"Oh?" she said, her voice cautious.

"Yeah," I pressed on. "We've got to. For me to really accept them, they have to be accepted at home—"

She cupped the mouthpiece and muffled a shout, "They *are* accepted at home, Cam!" Then she said, "Wait a minute," and dropped the phone to go close the bedroom door, and the seconds whittled away at my soul. She picked up the phone again and repeated a little louder, "Cam, they are accepted at home!"

"But they don't feel that way," I argued. "Kai panics whenever I switch and it makes them feel bad. You should have heard Clay—right on the tape—how bad he feels that Kai's scared of him. He wants to meet him—they all do—so they can feel accepted."

"We've been here before, Cam. Kai's . . . not . . . meeting them," she pounded, like a hammer on an anvil. I could feel her ferocity through the phone and it scared the hell out of me.

"But he's got—"

"This is not open for discussion," she snapped. "I'm not letting him meet your alters. That's it. He's too young! You said yourself how scared he gets. He's not ready! I'm sorry."

And then she was silent, and so was I, and the seventeen hundred and fifty miles between us stretched around the world, and around again, and around again, and my body felt cold, my stomach like stone, and I wondered for a second if I could stay in the hospital forever.

"Rikki," I said weakly. "We've got to go now."

"Okay, Cam," she said. "Goodbye." And her goodbye had the deadly shimmer of a bullet passing in slow motion through the muzzle of a gun.

I hung up the phone and, leaning against the wall for support, slowly sank to the floor, hugged my knees, and began to rock. My unblinking eyes locked onto the wavy pattern on the wallpaper across the hallway, and I began to disappear into it.

Lucinda came over from the nurses' station, touched me lightly on the shoulder, and said in her soft southern lilt, "Y'all all right, Cam?"

I looked up at her as I waded into the waves and said, "No."

Kai was tucked in and Rikki was lying next to him on his bed reading a Nate the Great mystery, mustering as much zeal as she could after the horrible phone call.

"Mom," Kai said, interrupting her reading, "is something wrong with you and Dad?"

That smacked her like a branch in the face. Rikki put the book down and thought fast. "Well," she said, trying to sound reassuring, "Dad and I've been having some disagreements about some stuff, that's all. Nothing's wrong."

"About Andy?" Kai asked.

"Why would we be disagreeing about Andy?" Rikki asked, surprised.

"Because you're dating him."

"I'm not dating Andy," Rikki said. "Did Daddy tell you that?"

"Uh uh," Kai said, shaking his head. "I thought it up. You go out with him like a girlfriend. You should be Daddy's girlfriend . . . I mean his wife."

"Is that what you think?" Rikki asked, amazed at what had been going on in Kai's young mind. "You think I'm Andy's *girlfriend?"*

"Yeah."

"Well, I'm not, sweetie. Andy's just my friend. Just because he's a guy doesn't mean we can't be friends. Right?"

"Well, anyway, he couldn't be like Dad. Nobody's as good as Dad." He took Rikki's hand. "Mom?"

"Hmm?"

"Do you love Dad?"

"Of course I love Dad, honey," Rikki said gently. "He's my husband. He's my *best* friend."

"What about me? Do you love me, too?"

"Aww, sweetie," she cooed. "You're my little man. I love you more than anything." Rikki squeezed Kai's small hand and kissed him on the head. His hair was a little damp and smelled flowery from shampoo.

"Good," Kai said. "Mom?"

"Yeah?"

"Multiple personalities isn't so bad."

For a moment Rikki was speechless while Kai's innocent words grappled with the ghosts in her heart. Then she propped herself on her elbow, turned to him, and gently stroked his smooth face. Their eyes met, and forcing herself not to cry, she said softly, "No, Kylie. It's not so bad."

Out in the cool night a neighbor's dog barked once, and then everything was still again.

"Mom?" Kai said, picking up the book and handing it to her. "Could you finish the book?"

Rikki looked down at her precious little man and gave him a squeeze.

"Sure," she said.

FORTY-SIX

The next morning I awoke leaden, draped in rags of utter confusion and despair. Acceptance and loss. Family inside and family outside. I couldn't even discuss it with the others in the journal. I'd already begun to shut them out again and was snagged in a trap it seemed I'd set for myself, or God had set for me. I was sure of one thing: I'd screwed up badly and couldn't get unscrewed by myself. *Maybe Steve can help. Yeah, we'll ask Steve to help. He can call Rikki and fix it somehow.*

I blurted the whole thing out the second Steve closed the door, tears flowing, snot flying, arms waving, begging him to call Rikki and fix it.

"Cam," he said calmly. "Of course, I'll call her if you think it might help."

"Oh, thank God. Thank you, Steve. Thank you."

"But—"

"But what?" I said, panicked.

"But . . . you need to tell me some things about Rikki."

"Oh, okay, sure," I said, breathing heavily. "What do you need to know?"

"First of all, I need to know if she accepts that you're a multiple? Is she committed to you and your healing?"

I calmed down a little. "Rikki is wonderful," I told him. "She's the finest person I know. She's been behind me all the way, and she's always been good to my guys."

"That's very good."

"Oh, shit, Steve." Despair grabbed me by the throat and I started to cry again. "She's gonna leave us for that guy, Andy. I've blown it and she's gonna leave us for him. She's—"

"But you just said she's been behind you all the way," Steve interrupted, confused.

"But there's this guy, Andy. He's a friend of hers. I think maybe she's gonna leave us for him."

"You mean leave you and Kai, or—"

"No!" I shouted, jabbing my thumb at my chest. "Us! She'd never leave Kai! She's the best mother you ever saw!"

"What makes you think she'd leave you for Andy?"

I sniffled and wiped my nose on my sleeve. "I don't know. She goes out to dinner with him. She swears they're just friends, but—"

"You don't believe her?"

I started to ramble. "Steve, I don't want to lose her. Where are we gonna go? We can't stay here forever. What're we gonna do?"

Steve put his hand on my arm. "Cam," he said firmly, "take a few deep breaths and listen to me."

I took some breaths and waited for Steve to speak. Thoughts were zipping around my head like fireflies in a jar, bumping into each other, blinking on and off.

"Now," Steve said, "I've got to tell you that I think you put Rikki in a very difficult spot last night."

I shook my head hard, trying to stop the flies. "How? How'd I do that?"

"Kai's not quite nine, right?" he asked. I nodded.

"Cam, Rikki's right. Kai is too young to understand all of this."

That startled me. "He is? But I thought—"

"What Clay and Per said on the video," he said, "maybe we should have talked about that yesterday. Maybe I was wrong to put that off." He leaned forward and leveled his gaze at me. "Cam, you put Rikki in a spot where she had to choose between comforting you and protecting Kai." He spread his hands. "She did the obvious thing any loving mother would do."

"Oh, shit," I said. "What do we do?"

Steve sat back. "We try to find some middle ground."

All the flies were glowing now. "Oh Jesus, Steve," I pleaded. "Call her. Please call her and see if there's some middle ground. Right now. Please."

"Okay. Is she at home now?"

"No, she's at work. I know the number."

Steve picked up the receiver, then put it back down. "Cam," he said, "I don't know what's happening between Rikki and Andy, and it's not really my place to ask. If she is actually thinking of leaving you for him, I can't stop it and neither can you. What I can do is talk to her about you and your guys. Explain some things to her." He picked up the phone again. "Do you have that number?"

I fed it to him as he dialed. I sat in that crummy steel chair, gripping those bile-green vinyl armrests I knew so well, hoping with all my soul that Rikki would be there and that Steve Sawyer could somehow change my fate.

"Rikki West's office," Janine answered. "How may I help you?"

Steve told her his name and asked to speak with Rikki. In a few sweaty seconds she picked up.

"Dr. Sawyer?" she asked, concerned. "Is everything all right?"

"Yes," he said. "Everything's all right. Cam is with me now, and he feels that by speaking with you directly I may be able to help clarify some things."

"Dr. Sawyer . . ."

"Call me Steve."

"Steve," she said icily. "I support Cam totally, but there is no way in the world I am going to put an eight-year-old boy in the position of trying to fully comprehend his father's condition. It's hard enough for me to grasp. I'm sorry, but there's nothing you can say that'll change my mind. I've been very careful to give Kai the information he needs and that he's asked for, based on what I feel he can understand at his age and level of development. And I don't believe that at this point in his life he needs to play Monopoly with Clay."

"Rikki," Steve said, "I agree with you completely."

"What?"

"I said I agree with you completely."

There was a pause on the line. Rikki's tone softened. "You do?"

"Yes," Steve said emphatically. "I agree with you that Kai is too young."

"I'm confused," Rikki said. "Then why did you call me?"

"Because Cam realizes that he put you in an awful position last night—"

"The worst."

"Yes, and it's partially my fault."

"Your fault?"

"Yes. You see, on the videotape he made of his alters, Clay said something about not wanting Kai to be afraid of him, and Per mentioned that he felt Cam should do something about that. I made the judgment call not to address that issue in yesterday's session, to focus instead on Cam's denial. I didn't anticipate that he might jump to the conclusion that Kai should meet his alters. Believe me, Cam's got a lot on his plate right now."

"Oh, I know."

"And I understand why he said that to you, and why his alters would want Kai to meet and accept them."

"So do I," Rikki said. "I understand that, too. And maybe eventually Kai will meet them. But he's too young to handle it now. He can't even tolerate when Cam switches, even without knowing the alters. I think that would put him over the edge."

"I agree," Steve said. "From what I understand, Cam's alters go back inside whenever Kai gets scared and calls for Cam to come back."

"That's right. They do," Rikki said. "Every time."

Steve said, "Rikki, do you realize how incredible that is? That means they're willing to subjugate their own desire to be out in order to put Kai at ease. That in itself shows a selflessness and an ability to cooperate that's way beyond that of most of the multiples that I've worked with. It's amazing, actually."

"That never occurred to me," Rikki said. "I just saw Kai being scared."

"Of course. That's natural. But you should understand and appreciate how difficult that must be for Cam's alters . . . what a strain it must put on him to have to disappoint them like that, and how that must contribute to his difficulty in accepting them himself . . . accepting that he is, in fact, a multiple."

Steve and Rikki were silent for a moment. I rocked back and forth, hugging myself, aching to know what she was thinking. Sweat poured out of me, stinging my eyes. I blinked hard, but it didn't help. There was nothing I could do so I just kept rocking, grateful Steve was there to pry up the boulders where the big snakes hid.

Rikki said, "I've never even considered how hard it must be for them to have to switch in when Kai calls for him. Cam doesn't tell me. I'm just this minute grasping how that must work on him." She was quiet for a few seconds. "I'd give anything if he could get better."

"Rikki," Steve said, "I think he can."

"You do?"

"Yes, I do. With your help and the help of his alters, I think in time he can heal and lead a pretty normal life."

"Really?" Rikki said.

"Really."

There was silence for a moment. "You know, Steve," Rikki said, her voice full of emotion, "it's been a long time since anyone's reminded me that Cam could actually get better. You really think he can?"

"I do," Steve said with conviction. "And there's a way you could help, if you'd be willing to."

Boy, did I want to hear what she said to that. "Of course I would," Rikki said.

"What if you agreed to spend time with Cam's alters, say, in the evening after Kai's gone to bed. Give them some time out in the house. Help them feel accepted . . . not just by saying they are, but by being with them. In exchange, we could ask them to wait until Kai gets a little older before they meet him."

I was jumping out of my skin, but I kept mum.

"What I'd like to do, Rikki," Steve continued, "is talk with Cam's alters, in particular with Clay and the other young ones, and see if they'd be willing to kind of watch out for Kai . . . be his protectors, and know that you'll be their friend and protector . . . after Kai goes to bed and when he's not around."

"Steve, that's an excellent idea," Rikki said excitedly. "I'd be happy to spend time with Cam's guys. I'd do it every night. I'd do just about anything if I could be sure Kai would be totally okay when I'm not at home. Will they agree to it?"

"I believe they will."

"Steve, you have no idea how relieved I am that you called," Rikki said. "I'm putting you up for sainthood."

Steve laughed. That was a good sign. A very good sign. Suddenly the world was in color again. Inside, Clay was telling Per yes, he'd do that, be Kai's protector, and Switch was saying the same thing, and Wyatt, too, puffing their chests like they were the new sheriffs in town. And Dusty was even saying she'd like to be able to talk with Rikki. I heard Bart say, "Night time is the right time," and Leif said, "Keep your eye on the road, pal," and Bart said, "Lighten up, Leif, I didn't mean anything by it."

Rikki said, "Thank you, Steve. Thank you so much."

Steve smiled broadly. "You're welcome, Rikki. Good luck to you. Would you like to talk to Cam now?"

"Very much," she said.

"Okay," Steve said. "I'll put him on." He took the receiver from his ear and looked over at me. "Rikki would like to talk with you."

Adrenaline shot through me and I felt faint for a second. Steve spotted it and told me to take a couple of deep breaths. I did, and it calmed me down some. I put my hand out and he passed me the phone. It felt warm where he'd been holding it.

"Hello?" I said cautiously.

"Hi, Cam," Rikki said, and there was sweetness in her voice. *My Rikki.* "You heard what Steve said?"

"Yes."

"Does it seem workable for you and your guys?"

"Yes, Rik, it does."

She said, "I promise to talk with everybody at night after Kai's gone to bed."

"Oh God, Rik," I said, tears forming in my eyes. "That'd be wonderful."

She said, "I want everyone inside to know that I'll appreciate it tremendously if they'll kind of watch out for Kai and go in when he's around, at least until he's old enough to understand a little better. And I'll be their friend and will talk to them when he's not around, even if it's during the day. Okay?"

Then Clay switched out and said in his little voice, "Okay. L-Like a sheriff, right, Rikki? To watch out for Kai."

Rikki laughed. "Yup, Clay. Just like a sheriff."

Clay switched back in and I came out. We were quiet for a few seconds while I worked up the nerve to ask her the big question. I swallowed hard.

"Rikki," I said carefully, "are you going to leave us for Andy?"

There was a desperate silence while I held my breath. And then Rikki said softly,

"No, Cam. I'm not. I love you. All of you."

And suddenly the harps glissandoed and the sun came out and birds started singing and balloons went up and Julie Andrews spun around and the hills were alive and so was I. I could breathe again. I believed her.

"Rik?"

"Yeah, Cam?"

"Your Buns in Space man's coming home."

Andy picked up on the first ring. "Andy Grumman."

"Hey there."

Andy knew immediately. "You're not coming," he said. After a pause

Rikki said, "No . . . I'm not coming." Andy sighed. "You love him, don't you," he said sadly.

"You know I do," she said. "I always have."

They were both silent for a moment and then Rikki said, "Andy, I think Cam's going to get better. I actually think he can recover from this."

"Really?"

"Yes," she said excitedly. "I spoke with his therapist at the hospital and he said that, in time, Cam could have a normal life. We could have a normal life."

"Aw, Rikki," Andy said. "That'd be great."

Neither of them spoke for a moment, the warm connection between them palpable. Andy broke the silence. "You can't break up your family."

"No," Rikki said. "I could never do that. Never. It's been broken up enough."

"Yeah," Andy said sadly. "I never had a chance. I always knew it."

Rikki didn't answer. She didn't have to. There was a heavy silence on the line while they dwelled in their own thoughts.

Then Andy said, "Well . . . I guess we won't be seeing so much of each other anymore, huh?"

"Sure we will, Andy. We're friends," Rikki said, but she knew it didn't matter.

"Friends," Andy repeated, with a sigh that filled the sails of a ship that was leaving for good.

After a moment Rikki said, "Andy?"

"Yeah, Rik?" Andy said.

Rikki opened her mouth to speak but no words came out, and in the silence that followed the ship sank below the horizon.

Andy said, "Don't say it, Rik. Just say goodbye."

With a tear in her voice Rikki said, "Goodbye, Andy."

FORTY-SEVEN

TCBY was still making parfaits when we got back to California. And it was a good thing, too, because on a bright, sunny day not long after we returned home, I drove over there to buy one for me and some of my guys. There was a bit of an argument over what to order, but we eventually settled on crunched-up Heath Bar on the bottom, chocolate frozen yogurt next, then butterscotch topping, then vanilla frozen yogurt, and mixed nuts on the top. Oh, and a dozen spoons . . . to go.

I put it all in a little purple cooler with an ice pack and drove over to Diablo. I parked, grabbed the cooler and a plaid blanket, and hiked the mile up to the top. I found a private spot overlooking the bay, spread out the blanket, and laid the spoons side by side. I wrote my guys' names on the handles of the spoons with a fine-point magic marker, and one at a time we took turns sharing the parfait. Right there in the world. Looking at the bay.

When I got home and told Rikki what we'd done, she cried and hugged us and said we'd done a good thing, and that made me cry, too.

Not too long after that, one of the people I'd interviewed for my dissertation study asked me if I'd be willing to speak at a conference for survivors of child abuse. The topic was "connectedness." For some reason

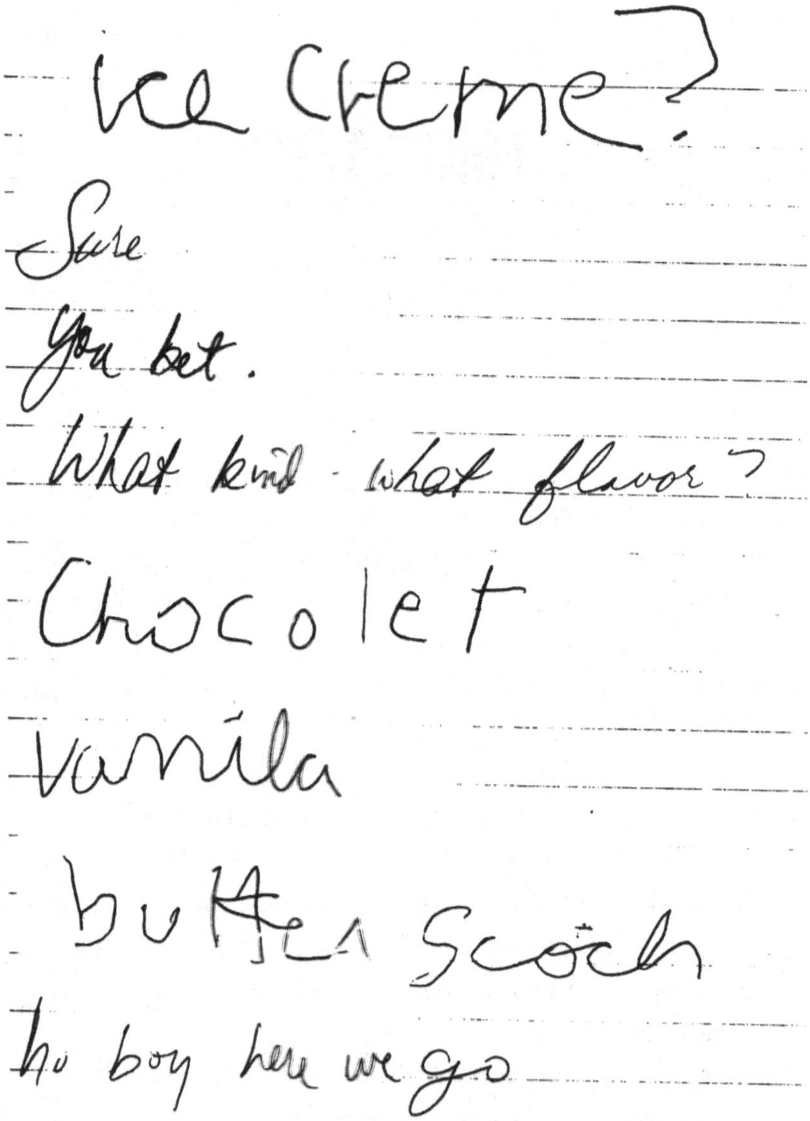
ice creme?
Sure
You bet.
What kind · what flavor?
Chocolet
vanila
butter scoch
ho boy here we go

Deciding what flavors to get at TCBY.

I accepted, but right away I started wanting to creep out of it, and every day until the conference I was kicking myself for getting us into such a mess when we had so much else going on, like the dissertation, and therapy, and being a dad, and eating parfaits. But Leif made sure I stuck to it and didn't grow feathers, and everybody agreed not to come out while I was giving the speech. So when the day finally came, I didn't shave any further than skin deep.

My sweet Rikki came along for support, and boy was I glad she did. She teased me a little while I drove to Oakland doing about forty miles an hour, saying, "Cam, you can go sixty-five here, you know."

The conference was held in a huge, beautifully restored Victorian house, and there must have been two hundred people there, many of them multiples and some of them therapists. When we walked in and I saw them all, I thought that I'd just as soon dive off the Sears Building into a brassiere full of tapioca as give that speech.

Rikki held my hand until I was called up to the podium and it was too late. I turned and glanced at her for a long second, like it was the last time I was going to see her, and she squeezed my hand and smiled wide showing all the china and said, "Honey, I'm right behind ya . . . like a jogger's fart." I cracked a smile at that, and it hurt my face because I was so tense. I walked up with my notes in my hand, hoping not to trip on the stairs, and said this:

I was invited to speak to you today on the topic of connectedness, and I accepted for two reasons. The first is that as a person with Dissociative Identity Disorder, achieving what I think of as real connectedness has been, and still is, the single greatest challenge of my life. It's what I strive for and want more than anything in the world. The second reason is to tell you about two connections I do have, to my wife Rikki and my son Kai. They give me strength and hope and have literally saved my life.

It seems to me I've spent my entire life having nothing more than a toehold in this world. That's all. Most of the time I feel like I'm just a piece of a human being, one of a bunch of jagged chips of glass from a broken vase, lying scattered on an old rug. I look over at the other broken pieces of glass and some of them look like me and some of them don't, but we're all just chips of glass on the same rug. And I say to myself, "Shouldn't we be closer together?" We'd look a whole lot more like a vase if we were closer together, you know . . . if we connected the pieces. And we'd be less likely to get swept up and thrown out with the trash.

I've got twenty-four alter personalities. I call them 'my guys' even though some of them are females, and we all live together in this body. We try to communicate with each other, try to get along and be concerned about each other's problems, but sometimes it takes so much energy that somebody who may be in real pain gets left out to fend for himself. And if we let that happen . . . if we don't tend right to it and stick together, we eventually end up having serious problems. Either this body gets sick or gets hurt, or I can't do what I'm supposed to do as a husband and a father. When my guys and I aren't connected, things get dark and pasty and hollow-sounding, like a damp cave in a scary forest. And I don't like caves. And I don't like trees with eyes that follow me and branches that turn into hands when I'm not looking. No, I don't like that at all. We *need* to stay connected. Then we'll be out in the warm sun with the palm trees swaying, and short-sleeved shirts, and melty candy bars. And that's much better.

I had a dream last night about me and my guys. In the dream we were all standing together barefoot on a deserted beach in the early morning fog with the sunrise poking through in soft yellow and orange streaks. Some of us were touching hands and catching glimpses of each other's eyes, and some of us were just looking down at our naked feet in the sand.

We could all hear the waves lapping up on the beach and smell the salt air and feel the dampness on our faces. Some of us felt the cold ocean water wash up over our feet as it crept up onto the sand; others saw it coming and took a quick step backward to avoid getting wet. We all knew we were together on that beach, but we didn't know why. Some of us knew they were in the present, some were sure they were in the past, and some thought they were far into the future. Some of us waited for the fog to lift . . . and some thought the fog was white cotton candy. Anyway, that was my dream. Twenty-five people connected by the sand, the sea, and cotton candy.

I don't just struggle with trying to be connected to my guys, the people in this body. Nope. I've felt disconnected from most other people for my whole life, too. For as long as I can remember, I've avoided looking too deeply into people's eyes, because I was afraid that if they really looked at me . . . if they really looked into my soul . . . they'd see that nobody was there.

But I desperately want to feel like I'm part of this world and somehow connected to the people in it. I guess that's why I'm here today. I'm hoping that somebody will look into my eyes and tell me they see somebody there, tell me they see Cameron West there. And if they see other people in there, well that's okay, too. It has to be okay. I'm through being disconnected from me. I am who we are, and it's got to be okay, or I've got no chance for a better life.

Over the past few years I've met a lot of people who, like me, had some really terrible things happen to them when they were young. And I know how damaging that can be, and how bad it hurts, and how hard it makes every aspect of your life. Child abuse is a dirty, oil-soaked jacket that's almost impossible to take off, so you just seem to wear it right into all your relationships, and every time you brush up against something, or hug somebody, or eye some clean sheets on a freshly made bed, you just know some of that foul stuff is gonna rub off and spoil everything. And it usually does. You can pretty much count on it. And it's a sad thing, because it keeps a lot of young relationships from growing up to be old ones. They just die young and sooner or later end up as tear stains in somebody's journal.

Somehow I managed to be one of the lucky ones, though, and my relationship with my wife Rikki didn't die young. It's lasted for sixteen years, and it's taken faith, and commitment, and Kleenex, too. I know it's been difficult for Rikki these last few years, and confusing too, living with a bunch of people who all look like me. You might say our life together is a real patchwork, and it's taken a lot of patching to make it work.

Rikki has lived in the tempest of a terrible war between the conflicting forces of will and pain, hope and uncertainty. Mine, and her own, too. And sometimes the smoke has gotten so thick we've almost lost the precious connection between us.

But there's always been a little boy there to blow the air clear, even though he didn't know he was doing it. His name is Kai and he's nine years old.

Now I think that being a parent isn't easy even for regular people. And I know that being a parent and being a multiple is harder than a Georgia peach pit. It's a source of both incredible joy and unspeakable pain for me. I know that Kai needs and deserves normalcy and consistency in his life in order to grow up well adjusted. And I'm one of the two people responsible for providing him with those things. And that seems sort of like a cruel joke to me, because the only thing normal or consistent about me is that I'm consistently abnormal.

With all my heart I want Kai to have a regular dad. And I want him to feel connected to his dad . . . someone he can count on and look up to, not a dad who switches and usually doesn't know what's going on. And I desperately want to feel connected to him. He's my son. My little man.

So every day I struggle to look Kai right in the eye . . . and in the heart . . . and be the same for him. And in that sameness, that repetition of daily stuff . . . reading to him, making his lunch, talking things over . . . that's where Kai and I connect. And that connection is its own gift. It gives Kai the fathering he needs, and it helps me to feel more whole.

The really hard part, the one that cuts me like the sun's glare off a shiny hood, is that as I'm doing that stuff, that daily stuff, trying to be a regular dad, I'm often looking at Kai and interacting with him from some tiny island in my mind. And Kai knows it, too. He knows it.

When an alter's out or there's some leakage going on between some of my guys, Kai says, "Dad. Can you hear me? Come back." And I'll hear his little voice come floating in on a bottle cap that drifts across my ocean, and I'll say to myself, "Damn, I've got to get back! I've got to get back!" And I'll jump in the cap and paddle with all I've got till I find my way back to this small person who's counting on me. Just knowing that Kai's at the end of the sound helps me to get back, but at the same time, knowing that I'm so far away, so much of the time . . . that I'm never really there . . . well that's almost more than I can take. I don't want Kai to grow up and think his dad was crazy—that Dad was howling in the attic when he should've been playing on the porch. I want to be the daddy on the porch.

But you know what the worst thing in the whole world is to me? It's not the thought that Kai will think I'm crazy, or that Rikki won't love me anymore, or that I'll have to go back to another psychiatric hospital. It's a rake. I call it Denial's Rake. And it's been dragged across my body, screeching its hideous tune, practically every waking and sleeping moment since I was half Kai's age. Denial about what happened to me, denial about the people who hurt me, and denial about being a multiple.

I've spent too long covering my ears and screaming, trying to drown out the ugly sound of Denial's Rake. And I've only just recently begun to understand that for all those years it was my own hand holding that rake, my own voice singing that screeching tune.

Well, I finally put that rake down, and it feels strange, too, because I'm so used to carrying it. And my inclination is to pick it back up. But I'm leaving it down, and I'm determined not to touch it again. And little by little I'm accepting and understanding who I am and how I got this way. I'm connecting to myself, or, I should say, my selves.

And though my life isn't easy, it isn't always hard, and lately it even seems to be getting a little easier. Why just this morning I told Rikki I haven't had a bad week in days.

And you know something? It's true.

EPILOGUE 2025

It has been twenty-five years since *First Person Plural* was initially published in the United States and throughout Europe and Oprah Winfrey introduced my little family to the world. When I say my little family, I'm speaking of my wife, Rikki, our son, Kai, me, and the twenty-four parts of me that I called my guys and mental health professionals refer to as alter personalities. I am a multiple, a person with Dissociative Identity Disorder.

Dissociative Identity Disorder is still intriguing and mysterious, but most people understand that the condition is the result of some form of trauma or abuse that happens early in life. The fact is that *First Person Plural* is not just a story about the consequences of some awful things that happened to me. It is a love story about a family struggling to overcome a challenge—an unusual challenge—but nevertheless just a human challenge. What many people have told us over the years is that they relate to our story because we faced adversity and kept our family together. That was Rikki's doing; she was our rock during the really hard times, and once I was able to face my denial, the difficult and lengthy process of healing began in earnest. As a twenty-fifth anniversary edition of *First Person Plural* is once again being made available in digital, audiobook, and hardcover formats, I thought this would be a good time to let people know how the Wests are doing.

This book tells the tale of the beginning of my therapeutic

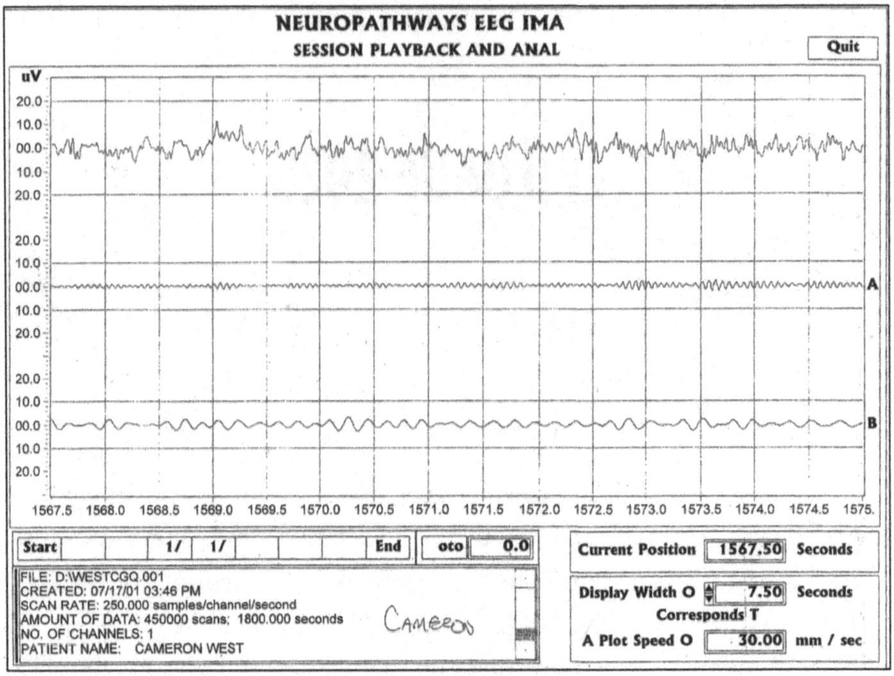
NEUROPATHWAYS EEG IMA
SESSION PLAYBACK AND ANAL
Quit
uV
A
B
1567.5 1568.0 1568.5 1569.0 1569.5 1570.0 1570.5 1571.0 1571.5 1572.0 1572.5 1573.0 1573.5 1574.0 1574.5 1575.
Start 1/ 1/ End
oto 0.0
Current Position 1567.50 Seconds
FILE: D:\WESTCGQ.001
CREATED: 07/17/01 03:46 PM
SCAN RATE: 250.000 samples/channel/second
AMOUNT OF DATA: 450000 scans; 1800.000 seconds
NO. OF CHANNELS: 1
PATIENT NAME: CAMERON WEST
CAMERON
Display Width O 7.50 Seconds
Corresponds T
A Plot Speed O 30.00 mm / sec

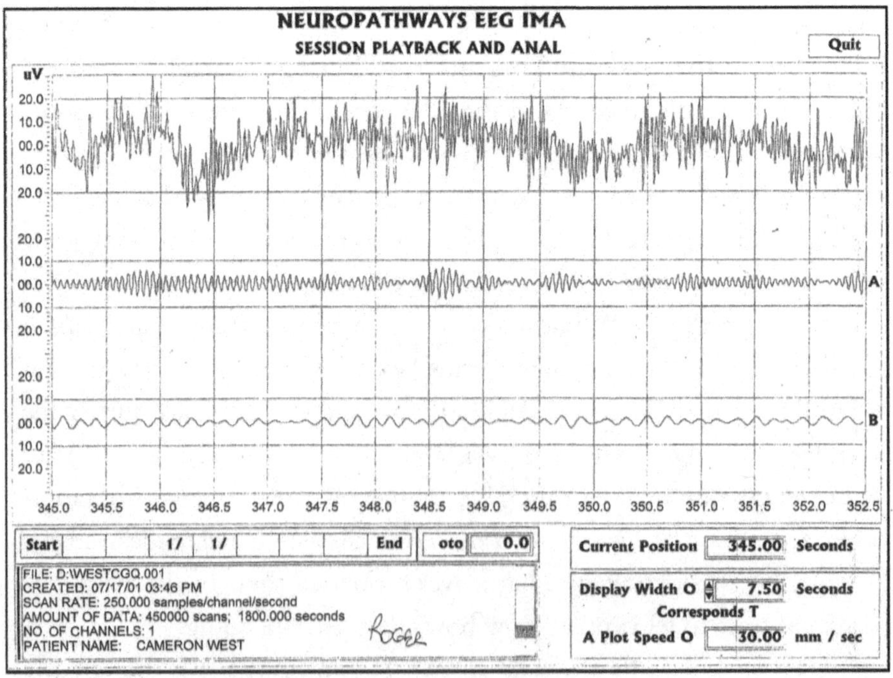
NEUROPATHWAYS EEG IMA
SESSION PLAYBACK AND ANAL
Quit
uV
A
B
345.0 345.5 346.0 346.5 347.0 347.5 348.0 348.5 349.0 349.5 350.0 350.5 351.0 351.5 352.0 352.5
Start 1/ 1/ End
oto 0.0
Current Position 345.00 Seconds
FILE: D:\WESTCGQ.001
CREATED: 07/17/01 03:46 PM
SCAN RATE: 250.000 samples/channel/second
AMOUNT OF DATA: 450000 scans; 1800.000 seconds
NO. OF CHANNELS: 1
PATIENT NAME: CAMERON WEST
ROGER
Display Width O 7.50 Seconds
Corresponds T
A Plot Speed O 30.00 mm / sec

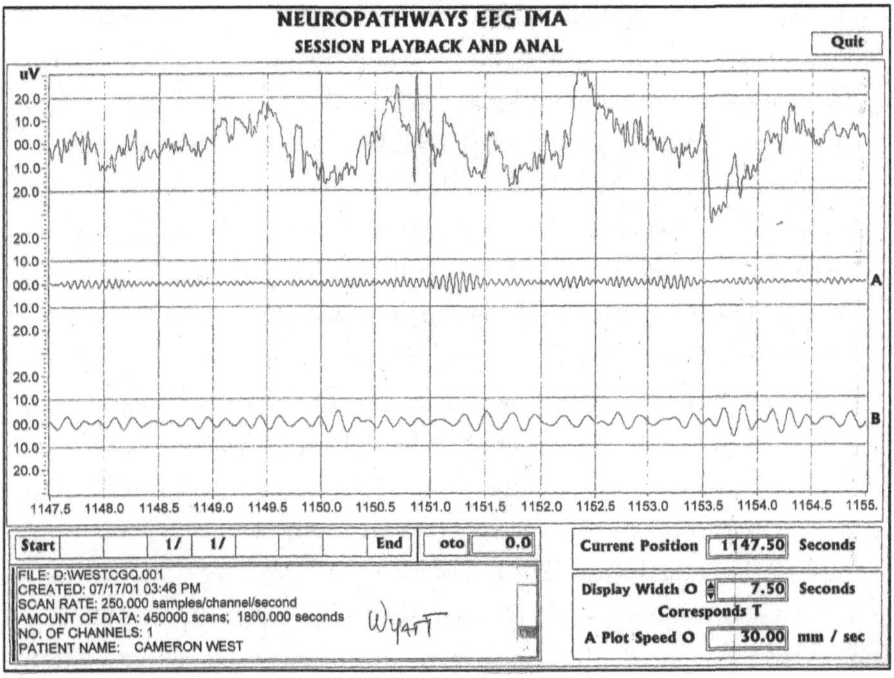

journey—from diagnosis to acceptance to starting the long and arduous process of healing my shattered psyche. I continued my therapy for many years, traveling sixty miles twice a week to spend two hours in the home office of Doctor Marilyn Rice, a specialist in treating people with dissociative disorders and post-traumatic stress. The specific treatment, called Eye Movement Desensitization and Retraining (EMDR), has been shown to be highly effective in helping war veterans and others who have experienced significant emotional damage to physically process the traumatizing events, thereby diminishing their potency. EMDR is based on the principal that traumatic events, when not fully processed, keep replaying over and over, causing an individual to react emotionally to memories, as well as sights, sounds, smells, and/or tastes occurring in the present that are associated with the past events that were the source of significant emotional or physical pain.

The therapy involves repeatedly taking the individual, or in my case, individual alter personalities, back to the original traumatic events, allowing them to be processed, using eye movement, until they no longer produce the unwanted emotional response. Essentially, EMDR, when carried out properly, clears away damaging mental debris and allows an injured mind to heal. For me, there was a significant pile of debris. Several of my alters had his or her own memories of abuse that had occurred many years earlier but were still causing emotional pain in the present. The work was extremely grueling, and the sessions left me totally drained of emotional and physical energy. But I was healing and, in the end, most of my alter personalities were able to rest; their jobs in my system were no longer needed. A few (Wyatt, Clay, and Roger) still reside quietly in a corner of my mind, although they have healed from the traumas from which they were created and no longer experience or cause me internal distress. The rest of my alters have integrated back into my core self, although Rikki says that she sees glimpses of some of those who have integrated. Lief comes through with his fierce determination when I have something difficult to do. Per is present in my quieter, more reflective moments. And Bart's sense of humor prevails, as laughter has always been a huge part of life in our household. I don't feel the need to fully integrate into a single personality, but if it happens, that's okay, too. I will always be a multiple and I will always appreciate the job that my alters did to save me from the disastrous consequence of childhood sexual abuse. I still feel the effects of my childhood trauma. Anyone who has been sexually abused knows that it is hard to ever feel truly clean. And I believe that there was some permanent damage done to my nervous system. But I have healed from much of the emotional pain and I have forgiven my abusers, which brings me a certain inner peace.

Denial was a major hurdle I had to overcome to begin the process of healing. It's a powerful defense mechanism that protects us from overwhelming emotional pain, and I felt its fierce pull as the nature of my abuse unfolded. Seeing my alters on video while in one of my hospital stays was a huge step toward accepting the truth of my abuse. Several years later I was asked by the Tokyo Broadcast System to participate in a documentary on the workings of the mind. As part of their program, I met with the late Dr. Margaret Ayers, a leader in the field of biofeedback and traumatic brain injury. Through EEG testing, Dr. Ayers recorded my brain wave patterns and those of several of my alters and the results were decisive and startling. My patterns differed distinctly from those of my alters and their patterns differed from each other. It was the first clear and undeniable physiological proof of the presence of alter personalities. The figures below are the actual readouts from the EEG tests performed. The testing served to allay any final doubts I had about the presence of my alters and the traumatic events that precipitated their emergence and should help to dispel any question of the validity of multiple personalities.

Having DID is, for many people, a very lonely thing. If this book reaches some people whose experiences resonate with mine and gives them a sense that they aren't alone, that there is hope, then I will have achieved one of my goals. A sad fact is that people with DID spend an average of almost seven years in the mental health system before being properly diagnosed and receiving the specific help they need. During that period, many of them are repeatedly misdiagnosed and incorrectly treated, simply because clinicians fail to recognize or understand the symptoms. If this book provides practicing and future clinicians certain insight into DID, then I will have accomplished another goal.

One of the areas of study that has helped to inform dissociative disorders is the understanding of trauma and, in particular, trauma from early childhood events. Post-traumatic stress PTSD has received considerable attention over the years, and theoretical constructs, treatment strategies, and psychopharmacological support aimed at trauma-based disorders provide clinicians with a broader toolbox for understanding, diagnosing, and treating dissociative disorders. Perhaps the most significant and far-reaching study informing our understanding of early childhood trauma is the Adverse Childhood Experiences (ACE) Study launched in the mid-1990s by Dr. Vincent Felitti of Kaiser Permanente and Dr. Robert Anda of the CDC. With 17,000 subjects, the ACE study examined how early childhood adversity such as neglect, abuse, and household dysfunction (before the age of eighteen) affects long-term physical and mental health. The results were startling. Two-thirds of the participants had at least one ACE. One in five people had three or more. The higher the number of ACEs the greater was the risk of mental health conditions (such as depression, anxiety, PTSD, dissociation, and suicidality), substance abuse, heart disease, cancer, diabetes, and autoimmune disorders.

The ACE study helped to shift clinical and public understanding of trauma-based psychological conditions such as DID from rare psychiatric phenomena to outcomes of childhood adversity. The study sparked a movement toward trauma-informed early assessment in schools and healthcare settings and trauma-based treatment modalities in clinical and residential treatment settings. Several studies followed linking dissociative disorders with early childhood adversity, and it is hoped that these along with the ACE study are providing clinicians with still more tools to aid in the diagnosis and treatment of clients presenting the signs of dissociative disorders. Sadly, early assessment has led to the discovery of dissociative disorders in a much younger population: teens and young adults. Early intervention can be a critical factor in recovery from trauma-based conditions making it even more urgent that clinicians be trained to see the signs and correctly diagnose young victims of abuse.

Fortunately, the study of the dissociative disorders has continued over the last twenty-five years. The literature has expanded, training for clinicians has increased, and conferences such as "Stronger Together: Dissociative Identity Past, Present, and Future" hosted by McLean Hospital and Harvard Medical School seek to improve the understanding of DID, reduce misdiagnosis, and dispel the myths that have hovered over this diagnostic entity. DID is increasingly more visible in popular culture and social media and on the internet, with lived experiences, resources, research studies, and a plethora of information, most informative and correct, some misleading and sensationalized. As with all content on the internet, the consumer must consider the source and search for accurate, research-based information by legitimate institutions.

Repressed memories, recovered memories, and even false memories are terms that are woven through the understanding of dissociative disorders. Clinicians, and all others whose lives are touched by DID, need to accept the fundamentally illusive nature of memory, because memory, or the lack of it, is an integral component of this condition. Our minds are stockpots that are continuously fed from many sources: parents, siblings, relatives, neighbors, teachers, schoolmates, strangers, acquaintances, books, radio, television, movies, and the internet. These are the ingredients of learning and memory, that change form over time as they are shaped by our experiences. In this incredibly amorphous neurological stew, it is impossible for all memories to be exact.

But even as we accept the complex and impressionistic nature of memory, it is equally essential to recognize that people who experience persistent and intrusive memories that disrupt their sense of well-being and ability to function, have some real basis for their distress, regardless of the degree of clarity or feasibility of their recollections.

We must understand that those who experience abuse as children, and particularly those who experience incest, almost invariably suffer from a profound sense of guilt and shame that is not ameliorated merely by unearthing memories or focusing on the content of traumatic material. It is not enough to just remember or even to process the memories. Nor is achieving a sense of wholeness and peace necessarily accomplished by either placing blame on others or by forgiving those we perceive as having wronged us. It is achieved through understanding, acceptance, and reinvention of the self.

At this point in time there are still people who question the validity of the DID diagnosis, though it is my great hope that the number of doubters has diminished significantly. The fact is that DID has its own category in the *Diagnostic and Statistical Manual of Mental Disorders* because, as with all psychiatric conditions, a portion of society experiences a cluster of recognizable symptoms that are not better accounted for by any other diagnosis. There will always be a few who will say that DID does not exist, and their words will be kindling for those whose fires are fueled by debate. As for me, for the most part, debate is what I use to catch de fish.

It is possible to induce the symptoms of DID, and, sadly, some people have experienced this at the hands of inept or untrained therapists. It is also possible to mimic the symptoms of DID, and a few have done so to seek some personal gain. Let the former be an arrow that points to a truth about all therapies, including that which you receive from your family doctor. There is a risk in saying, "Ahhh."

Regarding the latter, think for a moment about the boy who cried wolf. His false cries did not mean that there were no wolves. If you recall, there were—and there still are. That fable would have had a much happier ending if the people had paid attention to what really mattered: the boy was crying.

Back to the Wests, as if Rikki wasn't fully occupied with raising Kai and keeping me from emotional annihilation, in the early years of my struggles, she was diagnosed with breast cancer. Blessedly, it was Stage One, and we caught it early. She underwent a successful operation to remove the tumor and several lymph nodes, and she was bombed with chemotherapy and radiation. The treatment drained her life force dramatically over a period of a year and caused Kai and me no end of desperate worry. All the while, her spirit remained remarkably strong, even when she could barely lift her head from her pillow. It took at least another year for her to fully regain her precancer strength, which she did with exercise, diet, and a lot of laughter. My Rik, the love of my life, is strong and healthy today.

By far the most significant occurrence of the last decades was that my and Rikki's beloved son, Kai, grew up. Rikki and I raised him with the hope that he would pursue a life of artistic beauty and intellectual enrichment, of physical and spiritual health, of humor and of love, and he is doing that. The difficulties brought about by my condition, which he witnessed first-hand as a growing boy, caused him to develop into a kind and compassionate man, sensitive, perhaps overly so, to the emotional pain of others, but he did not emerge unscathed from his early experiences, and he underwent his own therapeutic healing journey over the years.

After high school, Kai attended a music conservatory in London where he specialized in the orchestral contrabass. He received an undergraduate degree and went on to complete his master's degree and two Fellowships to continue his studies. He has played with the London Symphony Orchestra, the London Philharmonic, and the Welsh National Opera, and was principal bassist for the world-famous violinist Nigel Kennedy on several international tours.

While studying abroad, Kai reconnected and fell in love with a friend from high school, and in 2011 Kai and the lovely Alexandra married and eventually returned to the States. Choosing to change direction from performing, Kai began an academic course of study at the University of Michigan and was recently awarded a Ph.D. in Musicology.

And the most wonderful news of all is that three years ago Alex gave birth to our precious grandson, August Reed West, whom we call Augie. It is our great pleasure to see Kai in the roles of husband and father, both of which he carries out with his full attention, tenacity, grace, humor, and a love that never skips a beat. And Rikki and I, having made the move to Michigan when Augie was born, find utter contentment in our new jobs as Gamma and Poppy to our sweet and silly and smart and hilarious little buddy.

We will all be heading back to California soon, returning to our comfy old beach house in a quiet spot on the Central Coast where we hope to remain permanently. I am happiest at the coast where sounds of the ocean refresh the soul and keep me calm. Families of dolphins swim casually by, sometimes leaping playfully to our delight. Seals pop their heads up to watch the surfers, and though Rikki and I have retired our boards, we look forward to seeing Kai paddling out with Augie at his side. Every so often, we see the high spray from the exhalations of humpback whales as they pass by in the distance. Occasionally a pod of whales will come close to shore to feed on the schools of anchovies that migrate by. What is certain death or a frantic escape from gaping jaws for the anchovies is, for the whales, just another lunch in a scene that has played out the same way in this beautiful place for millennia.

On many occasions I felt like the anchovy in the monster's jaws, and as significant as it was for me personally, and for my wife and son, it was also essentially insignificant. The fact is that bad things—dramatic life-changing things—happen to many living things, whether they are witnessed or not, and life continues. I survived unspeakable trauma that shattered my mind. I fought for decades to recover my sense of wholeness and self-worth. I healed from the grief and pain in a drama that began in my childhood and played out in my adult life, but I was also blessed with the love of a strong and emotionally healthy wife and a child who loved me and needed me, and they saved me from the huge jaws that threatened to take my life. And now I am a happy old multiple, and little boy loves me unconditionally and calls me Poppy.

So, to conclude, love yourself and others, appreciate beauty, art, and music or whatever brings you joy, laugh as often as possible, empathize with others' pain so that it may be diminished even if only for a moment, appreciate the flavors and textures of a finely cooked meal, let a cool breeze caress your skin on a warm summer night, and drift off to a peaceful sleep. Thank you for reading our story.

Cam West

ACKNOWLEDGMENTS

I would like to thank all the people at Hyperion who had a hand in bringing my story to life, in particular Brian DiFiore, Samantha Miller, my editor Laurie Abkemeier, and Mary Ellen O'Neill, who took the editorial helm with great enthusiasm after Laurie's departure.

A very special thanks to my agent Laurie Fox at the Linda Chester Literary Agency, for her vision, constant support, editorial expertise, and friendship. And many, many thanks to Linda Chester for her wisdom and guidance, and to her fine staff, in particular Joanna Pulcini and Gary Jaffe. Thanks also to Linda Michaels, Teresa Cavanaugh, and Anne Tente and Whitney Lee at Linda Michaels, LTD. It is my good fortune to have you all behind me.

For this twenty-fifth anniversary edition, I am utterly grateful to Daniel Ehrenhaft at Blackstone Publishing for bringing our story to a new generation of readers. Thanks also to Grover Gardner and to the incredibly talented narrators David Colacci and Susan Ericksen for producing an outstanding audiobook.

I would also like to express my deep gratitude to Dr. Linda Riebel and Dr. Frank Utchen for their friendship and encouragement and for proofreading the galleys.

I could not have written this book without two women who helped me to piece together the events that happened in either my physical or my emotional absence. I want to thank Janna Chase for her faith, skill, and patience, and for Clay's scarf and Switch's sheriff's star.

And, of course, my precious wife, who laughed when I wrote something funny, cried when I wrote something sad, and held me when I couldn't write one more word. I love you like ice cream on an August night.

Little Man, you inherited a scuffed-up, dented dad with busted shocks and four Elmer Fudds. I am sorry about that. But your light helps me shine, your heart gives me spring, and your wit and laughter keep my rubber on the road.

And finally, to all the guests in the Sad Hotel, there will always be comfort in the Comfort Room.

ABOUT THE AUTHOR

Cameron West was born in Chicago, Illinois. His family moved to a suburb of Boston when he was seven years old, and by the time he left for college he had moved six more times. He attended Berklee School of Music and Syracuse University and received his undergraduate degree in business and music from the State University of New York.

He met his future wife, Rikki, in 1978 in Boston where he was working as a touring musician, and they married in 1981. In 1987 while living in Nashville, Tennessee, where Cam was working as a recording artist and Rikki was attending graduate school at Vanderbilt University, Rikki gave birth to their son, Kai. Though Cam and Rikki had a strong relationship and a beautiful, healthy baby, Cam continued to suffer from a number of chronic illnesses that had plagued him since he was a teenager.

Cam loved his life as a new father, though his work, which required him to frequently be away from his family, quickly became a source of unhappiness. In 1988 he and Rikki made the decision to leave Nashville and the music business behind so Cam would be present while Kai was growing up.

They settled in a suburb of New York City and Cam went into business in sales. Though his business thrived, his physical health declined, and following a fourth failed sinus surgery in ten years, he was diagnosed with systemic candidiasis and a severely compromised immune system.

With Rikki's support and the help of a holistic medical practitioner, he was able to fight his way back to health over a period of almost a year. When Cam was finally physically healthy, his psyche started to crumble, and he began to show profound symptoms of dissociation. Rikki had worked with emotionally disturbed children and had been trained in counseling, and she recognized that Cam desperately needed the help of a mental health specialist. Cam was diagnosed with Dissociative Identity Disorder (formerly called Multiple Personality Disorder) in 1993.

Rikki moved the family to California in 1994 to make a new start. Although Cam was in regular therapy with a specialist in dissociative disorders, he was accepted into the doctoral program in psychology at Saybrook University in San Francisco and he earned his Ph.D. in 1997. His dissertation was a case study of the experiential aspects of switching and co-consciousness in three persons with DID.

First Person Plural: My Life as a Multiple (Hyperion, 1999) was Cam's first book. Oprah Winfrey took an interest in Cam and Rikki's story and invited them to be on her television show for a full hour. This appearance was the first of many (including *The Today Show* with Katie Couric, *20/20*, and *Entertainment Tonight*) for Cam and Rikki, and the book became a *New York Times* bestseller and was eventually published in more than two dozen countries. Movie rights were purchased by Disney Studios, and a draft script was written by Eric Roth (*Forrest Gump*, *The Horse Whisperer*), but the movie has yet to be made.

Cam wrote his second book, *The Medici Dagger* (Simon & Schuster, 2001), a novel about an orphan named Reb who became a stuntman and was drawn into a search for his hero Leonardo Da Vinci's legendary Medici Dagger to avenge his parents' deaths. The story involved long lost pages from Leonardo's notebook, which resurfaced and offered clues to the dagger's hiding place. The book, published in over twenty countries, was optioned twice by Paramount Pictures for Tom Cruise, but has yet to be made into a film. A sequel to *The Medici Dagger* called *Futurecard*, now in the works, finds Reb pitted against a new and formidable foe as nanotechnology meets terrorism and the threat is subliminal control.

Cam forayed for a time into academic research and writing on pain and toxicology, collaborating with world-renowned toxicologist Dr. Amadeo Pesce and a team of researchers on over thirty medical journal articles and a book chapter. These were published in the *Journal of Analytical Toxicology*, *Clin Chimica Acta*, *Pain Physician*, *Therapeutic Drug Monitoring*, *Journal of Opioid Management*, *Journal of Analytical and Bioanalytical Techniques*, *International Association of Therapeutic Drug Monitoring Compass*, *Toxicology and Testing*, *Medical Laboratory Observations*, and *Pain Medicine*.

Cam and Rikki live on the central coast of California. Though Cam's condition often limits his interactions out in the world and the degree to which he can tolerate external stimuli from loud and busy places, he and Rikki, married forty-five years, live a happy and peaceful life and enjoy their current job as daycare providers for their grandson, Augie.

RESOURCES

The International Society for the Study of Trauma and Dissociation: https://www.isst-d.org/

From their website:

> The ISSTD seeks to advance clinical, scientific, and societal understanding of chronic trauma and dissociation.

This organization offers resources for the public and clinicians, a training institute and certification program for clinicians, fact sheets, a list of web resources and a source for locating a therapist. For professionals they publish the *Journal of Trauma and Dissociation*.

Sidran Traumatic Stress Institute, Inc.: https://www.traumaticstress-institute.org/sidran-redirect/

From their website:

> Sidran Traumatic Stress Institute, Inc. is a nonprofit organization of international scope exclusively focused on educating patients, healthcare providers, and the public about recovery from traumatic stress (including Post Traumatic Stress Disorder). Sidran develops and delivers books and videotapes, assessment and teaching tools, and educational programs customized to meet

> the needs of specific consumer and professional populations. Sidran collaborates with other nonprofit organizations, private providers, government agencies (local, county, state, and federal), media, and industry to raise the level of understanding and competence in regard to traumatic stress conditions.

This organization provides training, a blog, resources, helplines, and books geared toward trauma informed care (TIC) directed specifically toward assessment and support for those who have experienced adverse childhood experiences (ACEs).

Dissociative Identity Disorder Research (DIDR): https://did-research.org/

From their website:

> This site aims to fill a void of comprehensive yet accessible resources pertaining to trauma and dissociation. It serves to promote awareness and understanding of a variety of topics related to dissociative identity disorder, other dissociative disorders, trauma, and trauma's effects. It achieves this by presenting current research and validated sources to the general public in a more easily understandable form. A secondary aim of this website is to promote connecting dissociative trauma survivors to research studies in order to contribute to scientific progress on these subjects.

This site offers a plethora of easily accessible information concerning DID, including definitions and descriptions, cause and comorbidity, differential diagnoses, treatment modalities, and resources.

Other websites that provide information on Dissociative Disorders:

NAMI – National Alliance on Mental Illness: https://www.nami.org/about-mental-illness/mental-health-conditions/dissociative-disorders

/Cleveland Clinic: https://my.clevelandclinic.org/health/diseases/9792-dissociative-identity-disorder-multiple-personality-disorder

Mayo Clinic: https://www.mayoclinic.org/diseases-conditions/dissocitive-disorders/symptoms-causes/syc-20355215

Sheppard Pratt: https://www.sheppardpratt.org/knowledge-center/condition/dissociative-identity-disorder-did/